AMERICAN REALITIES

HISTORICAL EPISODES

AMERICAN REALITIES

HISTORICAL EPISODES

*from the First Settlements
to the Civil War*

Second Edition

J. WILLIAM T. YOUNGS

Eastern Washington University

Cover and text illustrations by Cecily Moon

LITTLE, BROWN AND COMPANY
BOSTON   TORONTO

Library of Congress Cataloging-in-Publication Data

Youngs, J. William T. (John William Theodore), 1941-
    American realities.

    Includes bibliographies and indexes.
    Contents: v. 1. From the first settlements to the
Civil War — v. 2. From Reconstruction to the present.
    1. United States—History.   I. Title.
E178.6.Y68   1986   973   86-19984
ISBN 0-316-97740-3 (v. 1)
ISBN 0-316-97741-1 (v. 2)

Library of Congress Catalog Card Number 86–19984

ISBN 0-316-97740-3

9 8 7 6 5 4 3 2 1

MV

Published simultaneously in Canada
by Little, Brown and Company (Canada) Limited

Printed in the United States of America

Credits

To my mother
and the memory of my father

Preface

American history is an epic composed of many events: colonists made their homes in a new world; soldiers fought for independence; capitalists built giant industries; civil rights activists struggled for equality. In such episodes we encounter the emotions, thoughts, and experiences that made up the distinct worlds of the past. In the two volumes of *American Realities* my goal has been to recreate some of those worlds, to capture the immediacy — the reality — of life as lived in other eras. I have not tried to reduce all these events to a single pattern, but in the aggregate the chapters trace the course of American history from the distant past to the present.

Each chapter is designed to lead the reader to a better understanding of major themes in United States history. Each volume can be read by itself or in tandem with a conventional American history textbook. The standard surveys present the general patterns of the past; this book reveals in greater depth the life beneath those patterns.

Like ourselves the people of the past were immersed in the issues of their times. But even while living fully in their own worlds, they bequeathed us ours. Their stories reveal the broad contours of the saga as well as the illustrative particulars. The death of Thomasine Winthrop leads us to know Puritanism better, and the flight of the *Enola Gay* to Hiroshima exhibits the harsh outlines of total war. The Lewis and Clark expedition reveals the marvelous land upon which the nation developed, and Charles Coughlin's career illuminates the personal turmoil of the depression years.

While writing *American Realities* I have often wished I had the novelist's poetic license to fill gaps not covered by the sources. But fortunately, facts can be as engaging as fiction. Documents are often colorful and evocative, allowing us to listen to the deathbed conversation of John and Thomasine Winthrop, to see the light of the South Pacific from a B-29, to enter imaginatively into the realities of other men and women.

We can find historical kinship in the ordinary circumstances of daily life. George Washington is comprehensible because he was stunned when his army in Manhattan collapsed. John Muir is like most of us because he was troubled once about choosing a career. If you have never faced a similar moment, when all your plans went awry, you are indeed lucky.

My touchstone in choosing topics for *American Realities* was that each should suggest our common humanity even while revealing worlds distinct from our own. More simply, I had to care about the subjects and believe others could care about them as well. Through such sympathy we come actually to live in history and feel our involvement with the past: his story and her story become our story.

The second edition of *American Realities* includes four new chapters. The topics were selected to serve the same purpose as those of the other chapters, but their themes are new. In "Down the Santa Fe Trail" (Volume I), we explore the absorption of Northern Mexico into the United States during the era of "manifest destiny." In the chapter on Joseph McCarthy (Volume II) we investigate anti-communism in American life. The chapter on Lee Iacocca (Volume II) replaces an essay on the energy crisis of 1973–74, and in it we study the challenges facing industry in modern America. The final chapter, "From Seattle to Managua," brings American history to a current issue in foreign policy; in it we discover ways in which our own lives enter contemporary history.

The effort here to recreate history in words is supplemented by the imaginative drawings of Cecily Moon. Ms. Moon based her illustrations on careful reading of each chapter and on personal research in historical paintings and photographs. Each drawing highlights a major theme in the chapters.

For the instructor I have prepared a manual with chapter summaries, identification topics, multiple choice and discussion questions, and suggested research projects.

American Realities arrived at its present form with the help of many other scholars and writers. I am particularly grateful to Marian Ferguson, Dave Lynch, and Katie Carlone at Little, Brown for their help on the first edition and to Brad Gray, Barbara Breese, and Dave Lynch for their work on the second edition. A writer could not ask for more congenial and intelligent assistance in nurturing his ideas than these editors provided. The book also owes a great deal to the assistance of Claire Seng-Niemoeller and Frank Kirk; to Lois Banner, Ron Benson, Peter Carroll, Joseph H. Cartwright, David Coon, Doris Daniels, Emmett M. Essin, Don Glenn, James Hunt, Donald M. Jacobs, Maury Klein, Ralph Shaffer, and Julius Weinberg; and to Charles Baumann, Joseph Corn, James Gale, Richard Johnson, William Kidd, Nancy

Millard, Sue Murphy, Robert Toll, Albert Tully, and my students in
American history. For their help on the revisions I am particularly grate-
ful to Linda Stowe, Jay Hart, Russ Tremayne, and Madeleine Freidel.
I would also like to thank those reviewers who commented on the new
material for the second edition in its early form, August W. Giebelhaus,
Emmett M. Essin, Paul W. Wehr, and James L. Gormly. My wife,
Linda Youngs, who is both the sternest and most sensitive critic of my
work, gave me many valuable suggestions while pursuing her own busy
schedule as a mother and an attorney. Finally, in dedicating *American
Realities* to my mother, Marguerite Youngs, and to the memory of my
father, J. W. T. Youngs, I wish to recognize their part in helping me
find my own place in history.

Contents

VOLUME I

FROM THE
FIRST SETTLEMENTS
TO THE CIVIL WAR

NORTH
AMERICA

ATLANTIC
OCEAN

Timuquan

Tenochtitlán

Tulum

CUBA

Columbus's Route in 1492

HISPANIOLA

WEST
INDIES

Tulum

GULF OF
MEXICO

MAYA

1
THE NATIVE AMERICANS

October 11, 1492

American history did not begin with Christopher Columbus in 1492 or with John Smith in 1607. Long before Europeans reached the New World, native Americans settled the whole of the Western Hemisphere and created hundreds of civilizations, many as large and complex as fifteenth-century European states. They made pottery, built cities, founded empires, wrote poetry, and plotted the course of the sun and the stars. Eventually their lives would be changed by massive invasions of European soldiers and immigrants, but they did not exist simply to interact with Europeans. They began the human story in America long before 1492, and the story of their lives constitutes the first chapter of American history. They are indeed America's deepest roots.

On October 11, 1492, the people of Tulum on the eastern coast of Mexico's Yucatán Peninsula lived in an important coastal community, atop a high bluff overlooking the sea. On three sides stone walls marked the boundary between the town and the thick green bush beyond. On the fourth side limestone cliffs dropped away sharply to the white sands of a narrow beach and the warm turquoise waters of the Caribbean.

Compared with other Mayan cities, Tulum was built on a modest scale. Its *castillo,* or main temple, stood only forty feet high, less than one fifth the height of the great castillo at Chichén Itzá in the interior. The city housed no more than five or six hundred people, whereas tens of thousands had lived in the great Mayan cities of the past. These coastal Maya were nonetheless the heirs of a proud tradition. Their ancestors had charted sun and stars' course from great stone "observatories" and developed the world's most accurate calendar. They employed a sophisticated numerical system, chronicled their history in hieroglyphs, and honored their gods with elaborate carvings and massive temples.

Most of the ancient centers had been abandoned several centuries before when the Mayan people had come under the sway of invading Toltecs, and in 1492 the Maya were living in more than a dozen small states, their former glory long lost. But, in a few places like Tulum, whose neatly plastered and painted stone walls and buildings stood out brightly from the sea, something of that ancient splendor endured. Statues carved on building façades as well as frescoes testified to Mayan piety. The most striking figure was the "diving god," a divine figure apparently plunging earthward from the sky.

Tulum was a convenient embarkation point for trips in long wood canoes to the offshore island of Cozumel where pilgrims made offerings to Izchel, the goddess of medicine, sought out particularly by expectant mothers. They came before a large pottery figure representing the deity and were addressed by priests hidden behind the shrine.

The people of Tulum subsisted on generous crops of land and sea by raising maize, beans, squash, and chili, by hunting deer and turkey, and by taking fish, lobster, clams, and conchs from the clear waters of the Caribbean. They traded in canoes along the populous coast, exchanging native honey and shells for cacao (beans used to make cocoa), feathers, and other exotic products.

In 1492 trade and piety connected the people of Tulum with a wide area of Caribbean coastline and Yucatán interior. But their world was limited to the tropical skies of Meso-America. They were only one of hundreds of peoples who occupied the American continents. A thousand miles from the Mayan lands lay another world, impressive beyond what they could have imagined. Here, in the Valley of Mexico, the Aztec Empire was at its height; in contrast to its grand capital, a place such as Tulum was a mere village.

A traveler who approached the great Aztec city of Tenochtitlán for the first time must have been struck with wonder. Before him across a long causeway in the middle of Lake Texcoco lay a city of incredible size, home of some three hundred thousand people. On its fringes lay hundreds of small, man-made islands called *chinampas*, whose rich soil provided much of the city's maize.

Thousands of neat houses, made of adobe or stone and stucco, lined the streets, their whitewashed walls reflecting the bright sun and their flower-dense interior gardens filling the air with incense. Beyond these modest houses were larger buildings where the great lords and high priests lived. The greatest of these dignitaries was the emperor, a man elected from among the members of the royal family by the council of noblemen. He was venerated, almost isolated, by worshipful ceremony — riding from place to place in a litter carried by noblemen or walking on cloths cast before him to keep his feet from touching the ground. He ate his meals behind a gilded screen, shielded from the prying eyes of lesser mortals.

Near the palaces were temples dedicated to some forty major deities worshiped in Tenochtitlán. Some were traditional Aztec gods; others came from peoples conquered in the empire's endless wars. The greatest temple represented Huitzilopochtli, Left-handed Humingbird, whose pacific name seems ill suited to his stern character.

The hisory of Huitzilopochtli was inextricable from the history of the Aztecs. Long before being honored by a stone monument more than one hundred feet tall, he had been represented by a wooden image carried by four priests in the company of a wandering band of nomads. These were the original Aztecs, who, with their foremost god, had come to the Valley of Mexico several centuries before. Poor and despised, they were forced into a small section of desertland by their more prosperous neighbors, then driven even from this land into the marshes of Lake Texcoco. Here the god Huitzilopochtli told the priests to find an eagle perched on a cactus with a rattlesnake in its mouth and to build a city at that place. The foretold apparition was discovered on an island in Lake Texcoco, and in 1325 the Aztecs began to construct their great city.

It proved an admirable seat for the new empire. The lake was shallow, allowing the Aztecs to build up arable land from the silt and rocks of the lake bottom. Its waters discouraged attack by enemy tribes while enabling their own armies to set out and make war on neighboring tribes. As their power grew, braves from other tribes joined them, swelling their numbers and augmenting their power. By 1492 Aztec armies had marched hundreds of miles to the seas on the east and the west and into the interior both north and south, demanding and receiving tribute from dozens of neighboring states.

Throughout this period of remarkable growth, Huitzilopochtli, once the frail image of a wandering people, grew into a mighty god, with an insatiable need for human sacrifice. The Aztecs believed their god would make them victorious in battle if they offered him the hearts of captives. Hardly a week passed in Tenochtitlán without such a sacrifice. At the crest of the temple pyramid each victim was held over a sacrificial stone by four priests while a fifth cut the heart from the body with an obsidian knife.

Often the Aztecs made multiple sacrifices, and only a few years before 1492, at the dedication of the great temple, long lines of captives had gone one by one to the sacrificial stone, in rites lasting four days and consuming between twenty and eighty thousand lives. Often the victims accepted their fate with religious resolve, believing that their blood would feed the sun and unite them with the gods. Some even preferred death and refused the chance to live an honorable life among their captors. But many must have trembled as they began the long ascent up the stone steps of the pyramid on the way to the sacrificial stone.

Under the shadow of the temples one might think that life in Tenochtitlán had a ghostly pallor, that the proximity of so much death would distort the whole of life. But the city's daily routine does not appear to have had a morbid flavor. The people moved along the narrow sidewalks or through the smooth canals in brightly colored garments and gathered in huge marketplaces to exchange their wares. Aztecs engaged in dozens of trades — working as administrators, merchants, priests, goldsmiths, feather workers, painters, messengers, and teachers.

They exchanged their goods in such places as the nearby island of Tlaltelolco where as many as sixty thousand merchants and customers assembled on a single day. Here one could obtain corn, beans, venison, robes and other cloth, jewelry, swords, and spears. Because cacao beans, cloth, and gold dust were the only forms of currency, much of the trade was done by barter, and almost everyone was a merchant as well as a customer.

Although most of the citizens worked in such material occupations as raising crops or making jewelry, there was also an intellectual class in Tenochtitlán. The Aztecs possessed a considerable body of philosophy and theology, passed down from generation to generation in an oral tradition of poetry, song, and story. The priests taught the people rules

Maya boatmen in the Caribbean off Tulum. Along hundreds of miles of Yucatán coastline they traded and visited religious sanctuaries.

by which to guide their lives and furnished the ideological undergirding for an orderly world.

Aztecs kept their streets clean and conducted their transactions in the markets with decorum. They punished thievery, drunkenness, and adultery with death and raised their progeny in a strong home environment. When children were three years old, they received toys such as looms and grindstones to familiarize them with the tools of adult life. Their parents encouraged them to choose their vocations carefully and taught them a code of social conduct. One Aztec rule stressed the need to value goodness more than pride:

> Not with envy,
> not with a twisted heart,
> shall you feel superior,
> shall you go about boasting.
>
> Rather in goodness shall you make true
> your song and your word.
> And thus you shall be highly regarded,
> and you shall be able to live with others.

One of the most important social arrangements was marriage. Parents usually chose their children's spouses and taught young people to wait patiently for the proper moment for marriage. The priests declared:

> This is how you must act:
> before you know woman
> you must grow to be a complete man.
> And then you will be ready for marriage;
> you will beget children of good stature,
> healthy, agile, and comely.

Postponement was not a tremendous hardship, however, because most marriages took place when men were about twenty and women about sixteen.

On the evening of October 11, 1492, many wedding ceremonies must have been in progress during the twilight hours in Tenochtitlán. Each bride was carried to her groom's house; there she stood with him before the hearth, and friends tied his shirt to her dress as a sign of their union. After the ceremony the bride and groom burned incense to the gods for four days before being allowed to consummate their marriage.

We may imagine such a couple on this night, alone together, contemplating their lives and their gods, glad of each other's company in the crisp night air, anticipating with pleasure the time when they would "beget children of good stature, healthy, agile, and comely."

Several thousand miles away, in Florida, a region unknown even to the far-traveling Aztecs, the Timuquan Indians lived along what was later named the Saint Johns River. They inhabited small circular villages surrounded by simple log fortifications. Their houses were made of wood and thatch, and they wore simple loincloths. The Timuquans may seem at first to have been a simpler people than the Maya or the Aztecs. They did not build great stone cities, paint hieroglyphs, or accurately calculate the length of the year. Their culture had a richness of its own, however, reflected in their economy, recreation, and ceremonies.

Timuquans tilled the soil with hoes made of heavy fishbones attached to wood handles; the men hoed and the women planted beans and maize. They gathered fruit from the islands at the mouth of the Saint Johns and hunted the abundant wildlife of the region, including snakes, deer, and alligators. Pursuit of the alligator required the coordinated efforts of many men. First some of the hunters skewered the alligator through the mouth with a long, pointed log; then they flipped it over and other Indians shot arrows into its soft belly. These beasts, fish, and other game were carefully smoked over fires to preserve them through the winter. The smoked flesh was stored along with fruit and grain in large round buildings owned by the tribe or cooked in large earthenware vessels that could be set directly on a fire like an iron kettle.

A council of state assembled periodically on a long, curved wood bench with the chief at the center. The councilors approached cremoniously in order of age, and the chief listened to their advice. The council probably decided when crops should be planted, whether alliances should be formed, where the tribe should make its winter quarters, and other important matters.

Most of the tribe's business followed an orderly pattern determined by natural elements and native customs. Even warfare had a stylized, ritual quality. If one tribe wished to declare war, men were sent to post arrows in the paths near the enemy tribe. The leader then assembled his warriors and voiced incantations asking for victory. The bank of warriors marched out in an orderly procession, well armed with heavy bows and arrows or large wood clubs. At nightfall they made camp in regular lines divided into squads of ten. Often their only nourishment came from a drink called casina, carried by porters.

On the battlefield these tribes usually fought in large squares, with the leader protected in the middle and directing the action. If victorious, they dismembered their fallen enemies' bodies and carried home the limbs and heads as trophies. Even the wives of slain warriors had a ceremonial function to perform. They came before the chief to ask his protection and then went to their husbands' graves to mourn. They decorated the graves with drinking cups and weapons, as well as with most of their hair, cut short in a sign of sorrow. They were allowed to remarry only after their hair had once more grown to shoulder length.

In peaceful times the Timuquans enjoyed wading to the pleasant offshore islands carrying children and baskets of food in their arms. For sport they ran footraces and practiced with the bow and arrow. Their taste for beauty was reflected in the bright feathers worn in men's hair, the colorful ornaments in women's ears, and the animal skins that adorned the chiefs. The principal men and women of the tribe were decorated with elaborate tattoos; on important occasions the chief wore a brightly painted deerskin, and the women wore belts of silken moss.

The Timuquan existence was continually enlivened with rituals. In the spring a large stagskin filled with roots was placed atop a pole as an offering to the sun. The chief then prayed while the people made responses. After a victory in war the tribe assembled around the trophies and listened while a priest recited a victory chant to the accompaniment of the beating of gourds and a drum. During the greatest celebration of all, the marriage of the chief, the bride was brought forth on a litter behind heralds who blew through trumpets of bark to announce her coming. Then young girls, gold and silver ornaments

tinkling around their hips, danced before the couple, praising the king
in unison.

On October II, 1492, the Timuquans were probably occupied with
more practical matters, for they would soon move from their summer
dwellings into the forest to spend the cold months. Thus, they would
be busy gathering and storing as much food as land and sea would yield.

The Maya, Aztecs, and Timuquans were only three of the hundreds of cultures that flourished in the Americas in 1492. Some, such
as the Incas of South America, were great empires, as powerful as the
Aztecs. Others, like the Delaware, Abnaki, Hurons, Kickapoo, Sioux,
Nez Percé, Navaho, and Hopi were smaller tribes, but had nevertheless
created distinctive cultures.

Most of the tribes were familiar with only a small territory near
their own homes, but almost all of them traded with other tribes over
long distances. Thus, copper from the south shore of Lake Superior was
exchanged — through middlemen — for tobacco and shells from Virginia. Red pipestone from Minnesota found its way to upper New York;
unfinished blanks of flint were carried from Ontario to the Rockies; and
obsidian from the Rockies found its way to the Hopewell mounds in
Ohio. On a more local scale, fairs throughout the Americas periodically
attracted Indians from fifty to sixty miles away.

In 1492 there were approximately 100 million inhabitants in North
and South America; perhaps 10 million lived in the region that would
become the United States. Each tribe had developed hunting skills, and
most planted crops. Each built dwellings suitable to its own needs,
developed its own political system, and had its own religion. On the
night of October II that life was reflected in the thoughts of 100 million
human beings: a Mayan boy lay thinking about his plans to go diving
for conchs the next day with his father; an Aztec scholar contemplated
a sacred poem; a Timuquan woman silently mourned her husband killed
in a recent battle. Surely people had always had such thoughts, and
they always would.

A few miles away men of another civilization, economy, and faith
were preparing for their own night's rest in three crowded ships. Only
the captains had the privacy of sleeping berths; the crewmen slept in
their clothes wherever they could find space. The captain general, Christopher Columbus, had sailed many miles and would soon be a famous
man. But few men in history have ever been as lost as Christopher
Columbus was at that moment; he had miscalculated the circumference
of the world and believed himself to be on the edge of China, eight
thousand miles to the west.

Timuquan activities. This composite of Indian practices is based on drawings by a sixteenth-century French colonist, Jacques Le Moyne, and depicts a war council, meat being smoked, hunters disguised as deer, a native boat, and, in the far background, Indians offering a stag to the sun.

His small fleet had caught a last glimpse of the mountain of Tenerife in the Canary Islands on September 9 and had not seen land since. To the knowledge of the ships' companies, no other vessels had ever been so long at sea. The men had eaten nothing for days but peas, dried bread, and salt meat, cooked on deck over wood fires set in beds of sand, and they were rebellious.

Like the native Americans, they lived a life that was rich in sacred observances, and on these anxious days their accustomed sailors' pleas for divine assistance must have seemed more than routine. Each morning a boy awakened the crew with the verse:

Blessed be the light of day
And the Holy Cross we say.

He then recited the Ave Maria and the Lord's Prayer. In the evening the whole crew joined in reciting the Creed, the Lord's Prayer, and the Ave Maria and sang the Latin hymn, *Salve Regina.*

Many crewmen wanted to turn back before their supplies ran out rather than sail on day after day looking for land that might not exist. Even Columbus had been discouraged until signs appeared that land was nearby — branches in the water and flocks of migrating birds. On October 11 additional indications gave them even more hope: sandpipers flying overhead and, in the water, a branch covered with berries and wood that had apparently been worked with iron.

On the evening of October 11, Columbus reminded his men of a reward that had been promised to the first sailor who sighted land. Sailing that night over warm seas, with a strong following wind, Columbus thought he saw two lights flickering like wax candles in the distance. But they disappeared, and as the moon rose the ships were still in the middle of an empty sea.

Then at 2:00 A.M. on October 12 the lookout aboard the lead ship, the *Pinta*, cried "Land! Land!" Columbus came alongside in the *Santa Maria* and confirmed the sighting. The three ships hauled in sail and drifted south along the coast, waiting until dawn to seek a safe place to land. On the shore the Arawak natives, who called their island Guanahani, slept as the three boats approached on the moonlit sea.

The next morning Columbus found a safe passageway between the reefs on the western shore of the island and anchored his ships near a white coral beach. Ashore the men knelt and gave thanks to God for their safe voyage and named the island San Salvador (Holy Savior).

The natives, who had seen the three ships and run off in fear, were now subjects of the king and queen of Spain, according to the European explorers, who simply assumed lands not possessed by other European states belonged to the first "civilized" nation to visit them.

Fortunately, the Arawaks were unaware of the annexation, and the Spanish had no interest in backing up their claim with a garrison, so that Columbus's first meeting with these Indians of the New World took place in a peaceful atmosphere. After watching the strange men from the ships, some of the young men approached them cautiously. Each side wanted to trade, and soon a spirited exchange took place, the Arawaks exchanging parrots, darts, and cotton thread for red caps, glass beads, and hawk bells.

Columbus believed the natives were simple and innocent. They painted their bodies, wore almost no clothing, and were exceptionally friendly. He concluded that they had no religion of their own and could easily be converted to Christianity. The natives, of course, having seen the Spaniards only as traders, might as easily have concluded that these visitors had no religion and might benefit from being introduced to the Arawak faith.

From San Salvador, Columbus sailed west, always looking for indications that he was somewhere in the Far East. Guided by several natives from San Salvador, he sailed through more small islands, then reached the larger islands of Cuba and Hispaniola. He sought gold primarily, but was also interested in other products of the islands, including corn and potatoes — foods that in the long run would prove more important to Europe than all of America's precious metals. Columbus also became the first white man to observe the use of tobacco.

On Christmas Day, Columbus's flagship, the *Santa Maria*, rammed into a reef and sank. Columbus and his men were rescued by the *Niña*, and he regarded the event as a sign from God that he should found a colony on the shore nearby. After seeing that thirty-nine of his men were comfortably settled in the new colony, which he named Navidad, he boarded the *Niña* and set out on the long voyage home.

During his three months in the West Indies, Columbus had been warmly received by the natives on the islands he visited. He manifested no aggressive intentions and insisted that his men trade fairly, giving the natives something in exchange for goods they received. Toward the end of the voyage his patience was rewarded when chiefs on the larger islands gave him gold ornaments — treasures with which he could impress his sovereigns.

When Columbus returned to Spain, news of his achievement spread rapidly through Europe. Whereas the Viking "discovery" and colonization of America five centuries before had had a limited effect on Europe as a whole, the news of Columbus's voyage spread through a Europe that in the next century was capable of sending hundreds of expeditions to explore, colonize, and ravage the new land. Columbus himself led three more voyages, in 1493-94, 1498-1500, and 1502-3.

The joining of the Old and New Worlds in the years ahead would radically alter the history of both. American silver, gold, corn, potatoes, and tobacco changed the economic and agricultural history of Europe. Old World diseases, especially smallpox, decimated the native American populations, and European conquerors became the masters of lands once held by Mayas, Aztecs, Timuquans, Arawaks, and other peoples. Columbus died unaware that he had discovered a new world rather than a new route to Asia, and a mapmaker named Amerigo Vespucci named the region for himself when he drew a chart showing the New World as a separate geographical area. It was Columbus's daring voyage, however, that led to the merging of the two hemispheres.

If the Indians Columbus met on his first voyage through the Caribbean had been united into one nation, and if they had known that disease and conquest would follow in Columbus' wake, they might easily have prevented his return to Spain. His men might have been absorbed into the native cultures, their tales of the land beyond the sea drifting eventually into the world of Indian mythology. European monarchs, hearing of Columbus's failure, would not have sent another fleet into the unknown waters of the western seas, preferring instead to reach China by a new route around the coasts of Africa. Two or three generations might have passed before another explorer had the audacity — and the financial backing — to sail due west from the known world.

Even as it was, many Indians did not see a white man until long after the Columbus expedition. The Aztec Empire survived for thirty years before Hernando Cortés led a conquering army through the streets of Tenochtitlán. In the remote mountains and jungles of both American continents Indian tribes remained independent of Euro-American domination until the twentieth century. If the 100 million Indians alive in the Americas in 1492 had been told that they were about to be "discovered," they would have smiled in disbelief. Surely it was their own ancestors who first settled the land. Had they not reared families, formed governments, waged wars, manufactured pottery, constructed temples, conducted religious ceremonies, and speculated about the meaning and purpose of life — filled the land with human life?

From a European point of view, Columbus did discover America, but in a more meaningful way he began the long exchange between two worlds. Contact brought change, but the Indians were already familiar with change, with the ebb and flow of their own civilizations. Nor would the new conquerors and colonizers be immune from change. The English and Spanish nations would establish American empires, but these would crumble. The new American nations born in the revolts of the late eighteenth and early nineteenth centuries would in turn suffer shocks from economic growth.

At the height of the Aztec civilization a philosopher-king, Nezahualcóyotl, wrote a poem expressing his sense of the transitoriness of life:

Is it true that on earth one lives?
Not forever on earth, only a little while.
Though jade it may be, it breaks;
though gold it may be, it is crushed;
though it be quetzal plumes, it shall not last.
Not forever on earth, only a little while.

In such thoughts, as well as in the portraits we may construct of early life in the Yucatán, Mexico, and Florida, we are reminded that the humanity of American history had its beginnings long before ninety sea-weary sailors from another world fell to their knees on the island they called San Salvador.

QUESTIONS

1. Describe the principal political, economic, social, and religious characteristics of the three native American groups described in this chapter.
2. In what ways were the civilizations of America equal to those of Europe in 1492? In what areas were they more advanced? less advanced?
3. Why do we say that Columbus "discovered" America when the continent was already peopled and civilized?
4. In view of the damage Europeans would later do to Indians, why was Columbus allowed by the Indians to return to Spain?
5. Many people have a stereotype of the native American as uncivilized. Summarize the evidence against this view.

BIBLIOGRAPHY

BRANDON, WILLIAM. *The American Heritage Book of Indians* (1961). Lavishly illustrated and a fine narrative overview.

COLLIS, MAURICE. *Cortés and Montezuma* (1954). Stirring account of Cortés's conquest of Mexico.

CROSBY, ALFRED W. *The Columbian Exchange: Biological and Cultural Consequences of 1492* (1972). Describe changes in European and native American life resulting from contact between the two regions.

FARB, PETER. *Man's Rise to Civilization as Shown by the Indians of North America* (1968 and later editions). Interpretive history of Indian culture.

VAN HAGEN, VICTOR W. *World of the Maya* (1960). Standard popular survey of the Mayas.

JENNINGS, FRANCIS. *The Invasion of America: Indians, Colonialism, and the Cant of Conquest* (1975). Focuses on Puritan-Indian contact in New England.

LEÓN-PORTILLA, MIGUEL. *Aztec Thought and Culture* (1963). Sensitive analysis of Aztec intellectual life.

LORANT, STEFAN. *The New World* (1946). Includes seventeenth-century drawings and description of Timuquans.

MORISON, SAMUEL ELIOT. *Christopher Columbus, Mariner* (1955). Definitive account of Columbus's voyages.

2

THE FIRST
EURO-AMERICANS

Norsemen
in the New World

For thousands of years the peoples of America and Europe lived in separate worlds, as remote from one another as distant stars. Europeans came to America slowly, groping at the edges of the New World, touching the shores long before they penetrated the interior. Columbus sailed across the Atlantic four times but never realized he had reached new continents. England sent an explorer, Sebastian Cabot, to America in 1497, but established no permanent settlements for more than a century. There were, however, European settlements in the "New World" long before the voyages of Columbus and Cabot. One thousand years ago Norsemen colonized Greenland, on the fringe of North America. There they clung for almost five centuries, building farms and churches, trading with Europe, sending parties to the mainland. Their history shows in microcosm many elements of American history: a European culture being adapted to conditions in the New World, contacts between North America and Europe, and the hardships and rewards of the colonist's life.

Roughly a thousand years ago Europeans from Norway began settling Greenland, a rugged island on the edge of the New World. Their early contacts with North America did not lead to massive immigration by other Europeans; the distinction of starting that movement was left to Christopher Columbus. But the Norsemen did establish dozens of communities in this remote land, communities where life was as intense and varied as in any European town. Few records survive from these early societies, but we know enough to recognize that the story of the Norse settlements is one of the most interesting chapters in the history of European contact with America and anticipates, in some ways, the later history of European colonization. In order to understand this unique society, we will review the five centuries of Norse experience in Greenland, but let us first try to imagine the reality of these distant times by picturing a day in the settlements.

The year is 1150 A.D. In a small Greenland farmhouse a Norse family is beginning the day. The father, first to rise, leaves his bed of skins and steps to the firepit in the center of the room. Taking embers from a small hole beside the pit, he lights the fire. Although the room is chilly, he makes only a small blaze, for wood is precious in Greenland. To light the windowless room he touches a flaming twig to the seal oil in a small soapstone lamp.

His wife is now awake, nursing their four-month-old infant; she hears the other children beginning to stir. The father goes outside to check the late spring weather and is pleased with what he sees. Above the mountains the sun is just rising. Looking down over green sloping fields to the calm fjord below, he notices a few small patches of fog, but otherwise the air is clear. It will be a warm day.

From where he stands he can see green pastures, farmhouses, and a stone church. In the water perhaps a mile away a neighbor is heading out to sea to fish from a small wood boat. He hears the sea gulls' piercing cries and a bell sounding matins in the cathedral a few miles away. From the great manor at Brattahlid, where Eric the Red once lived, he can hear the sharp ring of a blacksmith's hammer.

Along the west coast of Greenland for several hundred miles are farmsteads like his own where other Norsemen are beginning the day. Some will go to the fields; some will fish or hunt along the shore. Directly across the open sea on the Labrador coast, some three days' sail to the west, Norsemen are felling trees to replenish Greenland's scant supply.

Returning to the house, the man finds that his wife has finished preparing the morning meal. His two-year-old son is playing with a chess piece; he takes it away, for the child may lose it on the earthen floor. The child starts to cry, but his older sister calms him by pressing in his hands a simple wood doll. Breakfast is a broth made from reindeer meat, a little bread, and some cheese. After breakfast the man goes outside again, his oldest son with him. During the day his wife will stay near the house with the children. She will weave the wool from their sheep into fine cloth for their best clothes and for export to Iceland and Norway. Later, when the children become restless, she will take them into the fields behind the house and gather berries.

Meanwhile, the father and eldest son take their bows and arrows, and leading a packhorse walk into the mountains along a glittering brook that splashes past their house. If they are lucky they will shoot arctic hares or even a reindeer, which will be slung on horseback. If the hunt is not successful, the horse will carry back hay from the upper pastures. They will also look for livestock — cattle, sheep, or goats — that may have wandered too far from the house.

In such activities as these, early Norsemen spent their years in Greenland. Settled on a great island that almost touches present-day Canada in the north, voyaging occasionally to the shores of the North American continent, hunting animals more American than European in origin, they may be regarded as the first European colonists in the New World. They lived in Greenland for some five centuries, longer than Europeans have been in America since Columbus came in 1492. And yet we know little about them.

The story of the Norse settlers begins and ends in mystery. We do not know why they came to America; we do not know what happened to them when their settlements were abandoned in the fifteenth century; and we know little about their five hundred years in Greenland. The Greenlanders did not leave the letters, diaries, and civil records historians must rely on to reconstruct the past. In fact, no written documents whatsoever survive from the Norse settlements. Fortunately, the settlers did leave other kinds of records. First are the sagas, tales told by generation after generation of Norsemen around fires in Greenland and Iceland and eventually written down. These tell us something about such people as Leif Ericson and Eric the Red. Then there are Icelandic and European sources — histories, annals, religious and trade records. But these few accounts are frequently inaccurate.

We have another kind of evidence, however. Even when people do not consciously record their lives for posterity, they do create objects scholars can study. During their lifetime they leave walls, churches, dwellings, remnants of tools and toys, fragments of furniture. When they die, their skeletons are left in the ground, clothed in costume of their day.

Studying these and other sources, archaeologists and historians have pieced together a picture of Norse settlement in the West. Their researches have been incredibly diverse. In assembling a history of the world's climate they have tried to learn what happened to the Greenlanders. They have used linguistic analysis and studies of local vegetation to determine what parts of America Leif Ericson visited. Radioactivity remaining in carbon from firepits indicates the age of settlements; animal bones furnish information about the Norse diet; and Eskimo legends suggest what happened to the settlers.

Even these sources, however, are constantly reevaluated. For many years "Vinland," the site of Leif Ericson's colony in America, was thought to have been in New England because grapes (from which the name Vinland comes) are found no farther north. But then it appeared that berries along the coast of Canada were sometimes called grapes and made into wine. Some scholars believed that bones of the Norse settlers show symptoms demonstrating that the Greenlanders' health was deteriorating in the later years of settlement; others disagree. A saga thought to be historically accurate today is supplanted tomorrow.

The historical record is complicated still more by the obscuring litter of forgeries. It is exciting to believe that the Vikings reached not only Newfoundland but also Rhode Island or Minnesota or Oklahoma. "Viking artifacts" have been found in all these places. For many years a tower in Rhode Island was claimed to have been built by Vikings, though it was easily proved that the construction was finished about 1675. Minnesota's Kensington Rune Stone, unearthed in the late 1800s, convinced many that Norsemen had reached the Midwest long before Columbus arrived in America. Subsequently, the stone proved to have been written much later than the date at which it was supposedly composed.

Studying these early men raises frustrating problems, but Norse research is so complex that it is remarkable how much we do know. The Vikings may not have reached Oklahoma or even Minnesota, but they did leave clear marks of their history in Greenland and Newfoundland. Their story begins far from the shores of North America, for the first Viking adventures were European exploits. The Vikings' ancestors had migrated to Scandinavia in ancient times. The Norsemen, inhabitants of modern Norway, lived on the fjords in small villages separated by mountains from the next cluster of setlements. The people farmed and grazed their livestock along steep mountain slopes and fished in the coastal waters.

In the early days the typical Norseman did not travel more than a few miles from his birthplace. His world was his fjord and perhaps the fjord next to it. But late in the eighth century Scandinavians began exploring and raiding hundreds, even thousands of miles from their homes. The word "Viking," which means sea rover, warrior, or pirate, began to be applied to them. The first known Viking raid landed three ships in Wessex, now a part of England, in about 787 A.D. Seven years later Vikings attacked and robbed the great British monastery at Jarrow, a center of European culture. During the next two centuries they conquered large sections of England, Scotland, Ireland, France, and Russia.

Historians have not yet fully explained this sudden change in the Scandinavian activities but find several probable factors. Famine and overpopulation may have incited some Norsemen to find new homes, and the ease with which Vikings could pillage other lands made raiding an attractive occupation. Accustomed to sea travel, they had the best fleets in Europe. Their ships were fast and maneuvered well. Driven by one sail and as many as thirty-two oarsmen, they could easily travel across the North Sea and up the great rivers into the heart of Europe.

Vikings were also great warriors, and they were armed with axes, spears, swords, and javelins. Protected by chain-mail shirts, they usually fought together in a wedge formation. Although they did not carry livestock on raids, they frequently "horsed themselves" — stole mounts from those they attacked. All in all, they were much better warriors than their opponents, easily overwhelming the isolated monasteries that dotted the European countryside. As their strength grew, they were able to assemble large fleets and conquer whole nations as well as great cities.

Once it was apparent that adventure and wealth were to be had on these expeditions, going "aviking" became almost a national pastime. Historians describe Viking expeditions as the chief national industry of the Scandinavian countries between 800 and 1100. The Viking character easily met the new opportunities and challenges. "Viking fury" was a common description. Vikings who attacked enemy troops single-handedly, as if in an enraged trance, were called berserkers. In one story a Viking insists that his friends tie him to a tree when a "fury" comes over him because he does not wish to harm them. At this period a new plea was added to many European prayers: "From the fury of the Vikings, O God, deliver us."

Viking love of exploration and conquest brought the first Norsemen to America. The same movement that planted Vikings in Normandy and Russia later peopled Iceland, Greenland, and Vinland. But the Vikings did not come to America from Europe in one nonstop voyage. Columbus crossed the unknown seas between the Azores and the West Indies in one two-thousand-mile voyage, but Vikings crossed the North Atlantic in relatively short hops. In the ninth century Viking ships raided and occupied Britain, Ireland, and two groups of islands north of Britain, the Orkneys and the Shetlands. From there only a few hundred miles separated them from the Faroe Islands. A few hundred more miles took them to Iceland, the same to Greenland, and finally another few hundred to Newfoundland.

But how did they find their way across the wild North Atlantic to these obscure places? Probably their "discoveries" and settlements were preceded by an accidental sighting in each new region. Ships were frequently blown off course, and in the crystal-clear air blowing from the Arctic they might have been able to see mountainous land more than a hundred miles across open seas. The Irish may have told the Vikings about the islands. In the seventh and eighth centuries Irish monks traveling in crude skin boats had settled religious communities in the Faeroes and Iceland. (These monks deserted Iceland when the Vikings arrived, and some may have gone on to America.)

The Vikings first visited Iceland in 860 and began to colonize after 874. Some of the settlers may have been Norse noblemen fleeing the rule of Harold Fairhair, who conquered all Norway at this time. Others were Norse refugees expelled from Ireland in the early 900s.

Unrest and conflict so disturbed early Iceland that in 930 a movement spread for "law and order." An *althing,* or legislature, was created, studied Norse laws, and adopted a legal code for Iceland. All free landowners could take part in the althing's annual proceedings. It is the oldest extant legislative body in the world.

Through the next four centuries, from 900 to 1300, Iceland continued to grow. In the eleventh century its population may have reached seventy to eighty thousand. The settlers prospered by farming and fishing and by trading with Europe. Then in the fourteenth and fifteenth centuries catastrophes afflicted the Icelanders: colder weather, the bubonic plague, volcanic eruptions, pirate raids, and unfavorable trading conditions in Europe. The plague alone may have killed half the population. Although the island was left poorer and less populous, the Norse Icelandic settlements have survived until today.

For more than a century Iceland was westernmost in the loosely associated Viking Empire, but farther to the west lay another, much larger island, soon named Greenland. Because climate and terrain formed the basis of the history of its people, we must pause to imagine Greenland a thousand years ago, shortly before the first European settlers arrived.

Greenland is the largest island on earth, approximately three times the size of France. Much of it lies north of the Arctic Circle; its northernmost point, Cape Morris Jessup, is only 440 miles from the North Pole. Almost 90 percent of the country is covered by a great ice cap, the world's second-largest glacier. This great mass of ice reaches elevations of ten thousand feet and lies as deep as five thousand feet below the surface of the water. The cap is almost perfectly smooth, completely hiding the mountains and valleys underneath. The glacier has been built up over thousands of years by falling snows, which accumulate on the surface and never melt. It is massive but not inert. Ever building weight at the top pushes down, forcing the ice outward. At the edge of the seacoast the ice may travel as much as one hundred feet in a day, forcing its way into the water and breaking off with a thunderous cascade that can raise great waves and send shocks that kill fish for miles around. The glacial wind worsens the harsh climate of Greenland, sweeping over its icy surface, down the mountains, and out to sea; such is the wind's omnipresence that Admiral Perry, the great nineteenth-century explorer, compared it to water flowing down a slope.

The ice cap is Greenland's most impressive geological feature, but there is another Greenland more hospitable to human life. Between ocean and mountains are many grass-covered valleys, intersected by deep fjords. In places, particularly on the southwest coast, the land is rich in flora and fauna. Meadows filled with flowers, wild berries, birch, willow, alder, and mountain ash lie beside the fjords. The animal life has diminished over the centuries; a thousand years ago the valleys and coastal waters were full of reindeer, arctic hare, codfish, seals, and whales.

Eskimos have lived in Greenland for thousands of years, but the first recorded European contact was Eric the Red's voyage of about 981. Eric, banished from Iceland for killing a man in a feud, might have gone back to Norway but decided to go west instead. We do not know why he made that choice, but he or other Norsemen had once been driven off course and seen the mountainous shores to the west. It is little more than two hundred miles from northern Iceland to Greenland; one can see one island from the other.

Yet it was a courageous voyage that Eric undertook. His vessel, like that of the other westward explorers, was probably a knarr, not one of the Viking raiding ships we associate with Leif Ericson. A trading vessel, the knarr was a broader ship than its sea-raiding cousin. It did not have the dragons or other figures at bow and stern that embellished combat ships. An ancient knarr was recently unearthed near Roskilde Fjord, Denmark. Reasonably well preserved, it helps us imagine what Eric's ship probably looked like. The restored vessel is fifty-four feet long and fifteen feet wide. Its keel and ribs are of oak, and its sides are pine planks caulked with twisted animal hair soaked in pine tar. The ships that sailed the Greenland waters a thousand years ago may have been slightly larger than this vessel and could have held thirty to seventy-five tons of cargo. They were open except for planking over the bow and stern sections for shelter from the elements. Carrying thirty or more people, they were propelled by a large square sail assisted by several sets of oars. The passengers sheltered in fur sleeping bags, which were also used to store their possessions.

In stormy weather with rain or snow falling on the boat and waves bursting over the sides, the vessels must have been hard to live in. There were no pumps and no decking, so that water had to be bailed to keep the vessel afloat. But in good weather with a following wind it would have been easy to forget the storms. We know something about how Viking ships sailed from an 1893 account of a voyage across the North Atlantic in the *Viking,* a vessel modeled on the "Gokstad ship," unearthed a few years before. This was a faithful reproduction, even to having the planks below the waterline tied with plant roots to let the hull flex as it moved through the water. The captain, Marnus Anderson, described the ship's progress sailing before the wind: "In the twilight the Northern Lights threw their fantastic, pale light across the ocean, while the Viking glided over the waves like a seagull. With much admiration we watched the graceful motion of the ship, and with great pride we noted its speed, which from time to time was as high as eleven knots."

Eric the Red left no log, but we can reconstruct his voyage from our knowledge of Norse sailing and from oral accounts of his trip that were later written down. Sailing west from Iceland, he would have been in open sea for several days. His crewmen, like those of Columbus five hundred years later, must have wondered if they would ever see land again, but Norse experience hinted that there was always more land to the west. With fair winds they could see the mountains of Greenland after only two or three days of sailing. Once across the open waters, they worked their way along the Greenland coast looking for good land, arriving finally near present-day Julienhaab. There fertile fields and mountainous fjords were like parts of Iceland and Norway.

It was probably in this region that Eric spent the next three years, his term of banishment. In 985 he returned to Iceland where he told the story of the new land. He was eager to persuade other Icelanders to come and settle with him — perhaps he wanted the prestige of leading a great migration, or perhaps he simply wanted Norse company. He was plainly hoping to promote settlement when he gave the region the appealing if somewhat misleading name of Greenland.

Eric managed to find several hundred Icelanders willing to accompany him to the new country. At the time the good land in Iceland was rapidly being filled. The sagas relate that Eric set out with a fleet of twenty-five boats, fourteen of which reached Greenland. Some may have sunk in the ocean, and others may have returned to Iceland. Once at sea it was not difficult for the Norsemen to find their way back to Green-

Norse ships. In the foreground with the high prow is a fighting ship. The other, in open cross-section, is a trading vessel called a knarr. *Most immigrants to Greenland traveled aboard knarrs.*

land. Although they did not have the compass or the astrolabe, which later navigators used to find their way at sea, they could determine longitude and direction by sun and stars and thus repeat the course of Eric's earlier voyage.

In Greenland the passengers scattered among the fjords looking for homesites. Eric set up his estate in Brattahlid, in one of Geenland's best pasturelands. His home was near the middle of a hundred-mile line of farmsteads, known as the Western Settlement. Other colonists went farther north to farm in an area later known as the Eastern Settlement. In the years that followed, hundreds of other Norsemen came to Greenland. During the eleventh and twelfth centuries the settlers numbered three to five thousand. Of these men and women, some went on to America.

Our first knowledge of the voyagers who went farther west is in the sagas. There are several versions, but the story of Norsemen in America appears consistently. In one of the sagas a man named Bjarni Herjulfson is the first to see America. A trader who carries goods between Norway and Iceland, he returns home to Iceland one winter and learns that his father has moved on to Greenland. Setting out to find him, Bjarni becomes lost. He sights land several times but refuses to stop because the country does not fit the description of Greenland, and he wants to get home. Another account has Leif Ericson, son of Eric the Red, blown off course and making the initial accidental discovery of America. In both versions, Leif makes the first settlement in the new land.

About 1002 A.D. Leif sets out with thirty-five men. He persuades his father to join him, but on the way to the boat Eric the Red falls and injures himself and must stay in Greenland. Leif then sails across the Davis Strait to the shores of North America. Continuing down the coast, he reaches a place abounding in grass, game, and salmon. Here the explorers carry their sleeping robes ashore and put up shelters. It is a fine, fertile land. A fish-rich stream runs through a meadow near the camp. There is plenty of timber to provide a cargo for the return trip, and one of the party even finds wild grapes. Leif and his men spend the winter there and return to Greenland in the next year. In subsequent years successive expeditions to America are led, in turn, by two of Leif's brothers and a sister. They explore other parts of the coast, but they apparently prefer his original settlement.

For centuries people have wondered where Leif's American settlement was. The description of the grapes suggested a location somewhere in New England, but until 1960 no remnant of Viking settlements had been found anywhere west of Greenland. Then Helge Ingstad, a Norwegian archaeologist, found ruins in Newfoundland that appeared to be the remains of the much-sought-after Viking settlement. For several summers he and a team of other archaeologists carefully dug through the site at a place called L'Anse aux Meadows. He found nine dwellings with firepits on the Norse pattern, a primitive smithy, scraps of iron, a stone anvil, and a Norse spindle whorl, used in spinning wool. These were clear indications of a Viking settlement. Moreover, the configuration of land and sea — the meadows, streams, fish, and coastline —followed the description in the sagas. Nearby they even found berries from which wine could be made. If Eric could make "Greenland" out of patches of meadow below an ice cap, certainly Leif could have made "Vinland" (Wineland) of a place with these berries.

In the years ahead other Norse finds may be made in North America. It is sure that many wood-gathering expeditions went to the Labrador forests after Leif's time, and other temporary settlements might have appeared. The location of Leif's colony has almost certainly been established — Samuel Eliot Morison wrote, "We believe Ingstad has it."

Now we have indisputable proof that the Vikings reached America. Both their ability to reach Greenland and their presence on the brim of the American continent for five centuries would make it strange if they had *not* reached America. The surprise is that they did not settle more extensively. Certainly Newfoundland and the land to the south is more hospitable than Greenland. The Indians whom the Vikings encountered in America were hostile, but surely the Norsemen, who had conquered large sections of Europe and had better weapons than the Indians, could have carved out colonies in America if they had wished to do so.

They did not create lasting settlements in Newfoundland and New England simply because they did not need to. They had found good places to live in Greenland, which was itself the outpost of an outpost. Overcrowding in Europe had instigated the migration to Iceland. Overcrowding in Iceland, in turn, had encouraged migration to Greenland. If tens of thousands of Norwegians and Icelanders had sought homes in Greenland, some of them might have gone on to establish permanent settlements in America. But they did not; there was land enough in Greenland.

And so it was on the fjords of Greenland, not the hillsides of New England, that the first European colonists in the New World established their homes. Let us examine their history. Greenland, we must recall, was not a short-lived colony. During the centuries of Norse colonization the earliest settlers had children, grandchildren, and great-grandchildren through ten generations and more. In that time they developed a distinctive culture, combining European and New World influences.

First we have the houses. Faced with winter temperatures of 40 degrees below zero, even on the seacoast, and with strong winds common, the settlers had to build dwellings that would be warm and solid. The early houses were chiefly great halls or main rooms, which served for living, eating, and sleeping. They were made with thick earthen walls and roofs of timbers, sod, and rocks. A central firepit provided warmth, light, and cooking.

These early halls resembled the dwellings of Iceland and Norway, but over the years a new pattern was formed. The large halls, probably too cold and drafty, came to be divided into smaller rooms. At first the great hall was split into two or three rooms. Late in the thirteenth century the "centralized farm" became common. These were large complexes encompassing from fifteen hundred to six thousand square feet and sometimes included rooms for animals. The precious cattle were placed at the very center of the structures.

Heat was provided by thick walls and furs and by modest fires. Probably the settlers spent most of the coldest days wrapped in robes, huddled together, fingers too chilled to spin wool or carve soapstone implements. The driftwood that was almost their only fuel can hardly have been plentiful enough to allow large fires every day. In especially cold times they must have been driven to cut scrub brush growing nearby, though it was needed to keep the winds from ripping away the pastureland. At times, winter isolation might be broken by a visit of neighbors, and in celebration a large fire and huge meal would be prepared. It was around such fires that tales were told that matured into the great Norse sagas. Then the guests would leave, and the family would be left alone in the wind and cold through the long dark winter.

Clothing, too, was influenced by the Greenland environment. Norse graveyards show us that the people sometimes dressed in the hooded, ankle-length woolen gowns worn in Norway. We know the settlements lasted well into the 1400s, because skeletons have been found clad in hooded capes and caps that were worn in Paris and Burgundy late in the fifteenth century. But one wonders if the Norse farmer wore a costume like that to tend the cows or his wife spun and cooked in her woolen gown. The day-to-day costume was more often made from the skins of deer, seals, or cattle. Sealskin trousers and heavy double fur coats were popular.

We know, then, that the Greenlander was well housed and well clothed. He also ate well, consuming the foods he took from the land and the sea. Goats and cattle provided milk that was processed into cheese in large tubs in rooms attached to the living quarters. For meat he ate mainly the flesh of birds, reindeer, and fish caught near the farm. In the summer there were wild berries in the fields nearby. The large number of grindstones found in their houses indicate that the Greenlanders had bread. Some historians contend that the grain must have been imported, but the settlers also grew some of their own and gathered wild grains from the fields and especially along the seashore.

Domestic animals weathered the North Atlantic passage along with their masters. The sheep were a particularly hardy breed, able to survive outside during the winter. The cattle were less sturdy and were housed for the winter either in stalls in the midst of human dwellings or in great long byres or stables, whose thick earth walls faced south to absorb the sun's rays. Some doorways may have been filled with sod after the cattle were brought inside for the winter. Their manure was probably left in the stalls to provide extra insulation against the cold. Their feed was hay, carefully stored from the previous summer, and dried seaweed from the coast. Even so, the cows lost so much weight during the winter they must have looked like skeletons when they finally came out to pasture in the spring.

An animal broth was probably the staple in the Greenlander's diet. People ate with large wood soup spoons; each had his own and carried it with him as a traveler today routinely takes his toothbrush along on a trip. After bones had been boiled into soup or gnawed through for their marrow, they were frequently thrown to the floor. Excavations show floors thickly littered with animal remains.

Making a living in Greenland meant performing a few essential tasks. The men spent their time on the farm in haymaking, herding, milking, and sheep shearing. They made implements from bones, including hoes and spades (from the bones of whales) and also buckles, knife handles, and even padlocks. They also made metal tools from local iron ore. Many of the larger farms had smithies where iron products were made and repaired, including axes, knives, scythes, sledgehammers, harpoons, fishing gear, arrowheads, and spears.

Men and women also spent time on finer crafts. Some carved walrus-tusk ivory into fine chess pieces. The women spun and wove wool from the hardy sheep, creating textiles that found their way from Greenland's fjords across the North Atlantic to Europe. Another necessary craft was carving of soapstone. The Greenland clay was not suitable for making pottery, and so the soft soapstone of the island was cut into bowls, spindle whorls or weights, oil lamps, and even large tubs holding up to forty quarts.

The average Greenlander probably spent most of his life near his own farm. But economic needs in the colonies took some Norsemen on long expeditions. The settlers were on hunting voyages far to the north where they killed walrus and narwhal. The walrus provided meat, ivory, and fur and the narwhal a spiral tusk that was marketed in Europe, sometimes as an alleged unicorn horn. The legendary unicorn was thought to have magical properties, and a powder ground from its "horn" was a popular apothecary item. The northern expeditions were frequent enough that parties were occasionally forced to winter far from the settlements, and at least one small church was built by Norsemen many miles north of the Arctic Circle. The Norsemen also sent expeditions to the coast of Labrador to gather timber and perhaps also to hunt black bear and sable for European trade. We do not know how often ships went to America. In time archaeologists may find artifacts left on the Labrador coast by such expeditions. They must have been common, because timber for houses, fires, and boats was in great demand in Greenland, and the three- or four-day voyage across the sea was relatively easy.

The hunt also took Norsemen on shorter expeditions down the fjords and along the coast. Seals were plentiful in most areas, and were valued for their skins and for their blubber, which could be boiled down into a fine oil for lamps and carried home in skin bags. On some expeditions the Norsemen must have traded with Eskimos, although such trade does not appear to have been an important part of their economy.

For several centuries trade was active between Greenland and Europe. The Norsemen probably imported some products, such as grain, honey, fine cloth, and tools. In turn, they exported many products. Besides woven fabric, walrus tusks, and narwhal horns, they shipped out the hides of walrus, seal, white and blue fox, and polar bear. They also exported some live animals. The Greenland white falcon was popular among European nobles and monarchs, such as Emperor Frederick II. On at least two occasions the Norsemen exported live polar bears; one went to a Norwegian king in appreciation for his appointment of a bishop for the Greenland church.

Norse trade kept the settlers in contact with Europe, and they appear to have traveled often between Greenland, Iceland, and Norway. Government, religion, friendship, and family ties united the far-flung settlements. One even learns of feuds begun in Iceland and concluded in Greenland. But for more than two and a half centuries Greenland was all but an independent country. Its laws were patterned loosely after those of Iceland and Norway. And like the Icelanders, the Greenlanders had an althing, a representative assembly that seems to have had both judicial and legislative functions. The althing at first was held at Brattahlid, ancestral seat of Eric the Red and Leif Ericson. Later it was moved a few miles south to Gardar near the Greenland cathedral. Outside Brattahlid archaeologists have found "booths," small dwellings that were probably used as guesthouses by representatives attending the althing.

In the middle of the thirteenth century Norway asked Iceland and Greenland to acknowledge her jurisdiction, and in 1261 after a long delay Greenland placed itself under the Norwegian crown. Thereafter the king had a representative in Greenland. Although Greenland records are lost, preventing close study of the representative's activities, at least we know he would have overseen the collection of taxes and the maintenance of civil peace. In practice, however, primary authority in the widely spread Norse communities was probably the local chief or the largest landowner.

During most of Greenland's early history the Catholic church was much stronger than the Norwegian government. The first settlers had been pagans, worshipers of Thor, Wodin, and other Norse gods, but the sagas tell how Leif Ericson was converted to Christianity while spending a winter with the king of Norway. The king asked him to take the faith to Greenland, and on his return Leif brought along a priest. His father, Eric, was unwilling to abandon the old gods, but Leif quickly converted his mother, who built a small church at Brattahlid. For a time Eric's wife left his bed, refusing to lie with a pagan. Perhaps to win back his wife, Eric converted to Christianity before his death in 1002.

Norse crucifix. No Medieval European lived farther from Rome, center of Christianity, than the Norsemen of Greenland. And yet for centuries they held on to their Old World faith in a harsh new land.

The new faith grew rapidly in Greenland. Midway through the twelfth century the Western Settlement had four churches; the Eastern Settlement, twelve. In the early years the church suffered from the lack of a local bishop. Only a bishop could carry out many religious functions, such as consecrating bread and wine, confirmation, administering penance, and ordaining priests. Finally in 1124 the king of Norway appointed a bishop for Greenland. The first appointee regretted leaving friends and family far behind but ageed to go to the distant territory.

When the bishop arrived, the Greenlanders built him a cathedral. He was also given his own farm, which became the wealthiest in the land. His residence, at first a large farmhouse, was expanded with a ceremonial hall measuring fifty-five by twenty-five feet. The three fire-pits in the hall included one that covered more than fifty square feet. The church building, ninety by thirty feet, was built of stone and eventually had glass windows. It, too, was heated by three fires and even then was bitterly cold in the winter. Apparently the bishop was allowed to wear gloves while saying mass, a luxury not allowed ordinary priests. The church was dedicated to Saint Nicholas, patron saint of mariners, bakers, and children. On his feast day there would be a torchlight procession to the church and a special service in his honor.

The bishop's influence must have been great in medieval Greenland. His wealth was reflected by the presence on his farm of a byre that could hold more than a hundred cows. The bishop was responsible for collecting church taxes, the so-called Peter's pence, which went to Europe. Most of the Greenlanders paid in "kind," the produce of their farms, and the bishop kept these products in storehouses in Gardar until they could be shipped to Europe. Thus, Greenland sealskins and walrus ivory found their way to Rome and helped pay for the Crusades and for struggles against heretics in Italy. The church now was so powerful that the parliament had been moved from Brattahlid to the great hall at Gardar. In this period two religious houses were also established in Greenland, a Benedictine convent in Siglufjord near a hot spring, and an Augustinian house in Kitisfjord.

These, then, are the outlines of life in the Greenland settlements. They were not mere colonial outposts like Raleigh's Roanoke, which lasted only a year or two, and yet the Norse settlements eventually did die out. Somewhere between 1341 and 1364 the Western Settlement was abandoned, and Greenland trade with Europe diminished. In the 1370s the last bishop who resided in Gardar died. Other bishops were appointed (the last did not die until 1540), but none again went out to his post. The last recorded voyage from Norway to Greenland was in 1410. In the sixteenth century and later, when ties with the New World were reestablished by sailors from France, England, Spain, and the Netherlands, parties of explorers occasionally touched Greenland. Some reported seeing Norse ruins, but none found any Norsemen. What had happened?

In spite of the scant records, we can trace some causes of Greenland's decline. Perhaps the most important one was a climatic change in the fourteenth century; we know that about this time the weather became a good deal colder. Such a drop in temperature must have strained Greenland's resources; more wood would be needed for heat, and the growing season would be shorter. It meant also that ice frequently blocked navigation to Europe. Trade was further inhibited by European conditions. Merchants in Bergen gained a monopoly on the Norwegian trade with the West and curtailed voyages to Greenland. The European market for walrus tusks also fell with an influx of elephant-tusk ivory from Africa. These may not have been the only problems. The bubonic plague, which ravaged Europe in the fourteenth century and struck Iceland and Norway in 1349 and 1350, may well have reached Greenland also. In the late 1300s pirates began raiding Iceland and may have struck Greenland. Locusts and soil erosion could have damaged the crops; and deficiencies in food, brought about by the shorter growing season, may have caused malnutrition.

Let us return, then, to the one thing that is certain: early Norse culture in Greenland did disappear. Many historians believe that the end must have come tragically when a brave people finally succumbed, ravaged by disease, malnutrition, and isolation. Samuel Eliot Morison talks of the last survivors as "hardly able to find enough food to keep alive, staring their eyes out all through the short, bright summer for the ship from Norway that meant their salvation." Gwen Jones speaks of the "inexorable and heart-chilling doom" of the Norsemen.

It is not certain, however, that the ending was so tragic. After all, the Greenland settlements did not disappear overnight. Well over a century passed from the time the Western Settlement was abandoned to the death of the last Norseman in Greenland. The settlements died out, but individual settlers were not necessarily helpless. They might well have chosen their own fates. As the climate deteriorated, many must have decided to go elsewhere. The plague that struck Iceland made land available on that somewhat more hospitable island. The Norse population probably declined steadily during the fourteenth and fifteenth centuries. From several thousand it probably dwindled to several hundred. Of these, some must have decided to stay in the dying settlements; others probably continued the movement back to Iceland; and quite possibly still others merged their lives with the natives of Canada or Greenland, who were now better able to survive than the Norsemen.

We know that assimilation into native populations was a Norse trait. The early Vikings who settled in Russia and France soon became more Russian or French than Scandinavian. As the climate grew colder the Eskimos who lived in the north of Greenland began to settle farther south, and there are indications that they intermingled with the Norsemen. Many Norse artifacts have been found in Eskimo sites, and in the

fifteenth century the Eskimos began building square houses on the
Norse pattern. Early post-Columbian voyagers to Canada mentioned
encounters with light-skinned, fair-haired Indians; some assimilation
may have occurred.

Finally, a few Norsemen must have clung to the old farmsteads
and died in solitude. We have evidence of one such death at a place
labeled Farm 167. Here in a fifteen-room house beside a secluded lake
a Norse skeleton was found by archaeologists. Most Norsemen were
buried in the consecrated ground of the local churchyard. But no one
was there to bury this man; he died alone, the last of his kind.

The final chapter in the history of the Norse Greenlanders is full
of interesting problems, but we should not allow it to obscure the important fact that the settlements survived for centuries before they were
abandoned. In this remote part of the New World, long before Columbus's voyages, Europeans had established their civilization. After 1492
Europeans would again come to America and would eventually dominate the new continents. But the post-Columbian settlements were not
the first Euro-American adventure. In the first the land and the natives
eventually prevailed, absorbing the Europeans.

QUESTIONS

1.   What kinds of evidence have scholars used to learn about the Norsemen in Greenland and Newfoundland?
2.   How did Viking experience prior to Eric the Red's voyage prepare the
way for the Norse discovery and settlement of Greenland?
3.   In what ways did the Greenlanders maintain contact with Europe?
4.   Why didn't the Norsemen establish more colonies on the North
American continent?
5.   In what ways did Norse life in Greenland perpetuate European culture, and in what ways did it respond to the American environment?
6.   What finally happened to the Norse settlements in Greenland?

BIBLIOGRAPHY

GAD, FINN. *The History of Greenland* (2 vols., 1971). Definitive history of
Europeans and Eskimos in Greenland.

INGSTADT, HELGE. *Land Under the Polar Star* (1966). Archaeological report
by the discoverer of Norse ruins in Newfoundland.

JONES, GWEN. *A History of the Vikings* (1968). Good general history of the Vikings.

_____ . *The Norse Atlantic Saga* (1964). Norse voyages to Iceland, Greenland, and beyond.

MORISON, SAMUEL ELIOT. *The European Discovery of America: The Northern Voyages* (1971). Beautifully written and scholarly account.

OLSON, JULIUS E., EDITOR. *The Northmen. Columbus. and Cabot* (1906). Original narratives, including Viking sagas.

QUINN, DAVID BEERS, *England and the Discovery of America. 1481-1620* (1974). England's entry into the New World.

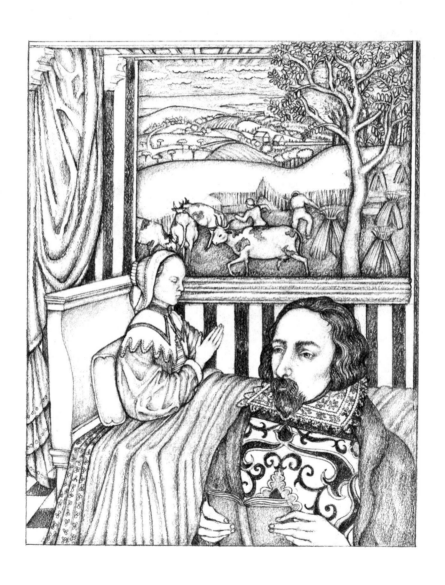

3

THE ENGLISH
BACKGROUND

A
Puritan Death:
John and Thomasine
Winthrop

The first European immigrants to the United States carried with them cargoes of Old World ideas and experiences that influenced the way they farmed their land, organized their governments, and worshiped their deity. One of these imported customs was the Puritan faith, a product of the Portestant Reformation. Nourished in thousands of European homes in the early seventeenth century, Puritanism grew to maturity in its native environment before it was brought to America. It taught men and women how to honor God and deal justly with one another, how to live fully on earth and prepare bravely for heaven. A living faith, it entered the lives of John Winthrop, a founder of Massachusetts, and his wife, Thomasine, molding their daily thoughts and preparing them for their separation in death.

In the fall of 1616 the county of Suffolk, England, was a region of great beauty and industry. The traveler walking or riding a horse along one of the narrow lanes that led from town to town would have been impressed by the meadows dotted with sheep, the fields of dark soil newly plowed for winter crops, and the fine villages. He would see men and women busy at their tasks: farmers plowing fields behind sturdy horses; dairymaids cleaning stalls and preparing milk, butter, and cheese; housewives making soap or gathering herbs from house gardens; woodsmen cutting timber; and townspeople making cloth. In a tavern the visitor might hear men discussing their fields, orchards, and livestock; the land dispute between Smith and Sibley; the marriage of the daughter of a local nobleman; or the religious situation in Germany.

If he had an eye for such things, the visitor could also see God in Suffolk County. The Lord was not as discernible as apples or woolens. But He moved over the land, preserving a good man from a bad fall, prospering the fruit crops, punishing a recalcitrant sinner, and engendering a sense of peace and joy in a believer's heart. It was possible, of course, to live one's life without being aware of God. Many men and women conducted themselves — their planting and harvesting, cooking and cleaning, begetting and child rearing — as if there were no God. But many others were aware of the presence of the Lord and worshiped him in their homes and churches. Occasionally one of the people of Suffolk left his trim cottage and pleasant fields to dwell in heaven with the Lord.

Such a person was Thomasine Winthrop, wife of John Winthrop of Groton Manor. In fall 1616 she would die in childbirth, a common event in seventeenth-century England. In those times one could not enter pregnancy without realizing that death, as well as new life, might be the issue. There is nothing unusual in the fact of Thomasine Winthrop's passing, but if her death in childbirth was commonplace, the record of it is not. Her husband, John, reported the incident in minute detail; his account allows us to stand beside Thomasine in her final days, see people enter and leave her chamber, and listen to the words and gestures exchanged between husband and wife. It also tells us something about the world Thomasine left behind and enables us to study a presence as real as any of these physical events, the relationship between John and Thomasine and their Puritan God.

John and Thomasine were both children of East Anglian gentry families. In the mid-sixteenth century John's grandfather, Adam, had purchased a church property known as Groton Manor when Henry VIII sought to further the Reformation and enrich himself by dissolving the monasteries. A second Adam Winthrop, John's father, inherited the manor.

John Winthrop was born in 1588, the year the English defeated the Spanish Armada. The England he grew up in was a scene of rapid change. In the half century after 1575 there was a fivefold to tenfold increase in the production of coal, salt, iron, steel, lead, ships, and glass. In addition, new industries were established producing copper, brass, paper, soap, sugar, and tobacco. The English began to form great trading companies to tap the wealth of Asia, Africa, and America. Economic historians generally characterize this era of growth as England's first industrial revolution. The energy and resourcefulness that sent miners into the bowels of the earth and drove merchant traders halfway around the world was also reflected in England's nationalism. The defeat of the Spanish Armada had established England as one of the preeminent powers in Europe. When Shakespeare's John of Gaunt called England "This dear, dear land," he was articulating the feelings of most of his countrymen.

These developments in the outside world were not all found, however, at Groton Manor. The Winthrops' involvement in the market economy was on a small scale. When John's mother, Anne, sent to his father in London a woolen shirt and five pairs of socks to sell, she added, "If you would have any for your own wearing, I have more a knitting." Such economic changes as the increase in paper and iron manufacturing might have made it easier to acquire a new Bible or plow, but most of the products at Groton Manor were made locally in ways that had changed little over the centuries.

The land where the Winthrops lived was in the southern part of Suffolk County, near the border of Essex. The rolling countryside was covered with rich farmland; green marshes; ponds; and forests of oak, beech, and willow trees. The county was the first in England to enclose its fields, and the land was intersected with innumerable hedgerows that served as fences. It was noted for its mutton, beef, butter, and cheese. It was a pastoral land, but the white gulls that fed at the Groton Ponds often reminded the people that the sea was only a few miles away.

The Winthrops produced most of the products they consumed. John's father, Adam, kept careful accounts of everything he bought and sold on the manor, most of his payments going to men who worked the land — a few shillings for mowing, digging a ditch, harvesting grain, or thatching a roof. They purchased only a few products: shoes, a plow, nails, paper. Income came from the lands they rented to tenants and from the sale of surplus agricultural produce such as grain, wood, and livestock. With these exceptions, the family produced most of what they ate, drank, and wore.

John was raised on the manor until age fifteen, when he went to Cambridge to attend Trinity College. He stayed at Cambridge for only

two years, returning at age seventeen to help his father manage Groton
Manor. He so impressed his parents with his maturity that they consented to his marriage to Mary Forth, the twenty-year-old daughter of
a neighboring gentryman. John and Mary lived together for ten years
until her death in 1615, when she left him with four children.

Although John lamented Mary's passing, in those days a bereaved
spouse seldom remained single for long. Marriage was a practical as
well as a personal and romantic relationship, for a wife's help was essential in raising children and overseeing a household. Thus, shortly after
Mary's death John began courting Thomasine Clopton, whom he undoubtedly knew already. She was the daughter of William Clopton,
squire of a nearby estate. The couple was married in fall 1615. Thomasine
was a good wife, "industrious," "plainhearted," and "patient of injuries." She showed her love of God in public and private worship and
cared for John's children as if they were her own. John was so attracted
to her that he would recall after her death their affection "had this only
inconvenience, that it made me delight too much in her to enjoy her
long."

During their year together John and Thomasine spent most of
their time in the day-to-day tasks of managing their country estate. The
Winthrop papers and descriptions of other households allow us to draw
a picture of their life. On a typical spring day they would awake with
the crowing of the cock. They would dress quickly in their chilly room
and hurry downstairs to a warm fire prepared by the servants. John's
four children would soon arrive and huddle near the flames to warm
themselves as servants came in from the kitchen. Each morning Winthrop read to the family from the Bible and offered a prayer asking for
God's favor in the day ahead.

After this simple service, parents, children, and servants sat down
at a large table near the fire and began to eat. The presence of servants
at the family table was customary in households like the Winthrops'.
It was only in a later period that the lives of the servants and masters
were sharply divided. Servants at Groton Manor were subject to the
same discipline and much of the same training as John's own children.
In many households servants were included in such family activities as
card games. Advertisements for help sometimes even stipulated that
the prospective employee should be adept at cards. In 1616 John had
decided that cards were not a proper pastime in a Christian household,
but he did share other activities with his servants.

At breakfast John and Thomasine might discuss the day's activities
with the children and servants. After they finished the meal, John would
be likely to tour the manor to see that all was in order, inspecting cattle

and pigs and supervising his servants in the fields or woodlot. On many spring mornings the air was damp and cold, but there were pleasant days when the sun broke through the clouds to the east and the wind bore the scent of salt water from the North Sea. Since most physical labor at Groton was done by servants, Winthrop could devote time to studying the Bible and performing religious works. We may imagine him retiring to his study after touring the manor.

Thomasine would probably supervise the domestic chores, seeing that the rooms were dusted, the floors swept, the butter churned, and the meals prepared. She might attend personally to a garden of flowers, vegetables, and herbs. Whereas the men supervised grain cultivation, English women usually planted radishes, beets, carrots, cabbage, cucumbers, onions, melons, parsley, cloves, and other garden crops.

At noon the cook would ring a bell summoning the household for the main meal of the day. Afterward, glad to have the excuse to ride through the country lanes, leading a small packhorse as he went, John might visit a neighboring tenant to collect rent in the form of grain. If the tenant were also a friend, they might discuss last Sunday's sermon, both men recognizing their Christian duty to extend the religious training of the Sabbath through the week.

At the manor Thomasine and the servants might spend the afternoon washing clothes, an arduous task performed only once monthly. They must first carry water by hand and then heat it over the fire and pour it into a large tub, where dirty clothes were soaped and scrubbed. The manor was virtually self-sufficient; even soap might be made from a combination of lye, leached from wood ashes, and household grease. Once Thomasine and the servants had thoroughly cleaned the clothes, they would put them in a second tub to rinse and hang them on a line. All the women, including Thomasine, would take turns at the work. At supper the family might discuss the day's events. John would again read from the Bible, and they would sing a psalm.

In spring 1616 Thomasine learned that she was pregnant. She and her husband must have often discussed the new baby, John wondering whether she felt well, and Thomasine worried about the older children's reaction to a new brother or sister. John might tell her, as he later wrote in his diary, that his children already loved her like a mother.

On the surface, life at Groton Manor seems a kind of agrarian paradise. The family is close; everyone is well fed, clothed, and housed; the men and women spend their days in honest toil. There is, however, another side to life at Groton. Like human beings of other times and places, John and Thomasine were troubled by domestic and political problems.

Most of the Winthrops' servants were reliable, but some were not. Thomasine characterized one as a "stubborne wenche" and believed another had been spoiled by a background of "badd servinge" in an alehouse. The world around them presented other problems. Families once wealthy were ruined by new economic forces. Changes in land use threw men out of work, and filled the roads with "sturdy beggars," men physically able to work but unable to find employment. Some turned to petty crime — John's father, Adam Winthrop, was robbed at least once by "false knaves." His diary includes frequent references to violence in the neighborhood — assaults, murders, suicides. Disease also scourged the country, sometimes killing large numbers in epidemics.

In a world full of confusion and change the Winthrops' God provided them with a sense of peace and stability. John and Thomasine believed that they should think constantly about their relationship to God rather than become overly absorbed in the joys and sorrows of everyday life. John and Thomasine believed in salvation by faith, the main doctrine of the Protestant Reformation on the Continent and in England. The Reformation had begun with Martin Luther's conviction than men must be saved by God's grace rather than by their own good works. The emphasis on grace was absorbed by John Calvin, who in turn influenced the early English Reformers. Under Queen Elizabeth, who ruled England in the latter part of the sixteenth century, and King James, who reigned in the first quarter of the seventeenth, the doctrine of salvation by faith held a high position in English worship. Some Englishmen did want further reformation of the church, but most were willing to accept the status quo. John Winthrop and others like him would eventually disagree with the church policies of the 1620s and identify themselves as "Puritan" opponents of the established religion, but in his early years his piety was nourished by Church of England ministers.

We can better understand Puritanism, and the elusive doctrine of faith, if we survey its influence on John Winthrop as recorded in his papers. At age ten he had come to have "some notions of God," but he characterized himself as being "lewdly disposed," "wild and dissolute," and dominated by a "voluptuous heart." This description does not mean that he spent his time drinking, whoring, and stealing. In fact, the only youthful sin he specifically mentions in his later writings is the theft of two books as a small boy. When Winthrop refers to himself as possessing a "voluptuous heart," he is probably describing his imagination rather than his actual behavior. Although such activity may not seem to qualify as "dissolute behavior" today, this failure to master his desires grieved Winthrop. He believed that a good Christian would discipline his heart and think about God in all his free moments. There was sin, he believed, in "all such works as are done to fulfill the will of the flesh rather than of the spirit."

By age eighteen John Winthrop was deeply perturbed about his spiritual condition. Now for the first time the word came into his "heart with power." He would walk for miles to hear a good sermon, and he developed a reputation for giving spiritual advice to others. But he also became too proud, and because he realized that without Christ's grace all his good works would not save him, he began to despair, feeling that perhaps he was only a hypocrite.

Throughout his twenties Winthrop's religious life consisted of alternating periods of assurance and doubt. He abandoned hunting and cards because he felt that they interfered with his religious life. He attempted to devote more time to prayer, meditation, and religious reading but frequently failed to meet his own high standards of conduct. He accused himself of having become too frivolous in his relationships with friends and of having eaten and drunk more than was appropriate. Once he condemned himself because during a church service his mind wandered to a journey he was about to taken into Essex, and soon he was "possessed with the world." He sought to "tame his heart" by regulating his diet, singing psalms while traveling, and reading religious tracts. But he found that complete abstinence from the pleasures of the world left him "melancholy" and "dumpish." He discovered that complete asceticism was as destructive to his spiritual equilibrium as excessive worldliness. The problem was to find a moderate course between these two extremes. The Puritans had a phrase that aptly described their relationship to material pleasures. "Wine," they said, "is from God, but drunkenness is from the devil."

The goal of Winthrop's constant self-regulation was a relationship with Christ that he could feel. Puritans believed that grace came when one preferred heavenly to earthly treasures. Moments of spiritual ilumination were rare but compelling. In 1612, for example, after comforting an old man with spiritual advice, Winthrop went to bed and dreamed that he was with Christ. "I was so ravished with his love towards me," he writes, "that being awakened it had made so deep impression in my heart, as I was forced to unmeasurable weepings for a great while."

Despite the experience of such periods of ecstatic acceptance, John often felt that he was too concerned with the world. His religious life was a constant struggle to "tame" his heart to complete service to God. On the manor he was responsible for overseeing a complex economy, planting crops, buying and selling livestock, gathering rents, and a dozen other duties. But important as these activities were, when he wrote about his own life or went to bed at the end of the day his greatest worry was frequently whether his rebellious heart had indulged itself too much in the world.

We know less about Thomasine's religious life than we do about John's, but it is apparent that she, too, was a serious Christian and believed that salvation came through God's grace. John later praised her for her reverent attention to religious services at home and in church and remarked that she avoided "all evil" herself and reproved sin in others. Undoubtedly on many evenings after they had discussed crops, children, or servants, they would end the day by praying or reading scriptures together. Together they would pursue the path of moderation.

John and Thomasine thus spent their days attending to matters temporal and spiritual. The year 1616 progressed from season to season. In the summer there were bright days interrupted by occasional sharp storms of thunder and lightning. Then came time to harvest and thresh the wheat. In October gray clouds hung over the countryside, and the crisp night air and the geese flying overhead announced the approach of winter. The hearth with its crackling fire drew the family to it in the morning. John and Adam dragged their main pond, catching carp for dinner. In preparation for winter the family salted fish and pressed apples into cider to store in the cold cellar.

Now that Thomasine was pregnant, she was less active. She spent time preparing for the new baby, making blankets and a bunting. She spent more time with the children, playing games and helping them read. In November she had difficulty moving and sleeping comfortably. Then on Saturday, November 30, she felt that her time had arrived. John summoned a midwife, who came to the house with several neighbor women. They heated kettles of water and encouraged Thomasine, who bore her pains patiently and asked constantly about the child. People would later remark "how careful she was" for the life of the baby in her travail. At last the infant was born, a tiny girl. She was washed by the women and then placed alongside her mother. John now entered the chamber and sat beside Thomasine and their new daughter. He offered prayers of thanks for the safe delivery.

That night John slept in a separate room, leaving Thomasine under the watchful eye of a "keeper," a woman who made sure that mother and child were well. On the following morning, a Sunday, John arose early and came to the room. When Thomasine awoke, he sat with her and prayed for the continuing health of his wife and daughter. After breakfast John, his parents, and the other children went to church.

Later that Sunday the child began to weaken, and on Monday morning the Winthrops' new daughter was dead. John later reported that Thomasine took the child's death with "patience," by which he meant that she accepted the loss as God's will. Thinking of Thomasine's earlier worry about the baby girl, people now "marvelled" at her ability to accept her death.

But John had little time to think about the loss of his infant daughter. Thomasine now became ill, suffering from a violent fever and a cough. The next morning these symptoms were allayed, but she was hoarse, her mouth was sore, and her throat bled. John began to fear for her life and on Wednesday sent for his cousin, a doctor.

When she heard that a physician was coming, Thomasine told John that she expected to die. His account of their conversation at this moment is so detailed that we can virtually hear their words. Frequently, ill persons were not told the truth about their ailments for fear of upsetting them, but Thomasine did not wish to be deceived. "John," she said, "when cousin Duke comes, I hope that he will deal plainly with me and not fill me with vain hopes."

Forced by his wife to acknowledge the seriousness of her condition, John began to cry. Thomasine was moved by his concern and begged him "to be contented" — to accept her condition with patience — "for you break my heart," she said, "with your grievings."

John replied, "I can do no less when I fear to be stripped of such a blessing."

Bedridden, seriously ill, Thomasine sought to comfort her husband. John later recalled that "always when she perceived me to mourn for her, she would entreat and persuade me to be contented, telling me that she did love me well, and if God would let her live with me, she would endeavour to show it more." She urged him to pray for her and stay as near as possible.

At noon Thursday the doctor arrived, and after examining Thomasine he declared that her condition was dangerous. When John told her this, she was "no whit moved at it, but was as comfortably resolved whether to live or to die." In this condition of resignation, of willingness to accept life or death from God, she fell asleep. She awakened at midnight, and feeling that death was near called to John to help her prepare. She wanted also to see her two ministers and other friends and so desired "that the bell might ring for her." In the early morning hours neighbors came one by one to talk by candlelight "quietly and comfortably" with Thomasine. Then the bell began to ring. John tells us, "Some said it was the 4 o'clock bell, but she conceiving that they sought to conceal it from her, that it did ring for her, she said they needed not, for it did not trouble her."

The ringing of the bell was a traditional way of telling a community that someone was critically ill. It allowed men and women in and around Groton who knew of Thomasine's illness to visit her or say prayers or simply think of her. The bell did not always announce a person's death — some for whom it rang recovered — but it always meant that the community might be losing one of its members. It was with this tradition in mind that the seventeenth-century English poet, John Donne, concluded a meditation on the interdependence of humanity with the line, "never send to know for whom the bell tolls; it tolls for thee."

In a small community like Groton, everyone knew for whom the bell tolled, and eventually the two ministers and more friends arrived. When the Reverend Mr. Sands appeared, Thomasine "reached him her hand, being glad of his coming." He questioned her about various religious matters and was surprised at the maturity of her answers. He said that he had "taken her always for a harmless young woman" but did not expect to find her so well "grounded" in religion. The second minister was impressed with her patience in the face of death and her "great comfort in God" and concluded "that her life and been so innocent and harmless as the devil could find nothing to lay to her charge."

At six o'clock the next morning the doctor came again. First he concluded that she had "received her death's wound" in the night but might languish for another day or two. Then, after feeling her pulse, he said that there was "some hope left." During the day Thomasine began to feel better and her next night was good; she "began to entertain some thought of life, and so," says John, "did most of us who were about her."

On Saturday, however, her condition worsened. She felt cold and told John to set his heart at rest; now, she said, "I am but a dead woman." She believed that her left hand was already dead and could not be persuaded that it was merely numb because she had slept on it. When John asked Thomasine to replace her gloves — in keeping with tradition, she was completely dressed — she at first refused, saying that it was vanity to cover a dead hand, but then she consented to please her husband.

In the next few hours she became increasingly disturbed. She complained of pain in her breast and appeared distracted. She believed that she was fighting with Satan; in her struggle she spat, clenched her teeth, fixed her eyes, and shook her head. Then she became calm, lifted herself in bed, and prayed "earnestly that she might glorify God, although it were in hell." She exhorted those around her to serve God and asked that the window curtains be opened. Formerly she had wanted them closed, but now she desired light.

Now certain that she would die, she asked to see each member of her family one at a time to give them her final advice. Her parting words to her sister included admonitions to serve God, marry for religious rather than worldly considerations, avoid lying, and raise her children well. Then she spoke to her mother, remarking that she, Thomasine, was the first child her mother would bury, and praying that she would not be "discomforted." Her mother, a pious woman, replied, "I have no cause to be discomforted. You will go to a better place, and you will be with your father again." The thought must have comforted the mother, but Thomasine, perhaps overly self-righteous now, said that since she would go to God she would be with "a better father than her earthly father."

She next spoke to members of John's family, thanking his parents for their kindness and blessing the children. She spoke to the servants, praising some and scolding others and encouraging them to behave well and to observe the Sabbath. Finally she told the woman who had served as her keeper not to blame herself if she died.

Thomasine was still in great pain. Her breasts were so swollen that her friends cut her waistcoat to give her some relief. She uttered many prayers and urged those around her to prepare to die, telling them they did not know "how sharp and bitter the pangs of death were." Reflecting on the church, she asked God to "bless good ministers, and convert such ill ones as did belong to him, and weed out the rest."

It was apparent that "God had given her victory" in her spiritual struggle. In the afternoon her pains lessened, and she told John she expected to live for another twenty-four hours. Through the afternoon and evening he read the Scriptures to her. Thomasine was attentive, asking John "earnestly" to read on whenever he paused and remarking on his texts. "This is comfortable," or "This is a sweet psalm," she would say.

In the evening the Reverand Mr. Sands came and prayed. Thomasine took him by the hand to say farewell. John retired, leaving his wife in the care of a woman who continued to read to her into the night. Thomasine frequently asked about John, and at two o'clock on Sunday morning he got up and came to her again.

At times Thomasine again had doubts about her conversion, saying that the devil wanted her to cast off her "subjection" to her husband. At noon, when others were at dinner, John and Thomasine continued to talk. John assured her of Christ's love for her and told her "how she should sup with Christ in paradise that night." From Groton Manor in Suffolk, England, she would actually go into the presence of Abraham, Isaac, Jacob, and the other prophets, apostles, and saints. This thought so encouraged Thomasine that she said, "if life were set before her she would not take it."

Thomasine and John conversed throughout the afternoon. He told her that the previous day had been the first anniversary of their marriage

Groton Church. In small English parish churches such as this men and women like John and Thomasine Winthrop first encountered the Puritan God. Many, like John Winthrop, took their faith to the New World.

and that now she was going to Christ, who would "embrace her with another manner of love." She misunderstood him and replied, "O husband, I must not love thee as Christ."

After a while she could no longer speak but lay back, her eyes "steadfastly" on John as he spoke to her about the promises of the gospel and the "happy estate" she was "entering into." If he paused, she would signal him feebly with her hands, urging him to continue. A minister came to pray with her at five o'clock on Sunday afternoon. At the end of the prayer she sighed and fell "asleep in the Lord." Three days later she was buried beside John's first wife in Groton chancel. Her child was taken from its tiny grave and laid by her.

Thomasine's death led John to a period of intense self-scrutiny. He regarded his loss as punishment from God. This was a typical Puritan response to the death of a loved one. One had to recognize his or her dependence on Christ in order to be saved. One sought, but frequently could not find, this sense of dependence. But the death of a loved one proved the frailty of human life and led one to seek the God who transcended human life. During Thomasine's illness John had felt his heart "humbled and God's free mercy in Christ more open to me than at any time before to my remembrance."

Although he does not tell us exactly what happened in the moments immediately after Thomasine died, we can readily imagine his behavior. He must comfort his children, who had come to regard Thomasine as their own mother. He would encourage and exhort everyone: Thomasine had died bravely; she was now in heaven; God had his reason for taking her and must be loved. As he spoke his mind must have been feverish with thought: *She is dead, God has punished me. I have relied too much on the creature, I will not set my mind on the world again. This life is transitory. Our home is in heaven.*

We know that in the days that followed Winthrop thought often about the course of his life. A small sin committed many years before troubled him. As a boy visiting a house he had spied two small books. Reasoning that the owner had thrown them away, he took them with him. The memory of that act grieved him, especially in times of affliction. Now, troubled once more, he made "satisfaction" for the books, probably by paying something to the former owner.

In January 1617 Winthrop attended a court session, usually an occasion for entertainment and frivolity as well as judicial business. This time he felt detached and was bemused by the respect paid by other men to wealth and pleasure. Later, on a trip to London, he mentioned that he used to "lose all my time in my journeys, my eyes running upon every object, and my thoughts varying with every occasion." But now he passed the time in prayer, psalm singing, and meditation.

In later years Winthrop would identify this period as his time of greatest piety, and he felt powerfully that Christ accepted and loved him. This was not merely an intellectual conclusion but rather a pressing conviction of Christ's presence. He wrote, "I was now grown familiar with the Lord Jesus Christ. He would oft tell me he loved me. I did not doubt to believe him. If I went abroad he went with me, when I returned he came home with me. I talked with him upon the way, he lay down with me and usually I did awake with him. Now I could go into any company and not lose him."

Thus, after Thomasine's death John Winthrop spent many hours meditating about a being whom he could love without fear of loss. He took comfort in the belief that there is in this world a reality that transcends human life. Some men and women who have been possessed by this realization have concluded that they should withdraw from the world and worship God in a monastery or convent. Some, like Thomasine, have anticipated a moment when their spirit would leave the world and actually dwell with God. But John Winthrop did not withdraw from the world. Another aspect of Puritanism helped him find his way.

Puritanism taught that life was precious as well as transitory, that men have a duty to make their lives and their societies conform to the will of God. This perception carried Winthrop into the Puritan opposition to the religious policies of King Charles and Archbishop Laud in the late 1620s. Because he was intelligent, energetic, and persuasive, he would become the leader of a group of Puritans who decided to go to America and form there a "Holy Commonwealth," conforming to God's will.

Eventually John, too, would leave Groton Manor, consoling himself for the loss of his home by recalling that all life is transitory and that man finds fulfillment only in the life of the spirit. Thus, the piety that prepared Thomasine for death also prepared John for America.

QUESTIONS

1. The Puritans believed in salvation through Christ's grace. How did they attempt to bring themselves closer to Christ?

2. What kinds of thought and behavior did Puritans discourage? Give specific examples and explain the reasoning behind each.

3. What did Puritans mean when they said that wine is from God but that drunkenness is from the devil?

4. What are the chief characteristics of Puritan family life as exemplified by the Winthrops?

5. How did Thomasine's behavior in childbirth and death reflect her Puritan piety?

6. Explain this statement: "The piety that prepared Thomasine for death also prepared John for America."

7. The Winthrop household was typical of preindustrial households in England and America. Describe the "economy" of the household (how products

were produced, exchanged, and consumed) and describe the roles of husband and wife in the household.

BIBLIOGRAPHY

BREMMER, FRANCIS. *The Puritan Experiment* (1976). Historical survey of Puritanism.

BRIDENBAUGH, CARL. *Vexed and Troubled Englishmen* (1967). English society on the eve of the Great Migration.

HAMBRICK-STOWE, CHARLES E. *The Practice of Piety* (1982). Excellent account of Puritan devotional practices.

MIDDLEKAUFF, ROBERT. *The Mathers: Three Generations of Puritan Inellectuals* (1971). Intellectual biography of three Puritan ministers.

MILLER, PERRY. *The New England Mind* (2 vols., 1939, 1953). Standard intellectual history of the Puritans.

_____AND THOMAS H. JOHNSON, EDITORS. *The Puritans* (2 vols., 1963). Anthology of Puritan writings.

MORGAN, EDMUND S. *The Puritan Dilemma* (1958). Excellent short biography of John Winthrop.

_____ . *The Puritan Family* (1966). Survey of domestic life.

MORISON, SAMUEL ELIOT, ET. AL. EDITORS. *Winthrop Papers* (2 vols., 1929, 1968). Includes John Winthrop's spirtual musings and his account of Thomasine's death.

STANNARD, DAVID. *The Puritan Way of Death* (1977). Provocative but misleading description of Puritan encounter with death.

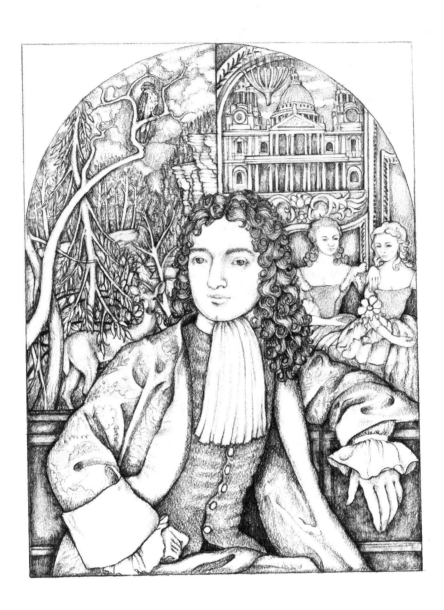

4
THE BRITISH
AMERICAN

William Byrd
in Two Worlds

Europeans lived in the New World for several generations before they began to think of themselves as Americans. Britain dominated their government and culture: the colonists honored a British ruler and admired British literature, music, and architecture. By 1700 Americans possessed most of the coastal regions but looked eastward across the Atlantic rather than westward over the Alleghenies to discover who they were. William Byrd's career demonstrates the colonists' tendency to regard England as home. He spent much of his life in England pursuing his fortune. Finally, however, it was in America rather than in England that he and other settlers found the greatest use for their talents.

The sun went down behind the steep, forested ridge of the Alleghenies. Resplendent stars shone brightly in the clear autumn sky while bear, deer, and opossum foraged among the darkened trees. In the midst of a vast and potent wilderness there glowed a solitary campfire, a flickering circle of light illuminating tents, horses, and a cluster of men.

The men standing by the campfire were working their way through swamps and brush surveying a dividing line between the colonies of Virginia and North Carolina. Their supplies had long since run low, and most of their horses were lame. Nonetheless, their camp was festive: this was October 30, 1728, the king's birthday, and patriotism led them to consume spirits and discharge fireworks in celebration of their nationhood. The men were doing their best, toasting King George II with the last of their liquor, a bottle of cherry brandy carefully preserved by their leader, William Byrd, and drinking to the queen and all her royal progeny with drafts of pure water from an Allegheny tributary. To complete the celebration, they set off explosives, fashioned of green cane from a nearby field, and laid in the fire. The air within the cane joints expanded and punctured the night air with loud and satisfying bangs.

When William Byrd recorded this episode, he considered it natural to honor the English king. Although he was a third-generation Virginian out in a land of American Indians and American forests, he regarded himself as an Englishman and was accustomed to celebrating his transatlantic heritage. In the middle period of colonial history, Byrd lived in two worlds — provincial Virginia and Georgian England. It was as natural for him to observe the king's birthday in the American wilderness as for any British subject in London.

Byrd's history, remarkable for his dramatic and wide-ranging achievements, highlights important features of British-American life. Byrd was many things — planter, gentleman, politician, writer, and lover. A contemplative as well as an active man, he sought to live a full and dignified life alternately as a London gentleman and as a southern planter. In certain respects he succeeded in standing astride the Atlantic, half British and half American; yet his life also exhibits a tension between the two worlds. As a colonial American he was unable to achieve the stature he sought in London; as an Englishman he had difficulty feeling at ease in provincial Virginia.

Byrd's history can be seen as the story of a man seeking to locate himself, to find a "home." His quest for personal satisfaction in two worlds was full of contradictions. He was a moralistic libertine, a contemplative gadabout, a provincial cosmopolitan. In some ways he was an unattractive figure; he was arrogant, undisciplined, insensitive. But at the same time he was peculiarly open, forthright, and perceptive. Because he lived fully and left accounts that reveal his multifaceted personality, he appears to us as a peculiarly vital and accessible human being, a representative figure in an America that did not yet know itself as America.

The William Byrd of our story was the second Virginian of that name. His father and namesake, William Byrd I, was the son of a prosperous London goldsmith named John Byrd. The elder William, born in 1652, might well have stayed in England and followed his father's trade, but he was drawn to Virginia in 1670 by an invitation from his uncle, Capt. Thomas Stegg. It was through the Stegg family that the Byrd dynasty in Virginia made its start. Capt. Thomas Stegg was the son of an earlier sea captain of the same name, an Atlantic trader, who was appointed by Parliament during the English Civil War to sail to Virginia and demand that the colony acknowledge the rule of Oliver Cromwell. Stegg completed his mission but was lost at sea on his return passage in 1651. He left his property to the younger Cap. Stegg, whose sister married John Byrd and bore the nephew whom Thomas recalled in his later years. Because he lacked an heir, he invited this nephew, William Byrd I, to come to Virginia and, by implication, to take over his land.

Thus, as a youth of eighteen, William Byrd I went to Virginia to seek his fortune. Unlike the original southern pioneers who died by the hundreds from starvation, disease, exposure, and Indian attacks in the first bleak years at Jamestown, and unlike the Pilgrims of Plymouth Rock who found no "inns to refresh their weather-beaten bodies," William Byrd I arrived in a wilderness that was already somewhat civilized. He sailed up the James River in 1670 and landed near his uncle's substantial two-story stone plantation house.

William Byrd I hardly had time to settle into his new surroundings before his uncle died, leaving the young man a Virginia estate. Byrd took good care of his inheritance, thanks in part to the help of a young woman named Mary Horsemanden Filmer, whom he married in 1673. She was the daughter of Sir Warham Horsemanden, a staunch supporter of King Charles II. Her family would supply the Byrds with valuable connections in England.

In 1674 the couple's first child was born. Named William Byrd II, he spent his early years on his father's Virginia plantation, the hub of extensive agricultural and trading activity. The elder Byrd raised tobacco, which he exchanged for African slaves and English manufactured goods. His plantation was an entrepôt for trade with smaller planters and with remote Indian tribes. As a boy, William could watch large packtrains with several score horses forming near his house in preparation for their journey along the Trading Path four hundred miles into the interior to the lands of the Catawba and the Cherokee. In those distant regions they exchanged cloth, blankets, beads, pots, pans, hatchets, guns, lead, and rum for the hides of bear, deer, beaver, otter, mink, and buffalo.

By engaging in such activities the elder Byrd increased his fortune, and in colonial America wealth generally led to political influence. The colonists had already broken with some of the aristocratic traditions of England. The colonial electorate was proportionately larger than the English. In both regions one must be a free adult male with fifty acres of land or fifty pounds in property in order to vote, but in America the widespread availability of land made it much easier to acquire the fifty acres. Although one could not vote for the governor or for members of the upper house of the legislature — in most colonies they were appointed by the crown — one could elect the lower house, called in Virginia the House of Burgesses.

Widespread political participation did not, however, undermine the relationship of wealth, social position, and political influence. The colonial ruling elite as well as the English aristocracy assumed that these forms of power belonged together. The upper house of the colonial legislature consisted of the wealthiest colonists, and even the House of Burgesses was mainly composed of well-to-do planters. They alone could afford to leave their plantations in the care of overseers and serve without pay in the legislature. It was generally assumed that the wealthy were the fittest to rule. Their plantation experience educated them in government, and their superior social position reminded colonists of their accustomed rulers in Europe. It seemed natural to think of such men as leaders.

With his success as trader and planter, it was inevitable that the elder Byrd should join the provincial elite. But his career was almost ruined by an event that occurred while he was still in his twenties, a curious episode in Virginia history known as Bacon's Rebellion. In 1676 an unauthorized frontier war against Indians culminated in a revolt against the colonial governor, Sir William Berkeley. The revolt was once interpreted as a democratic upheaval, but is now generally understood as having been a conflict for privilege among factions of Virginia gentry. The minor reforms that followed the fall of the rebels somewhat broadened the circle of privilege in Virginia, but it did not end the assumption that wealth and power should be closely intertwined.

William Byrd I nearly became one of the victims of the rebellion. A frontier planter, he was so worried by the Indian attacks that in 1676 he sent his wife and child to England to escape the conflict. In their absence he joined rebel Nathaniel Bacon's attacks on the Indians.

But when Bacon waged war on the governor, Byrd wisely sided with Berkeley.

His wife and son returned from their short exile in 1677 to find that Byrd had chosen the winning side and had thus launched a political career that would take him to the House of Burgesses, the Provincial Council, and in 1687 to the position of auditor of public accounts and receiver general of Virginia. When his son reached age seven, Byrd sent him to England to attend school, as was customary among the Virginia gentry. Lacking a local college, the Virginia aristocrats assumed that a child must go abroad to receive a good classical education and become familiar with the larger world. Thus, in 1681 William Byrd II left home on his first long pilgrimage to England.

In London he was placed under the care of his maternal uncle, Daniel Horsemanden, who sent him to Felsted School, thirty-five miles northeast of London. Felsted was a tiny island in the rolling fields of Essex but was well respected because its headmaster, Christopher Glasscock, was reputed to be one of the best schoolmasters in England. William Byrd passed his early youth at Felsted. In the chill fogs of rural Essex, far from the hot sultry air of plantation Virginia, he learned, played, ate, and lived in a world of boys; his earlier world, the place of father, mother, servants, slaves, and traders, must have seemed as remote and unreal as a dream.

William Byrd's classical education influenced his thought and behavior for the rest of his life. Felsted taught him Latin, Greek, and probably Hebrew. It introduced him to the history of ancient civilizations and grounded him in biblical and classical philosophy. In later years he read the ancient tongues almost daily, perhaps because he had first met them after he had lost his family and his native land. They may have given him a sense of continuity and stability in the changing environments, cultural as well as personal, of his existence.

In 1689, at age fifteen, Byrd was ready to leave Felsted to embark on the second phase of his education. His father was eager that his son, who would inherit the Virginia estate, should not be an untutored provincial in the world of commerce. Thus he sent him to the Netherlands to learn the "fine business sense" of the Dutch merchants. In the following year, he transferred the boy to the London firm of Perry and Lane, merchants who handled the family dealings in tobacco and furs.

Byrd's education took another turn in 1692 when he entered the Middle Temple in London to study law. The Temple, one of the most ancient and respected educational institutions in England, was a school for dramatists, scientists, and merchants as well as lawyers. Its emphasis on culture and gentlemanly behavior attracted the sons of many leading English families. At the Temple, Byrd studied the law and qualified for the bar in 1695; during this time he also developed a taste for drama, science, conversation, and women.

His interest in the drama was encouraged by three of the leading English dramatists of his generation, William Wycherley, William Congreve, and Nicholas Rowe, all of whom studied with Byrd at the Temple. Many great plays, including Shakespear's *Twelfth Night*, had premiered at the Temple Theatre. Byrd's devotion to drama continued through many evenings at Drury Lane and the Queen's Theatre in London; in later years his extensive library in Virginia would include several hundred plays, probably the largest collection in America.

Byrd also maintained an active amateur interest in science. Through a family friend and personal confidant, Sir Robert Southwell, he was admitted to the Royal Society in 1696. This organization brought together the greatest scientific minds in England; Byrd's colleagues included such eminent men as Sir Isaac Newton. Byrd's contributions were limited, but he maintained an avid interest in the society throughout his life and corresponded for many years with some of its members, including Charles Boyle, Earl of Orrery.

Science and drama contributed to a third area of activity in London — Byrd's interest in polite conversation. If one activity stands out above all others in Byrd's life, it is human discourse. Many of his days seem to have been spent in talking with friends about literature, drama, science, and society. They met in each others' rooms, in coffeehouses, and at fashionable spas, such as Tunbridge Wells.

Finally, Byrd was interested — to the point of obsession — in the opposite sex. Many years after he left the Middle Temple he recalled his youthful "intrigues" with "naughty jades" in a letter to his former partner in lust, Benjamin Lynde, a staid and proper chief justice of Massachusetts. The dramatist William Wycherley, another Temple friend, is supposed to have introduced Byrd to the taverns, gambling, and women that made up much of London's night life. We have no diary of these early activities, but Byrd hints at them in a letter to a godson, whom he counsels: if you must be punished at school, don't let it be for failure to study, "but for some sprightly action or gaiety of heart." Byrd's own sprightliness is indicated in a brief autobiographical piece entitled "The Enamored Bird." Writing of himself in the third person, he says, "Love broke out upon him before his beard, and he could distinguish sexes long before he could tell the difference betwixt good and evil." He continues that it is fortunate that he did not have a twin sister, for he might have had an affair with her in their mother's womb.

There were many opportunities for a young man to find sexual companionship among London's prostitutes and with women looking for temporary alliances, and Byrd appears to have known many of them during his twenties. But as he neared his thirtieth birthday he began to think of marriage. Lady Elizabeth Cromwell, a bright, clever, attractive young woman, seemed a likely candidate. She promised to be a stimulating companion to a successful suitor, and she would bring her husband an annual income of £2,000 a year, enough to enable Byrd to live easily in England for the remainder of his life. But Lady Elizabeth had other plans. In summer 1703 she went to Ireland, leaving Byrd, as he complained to her, with his soul "perfectly out of tune." He wrote that she was wasting herself on Ireland, a country "so disagreeable that even toads and spiders disdain to live in it." But this effort was all to no avail: she married another man.

In disparaging Ireland, Byrd revealed sentiments he may have harbored toward his remote homeland in America. He had learned to take a cosmopolitan view of distant regions. But Virginia could not be entirely forgotten. In 1695, after completing his studies at the Middle Temple, he had made a short visit to his family. He might have settled then in America had the colony not needed a representative in England. Young William Byrd was a natural choice for the business because of his legal training, his familiarity with London, and — most likely — because he was glad enough of an excuse to return to the great metropolis. He had arrived back in England in 1697 and argued the colonial side on such questions as whether Virginia should help New York fight an Indian war and whether the colonists should be prevented from planting flax and cotton. For a time he had the title of "agent" of the Virginia Assembly, but in 1702 the position was abolished, leaving him free to return to America in 1705 when he received the news of his father's death.

Upon his return William Byrd took up residence at Westover, a large wood house overlooking the James River and commanding a plantation of six thousand acres. In addition to Westover, he inherited another house on the James and an additional twenty thousand acres. Byrd was immediately occupied with the innumerable details of plantation life. He supervised the planting and harvesting of tobacco and other crops, designed a garden, planted orchards, and experimented with new agricultural techniques. By studying English agricultural tracts he became one of the best farmers in Virginia. He also ran the plantation's many trading enterprises — importing manufactured goods and distributing them to the smaller planters and exporting furs and tobacco. In addition he had to make frequent trips into the interior to inspect the work on his other plantations.

His early months at Westover must have been lonely. He met other gentry on visits and at church, but he lived in isolation. It was time to find a wife, and Byrd's position as a suitor was now much

stronger than it had been in England, where he was easily overshadowed
by men of greater wealth and higher rank. In Virginia he was head of
one of the colony's foremost families. He was personally attractive as
well. His pleasant face, long aristrocratic nose, heavy dark brows, and
sparkling eyes reflected a captivating good humor. He was a dazzling
conversationalist and a charming escort.

He easily won the attention of Lucy Parke, the pretty daughter of
Col. Daniel Parke, who would later become governor of the Leeward
Islands. Her membership in the colonial aristocracy was a necessary
element of their courtship. Conscious of their status, the members of
the Virginia elite insisted upon marriage within their own class. Byrd's
acceptance of this code was apparent many years later when he met a
gentry couple whose daughter had run away with an Irish overseer. He
heartily agreed that she should not have married a "dirty plebeian."
Certainly Byrd, although only one generation removed from London
trade, would mingle with only the bluest blood in Virginia.

But the wedding of William and Lucy was not merely an alliance
of social convenience. The marriage roused the passions of both parners.
Variety was the hallmark of Byrd's character as well as Lucy's. Their
volatile personalities gave off sparks of anger as well as love but never
receded into boredom. That we can speak with such confidence about
the love affair of a husband and wife who have been dead for more than
two centuries is one of the wonders of Byrd's story. Most private emotions are lost with the lives that supported them. A person's house,
furniture, or portrait can easily survive. But his emotions seldom leave
a mark. Even letters between husband and wife most often describe
their hours apart rather than their hours together; and a diary is seldom
candid about a matrimonial partner, who might glance at its pages at
any moment.

It is against all odds, then, that William Byrd should have left
an intimate account of his life with Lucy. But he did and solved the
problem of privacy by a simple stratagem: he used an obscure form of
shorthand that he probably learned in London. Not only did it ensure
confidentiality, but it also alleviated a common problem of the diarist,
that of finding time for daily longhand entries. After Byrd's death the
diaries vanished into obscurity for almost two hundred years. The volumes that are known to have survived were published in this century
when Marion Tinling, a specialist in early forms of shorthand, transcribed Byrd's diary for 1709-12 at the Huntington Library in California.
Two other portions of the diary, covering the years 1717-21 and 1739-41,
were subsequently transcribed and published. Although they cover only
one seventh of William Byrd's life, they reveal the contours of his personality and experience with remarkable clarity.

It is through the first diary that we come to know the relationship between William Byrd and his wife. In a plantation society, remote from their neighbors, William and Lucy spent many days as one another's only companion. Some of their hours were, of course, spent separately. The husband had to supervise the plantation; the wife ordered household affairs. But they passed many hours entertaining one another, playing cards or billiards or reading books together, especially volumes of sermons by the great English churchman, Archbishop Tillotson. They danced or walked in the garden among William's well-pruned trees or went down to the bay to watch the fishermen. They tended each other in their illnesses and shared meals of beef, venison, pigeon, or turkey. In the evening Lucy sometimes sang to her husband.

William Byrd especially enjoyed these companionable times, but they were often interrupted by periods of violent quarreling. Byrd frequently blamed their disputes on Lucy's feminine "weakness," but it is evident he could be a difficult husband. He enjoyed cheating her at games, amusing himself but annoying Lucy. He teased her by caressing other women and found it difficult to understand her annoyance when he and a house guest began discoursing in Latin, edifying one another but excluding Lucy from the conversation.

From the diary it is evident that William Byrd expected to govern his wife. Such indeed was the current convention, and it is doubtful that Lucy expected to participate in such "manly" affairs as politics and plantation management. But in some domestic affairs, where she felt she should be respected, her husband seemed unreasonable. He regarded the library as his own province and refused to allow her to take a volume from there without his permission. Intervening in household affairs, he criticized her handling of servants or the family larder. Once when she secretly ordered some personal goods from England, he intercepted them, remarking in his diary that the extra expense was "enough to make a man mad." A few days later he sold most of them, leaving Lucy in tears.

She was not even given free rein in matters of appearance. It was fashionable at that time for women to pluck their eyebrows; but for unknown reasons William Byrd opposed the custom. When he discovered his wife about to remove her brows on the eve of a trip to Williamsburg, the provincial capital, he told her to stop. She protested but finally accepted his judgment. Byrd summarized the incident in telling words; I "got the best of her, and maintained my authority."

Lucy Byrd did not write a diary, but from her husband's notes it appears that she was eager to find some segment of life that she could nourish and control in the way William governed the plantation. She bore four children, but two died in infancy. The other two were reared as much by servants as by their mother. She could of course govern the servants, who looked after the children and did the household work. But William would not give her a free hand even in domestic affairs. In one particularly violent encounter when Byrd intervened while she was punishing a servant, Lucy was so frustrated that she attacked him with a poker.

The relationship between William and Lucy Byrd was obviously changeable and passionate. It would be inaccurate to describe it as either a wholly "good" or a wholly "bad" marriage. Like many another union of man and woman, it had periods of mutual tenderness and times of reciprocal hostility. It seems probable, however, that both partners were frequently stimulated and comforted by the companionship and that they enjoyed a satisfying sexual relationship.

Again, it is William Byrd's diary that allows us to make such an observation. In it he recorded, not only his discussions and his arguments with his wife, but also their sexual activities. Mingled with the entries on weather, plantation affairs, reading, and politics are dozens of brief notations on lovemaking. William Byrd used two common words of the times, "roger" and "flourish," to denote an act of sexual intercourse. He did not describe these intimate moments explicitly, but even in its stark simplicity the diary indicates the many moods of the couple's love. That range is suggested by these entries:

> About 10 o'clock we went to bed, where I lay in my wife's arms (April 19, 1709).
>
> In the afternoon I took a flourish with my wife and then read a sermon in Tillotson (September 10, 1710).
>
> About 11 o'clock I went to church and heard a sermon from Mr. Anderson. . . .I gave my wife a flourish on the couch in the library (August 3, 1710).
>
> I gave my wife a flourish in which she had a great deal of pleasure (November 4, 1710).
>
> In the evening we drank a bottle of mead, and I ate some toast. . . .I rogered my wife with vigor (May 29, 1711).
>
> In the evening I took a walk about the plantation and found things in good order. . . .I gave my wife a powerful flourish and gave her great ecstasy and refreshment (April 30, 1710).
>
> In the afternoon my wife and I had a little quarrel which I reconciled with a flourish. Then she read a sermon in Dr. Tillotson to me. It is to be observed that the flourish was performed on the billiard table (July 30, 1710).

And so it went. In bedroom, library, and billiard room; with tender pleasure or wild ecstasy; after quarrels, separations, and companionable moments William and Lucy thus consummated their love. There were long periods in which their physical relationship was interrupted by childbirth, sickness, or distance, but sex was there to comfort and thrill them during ordinary times. Byrd continued to have a wandering eye and occasionally allowed himself to fondle one of the chambermaids when he was away in Williamsburg. But if he lusted after other women with his heart and even now and then with his hands, he appears to have confined the ultimate expressions of his ardor to Lucy. He was, in the fashion of the times, a faithful husband.

In his thirties, then, William Byrd discovered the pleasure of commitment to work and marriage. But he sought something more: greater wealth and power. Byrd purchased large tracts of Virginia and Carolina wilderness, and when Lucy's father died, killed in an insurrection in the Leeward Islands, Byrd gained his father-in-law's Virginia lands by assuming his debts.

His desire for power was even greater than his thirst for land. At its most primitive level, power in plantation Virginia meant power over black slaves. At home in Westover, William Byrd had more authority than a medieval baron and treated his slaves with a combination of sensitivity and brutality. He always referred to them as "my people" and was frequently among them, talking with them in the evening, caring for them in sickness. But if a slave seemed lazy, careless, or rebellious, Byrd did not hesitate to administer a beating designed to discourage his misbehavior.

He also was a power among the local planters. Soon after his marriage he was assigned the best pew in the local church, much to his pleasure. In his mid-thirties he became commander of the Virginia militia in a two-county area. Occasionally he reviewed his citizen soldiers and supervised training days when the men drilled and held contests at wrestling and marksmanship. He was treated as the great man of the region. As he confided to his diary after one review, "Everybody respected me like a king."

William Byrd enjoyed the deference of slave, pastor, and militiaman. But he knew he was not a king. Power in the provincial world of rural Virginia was a pale imitation of power in London or even in Williamsburg. Byrd could not forget the greater world, even while enjoying preeminence on its fringes. His ambition as well as his sense of duty often took him to Williamsburg. In 1705 he had inherited the position of receiver general from his father, just as an English aristocrat might follow his father in office. The passing on of an office was not as certain as the willing of land, but because property and office were

closely associated a man who inherited land frequently acquired a con-
comitant political role. Byrd had to wait five years after his father's
death before he acquired a second family office, a seat on the Governor's
Council, but it was assumed from the start that the new squire of Westover would eventually have that position as well as that of receiver general.

Byrd also sought to win the highest office in the colony, the position of lieutenant governor. (The lieutenant governor served in the stead
of a titular head, who held the office of governor but resided in England.)
Through his London connections Byrd came close to winning the position, but it went instead to Alexander Spotswood in 1710. Thwarted,
Byrd became an ardent supporter of the council against the chief executive. He opposed Spotswood's efforts to change the way the receiver
general collected taxes, and with his fellow councilors he fought the
creation of a new court system that would undermine the judicial functions of the council. Byrd was further annoyed when in 1714 Spotswood
established a monopoly over the colony's Indian trade.

Unable to prevail in Virginia, he decided in 1715 to return to England as an agent of the council to seek Spotwood's recall, perhaps even
to replace him. He intended to remain in England only a short time,
but it was soon apparent that business and politics would keep him
longer, and he sent for Lucy. She arrived in summer 1716 and was
warmly received by Byrd's old friends, who called her "an honor to
Virginia." Lucy's presence in London was a reminder of all the proud
Byrd had achieved during the past ten years in Virginia. But, unfortunately, her career there was as brief as it was satisfying. Lucy contracted
smallpox and died on November 21, 1716.

Byrd had little time to regret his wife's death. Even as he was
burying her, he was engaged in his struggle against Governor
Spotswood. He testified to the Board of Trade, the English agency most
responsible for colonial government, that Spotswood had threatened
colonial liberty by taking upon himself the power to appoint judges.
In response, Spotswood wrote from Virginia that the real threat to
proper order came from the council itself. Citing the ambitions of Byrd
and several of his fellow councilors, he warned that unless such men
were thwarted Virginia would soon be ruled by "the haughtiness of a
Carter, the hypocrisy of a Blair," and "the malice of a Byrd." He almost
succeeded in having Byrd removed from the council. Clearly, the lust
for power was not confined to the lords of Westover.

Byrd was able to prevail on one of the specific issues in the conflict
but was defeated in a second. In 1717 the Board of Trade repealed the
law that had allowed Spotswood to establish a monopoly in Indian trade
but upheld the governor's prerogative in the important area of special

courts. The council's reaction to this news was so hostile, however, that the board became uneasy about the colony's stability. In 1719 the board asked Byrd to return to Virginia to heal the breach.

He arrived at Westover in 1720, and soon afterward, much to everyone's surprise, he and Spotswood came to an understanding, perhaps because they had much in common. The conflict between governor and the council had hardly been a democratic protest against royal authority. The councilors sought mainly to protect their status as a provincial elite. Their cause was neither antiaristocratic nor anti-British; in the fight against the governor, they had appealed to the crown rather than to the people. The road to influence and respectability in 1720, whether for an individual or for an institution, lay in association with British authority.

Certainly this was William Byrd's belief, for after setting his plantation in order he returned once more to England, apparently hoping to use his position in Virginia to gain status in London. In this spirit he courted "Sabina," his pseudonym for Mary Smith, the daughter of a wealthy commissioner of excise. She lived across the street from Byrd in London and had caught his attention shortly after Lucy's death. She was young, lovely, witty, and wealthy — everything Byrd could hope for in a second wife. Their courtship lasted more than a year. At first they courted in secret, even communicating in invisible ink — an awkward arrangement, because sometimes they themselves couldn't read their messages. Finally Byrd worked up his courage and approached Sabina's father. He tried to impress on this rather forbidding parent that he, Byrd, was a man of great property in Virginia; he owned 43,000 acres, 220 slaves, and prodigious quantities of livestock. But Mary Smith's father was unimpressed with an estate so far from London. He told the crestfallen planter that all his possessions were "little better than an estate in the moon." Never before had Byrd been made to feel more like a provincial, an outsider in London's attractive society.

He was despondent for several months. He tried to persuade Sabina to marry him against her father's will, but she refused. He clung to her in his imagination, seeing her in the window across the street and making "distant love to her." When he received her final note of rejection, he "cried exceedingly." Mary Smith had offered him something more than beauty and wit. She would have brought him great wealth and a fixed place in London society. With her he might have remained permanently in England as an Englishman. Without her he had lost both a woman and a world.

Of course, few such momentous turning points in life are recognizable at the time. Often we are not even aware of our limitations; we reflect that what could not be achieved today might still be gained

Westover. William Byrd, told in London that a Virginia plantation was "little better than an estate in the moon," built this house in America.

tomorrow. In this spirit William Byrd continued to seek a wealthy spouse while doing his best to lead the life of a bright London socialite. He met with friends at Will's Coffee House almost daily; played at cards, billiards, and bowls; and gambled at the residence of the Spanish ambassador. He attended plays and went to masked balls, took walks with the fashionable ladies and gentlemen in St. James's Park, and visited friends at fine country estates.

Byrd kept busy with these activities, but his life in London gives an impression of excessive frivolity. He might try to appear lively and gay, but he was a man approaching fifty and yet was exhibiting the rootless passion of a much younger man. He had no spouse and no employment. The Virginia gentleman had become a London gadabout, and his sexual life is a barometer of his condition. The second of his surviving journals covers the years 1717-21 and is mainly about life in London. With his usual candor he describes an astonishingly intricate love life. Arranged in order of stability, there were three tiers in his relationships. First there were his mistresses. These were usually older women whom he would visit every week or so; sometimes he kept two or three of them simultaneously. Their alliances appear to have been based on mutual affection as well as on monetary compensation. Then there were prostitutes, some of whom he met at a fashionable house run by a Mrs. Smith; others, in the park. Finally, there were contacts with maids, cooks, and women encountered at masked balls.

These companions parade through the pages of Byrd's diary in a seemingly endless procession, reminding the reader of his description of himself in "The Enamored Bird." In that autobiographical sketch Byrd had said: "He would follow a scent with great eagerness for a little while, but then a fresh scent would cross it and carry him violently another way." One evening Byrd might take a prostitute to the Three Tuns Tavern for pheasant and woodcock, then retire with her to an upstairs room. A few days later he would find another woman and make love in a park or a coach. He went to see his friend Lord Orrery; finding him not at home, he kissed Lady Orrery for "half an hour." Another time he kissed Lord Orrery's housekeeper. Apparently never at a loss in such matters, he once visited a mistress and, finding her not at home, caressed the maid; then upon his mistress' return, he retired with her to the bedroom for more serious lovemaking.

Although William Byrd took some satisfaction in his hectic love life, he recognized the disadvantages of these brief encounters. There was always the danger of venereal disease, which he had already contracted at least once. Then, too, his conscience, while permitting him his mistresses, rebelled at his use of prostitutes. He frequently asked God's forgiveness after a furtive meeting with purchased flesh or thanked God for preserving him on evenings when none of the women on the street suited his taste.

Hoping to find stability again in marriage, he continued his quest for a wellborn English lady, proposing three times unsuccessfully to a widow Pierson and once to Lady Elizabeth Lee, an illegitimate granddaughter of King Charles II. Finally in 1724 he won the hand of a woman twenty-five years his junior, Maria Taylor. She was sufficiently wellborn to satisfy his social ambition and attractive and clever enough to win and hold his attention. But although she was an heiress, she was not wealthy enough to allow Byrd to retire in England.

Byrd would have to turn his attention once more to earning a living. His Virginia plantations were in the hands of overseers, who could not be efficiently regulated at a distance of three thousand miles. The lands yielded enough revenue to keep him well as a bachelor, but they would now require his personal attention. Thus, he and Maria went to Virginia in 1726. Byrd probably expected to return shortly to England, for he held on to a fashionable apartment at Lincoln's Inn.

In Virginia, Byrd supervised the management of his main estate at Westover and made frequent inspection tours of the other plantations. Hoping to increase his income, he experimented with new crops such as hemp, grapevines, and ginseng — a medicinal root — and sought new offices in the provincial government.

As the months in America turned into years, William Byrd clearly missed England. In 1727 he wrote a friend telling him that his daughters by his first marriage had difficulty adjusting to their "retirement" from London. "They can't get the plays, the operas, and the masquerades out of their heads," he said. He did not complain about his own isolation but did his best to carry parts of the great world to Virginia. He continued to build up his library and read almost daily in Latin, Greek, Hebrew, and French; and he surrounded himself with the most cultivated and interesting minds in Virginia, including ministers, professors, sea captains, and English visitors. He kept up a correspondence with his old friends in London and devoted a room at Westover to portraits of English grandees he had known.

Byrd carried his London years with him even on journeys to remote sections of Virginia. On one trip, for example, he was delayed by rain at a plantation house, and finding that his hostess enjoyed plays, he read to her from *The Beggar's Opera* and told her how the play had captivated London a few years before.

In such activities Byrd showed his continuing interest in the wider world that he had known for so many years. Nonetheless, as the years passed, he found himself more and more rooted in American soil. Life with Maria was less exciting than with Lucy, but it brought a domestic tranquility that he now enjoyed. For the first time in his life he was surrounded by a family. His daughters by Lucy had been reared by relatives in England; now they came to live at Westover. In addition, he had three daughters and a son, William Byrd III, by Maria.

He turned his literary genius for the first time to American materials. In England he had written fashionable, witty prose of no great importance, including a poem entitled "Ode to a Fart." His American writings were lighthearted without being frivolous. They included many fine descriptions of the locales and peoples of the region. The so-called Westover Manuscripts — three books Byrd wrote to circulate privately among his friends — are among the best literary products of colonial America.

The first and best of the manuscripts grew out of his participation in the 1728 expedition to survey the Virginia-North Carolina dividing line. The *History of the Dividing Line* contains witty character sketches of Byrd's fellow commissioners, whose virtues and foibles he revealed perceptively. It also contains engaging portraits of local persons, including the backwoods squatters who made their women do all the work, rising late in the morning "after stretching and yawning for half an hour." He got to know the Indian guide, Bearskin, and wrote a long passage describing the man's religious beliefs.

The other commissioners often chased after women, but Byrd refrained from such activities and did his best to prevent abusive behavior. In an earlier version of the *History* he referred to all the men by pseudonyms; it is symptomatic of his new maturity and self-control that he gave himself the name "Steady."

After returning from the dividing line, Byrd apparently decided to stay in Virginia. In 1729 he sold his London chambers at Lincoln's Inn. A year or two later he began work on a magnificent brick mansion to replace the old wood house at Westover. In many ways the new house was a reminder of England and may have been modeled after the country estate of one of his English friends. A formal garden with gravel paths, gates, fruit trees, cedars, and hedges and its rooms crowded with English furniture, ornaments, books, and portraits were reminders of the Old World. But it sat on a Virginia hillside overlooking a Virginia river, an English home in an American setting. If it reflected Byrd's continuing respect for things English, it reflected also his willingness finally to live his English life in an American environment.

A letter written several years before to Lord Orrery suggests that he could take a positive outlook on his Americanization. "Like one of the patriarchs," he said, "I have my flock and my herds, my bondmen and bondwomen, and every sort of trade amongst my own servants, so that I live in a kind of independence of everyone but Providence." Byrd emphasized the simplicity and innocence of plantation life. "Half a crown," he said, "will rest undisturbed in my pockets for many moons together." There was no need to fear "public robbers nor private." Certainly Virginia was not London, but there were compensations. "We are happy in our Canaans," he said, "if we can but forget the onions and fleshpots of Egypt." He wrote in the same vein in a letter to another English friend. "A library, a garden, a grove, and a purling stream," he said, "are the innocent scenes that divert our leisure."

In these letters Byrd struck a note that others would sound again and again in descriptions of America. If Europe could offer great cities, historic buildings, and sophisticated company, America could make a virtue of the absence of these things. Simplicity, innocence, and nature were abundant in the New World. And weren't they as attractive as crowded theaters, busy streets, and noisy masquerades? Byrd was still too attracted to the cultural advantages of London to belittle her achievements. But in coming to appreciate American nature and customs, he deepened his accommodation to his native habitat.

In one respect, however, these letters are misleading. They suggest that Byrd was able to live a life of endless leisure. In fact, he worked much harder in Virginia than he had in England. As he said in his letter to Lord Orrery, "I must take care to keep all my people to their duty, to set all the springs in motion, and to make everyone draw his equal share to carry the machine forward." Byrd had to supervise the work at Westover and the other plantations. Additionally, his ambition and his debts kept him busy seeking new ways to earn money. These activities led him to become increasingly involved in the government and economy of the region. His thirst for land was inexhaustible; he built up his inherited estate of 26,000 acres to almost 180,000 acres and forged closer ties with other great Virginia landowners. His chief rival for preeminence among the planters was Robert ("King") Carter, who accumulated three hundred thousand acres before his death in 1732. Two of Byrd's children married Carters.

Byrd's final years had a serene quality. He and Maria governed their beautiful Westover in harmony. He read his Latin and Greek, walked in his garden, visited his people, and entertained his friends. As he approached his seventieth year he had a wry sense of humor about his own mortality. In 1741 he wrote to a friend in London, "I am alive, and by the help of ginseng, hope to survive some years longer." He was lively enough in his late sixties to "play the fool" now and then with the maids but was not virile enough to give Maria much worry. In 1743 his political career was crowned by his appointment to the presidency of the Virginia Council.

He died a year later and was buried in the garden at Westover. The epitaph on his gravestone called him a "hearty friend to the liberties of his country." In 1776 that description would acquire a meaning that would have been incomprehensible to William Byrd. During Byrd's lifetime, love of America and loyalty to England were part of a single fabric of patriotism. His home was in a place that no longer exists, where colonists in a New World still looked to an Old World to discover who they were.

QUESTIONS

1. How did William Byrd's life in Virginia reflect British influences? How did it reflect American characteristics? (Mention pertinent customs, interests, institutions, and objects.)

2. In what respects was colonial Virginia an aristocratic society? In what respects was it democratic?

3. The author suggests that in England, William Byrd was something of a gadabout, whereas in America his life was more stable and constructive. In what ways to Byrd's vocational, intellectual, and sexual activities support this argument?

4. This chapter describes several levels of authority in colonial Virginia. Describe the distribution of power in each of these relationships: husbands and wives, masters and slaves, local gentry and average colonists, Virginia and England.

5. William Byrd's career reveals both the satisfaction and the frustration of being a British American. In what ways were the two identities compatible? In what ways did they come into conflict?

BIBLIOGRAPHY

BOORSTIN, DANIEL. *The Americans: The Colonial Experience* (1968). Provocative discussion of the ways in which American experience altered Old World customs and institutions.

BRIDENBAUGH, CARL. *Myths and Realities: Societies of the Colonial South* (1952). Narrative history of southern colonial societies.

MARAMBAUD, MARION, *William Byrd of Westover. 1674-1744* (1971). Topical account of Byrd and his world.

TINLING, MARION, EDITOR. *The Correspondence of the Three William Byrds of Westover. Virginia. 1684-1776* (1977). Fine collection of letters to and from the Byrds.

WOODFIN, MAUDE H., EDITOR. *Another Secret Diary of William Byrd of Westover, 1739-1741* (1942). Covers later years in Virginia and includes letters and iterary exercises.

WRIGHT, LOUIS B. *The First Gentlemen of Virginia* (1940). Biographical sketches of colonial gentry.

_____ AND MARION TINLING, EDITORS. *The London Diary (1717-1721) and Other Writings* (1958). Includes the Westover Manuscripts.

_____ AND MARION TINLING, EDITORS. *The Secret Diary of William Byrd of Westover. 1709-1712* (1941). Covers early years in Virginia and marriage to Lucy.

5

DIVIDED
LOYALTIES

Jonathan Boucher
and the
Pre-Revolutionary
Crisis

In the turbulent years preceding 1776 many Americans opposed the revolutionary movement. Some were attracted to Britain by political, cultural, economic, and religious ties; others feared that independence would produce chaos or oppression. Jonathan Boucher was one of the many Americans who opposed the Revolution. He was a constructive and imaginative citizen, but when he criticized the patriots, he was forced into exile. His career demonstrates the continuing hold of Old World loyalties on settlers and suggests the difficulties many colonists faced in choosing between loyalty and rebellion.

On May 4, 1775, George Washington boarded a ferry at Alexandria, Virginia, to cross the Potomac River. The Battles of Lexington and Concord had been fought two weeks before, and he was now on his way to the Continental Congress at Philadelphia. As his boat crossed the river, Washington spied an old friend, the Reverend Jonathan Boucher, on board another ferry. The people on Boucher's boat gave Washington three cheers, and he, in turn, beckoned them to stop so that he could come aboard and shake their hands. According to Boucher, "Everybody seemed to be on fire, either with rum, or patriotism, or both."

As Boucher greeted Washington, he was afire with neither rum nor patriotism. Instead, he was worried about the events that threatened to divide Britian and America. In a "few disturbed moments of conversation" he warned Washington that the troubles between England and America would surely lead to civil war and colonial independence. Washington tried to reassure Boucher, telling him that his fears were groundless and that if Boucher "ever heard of him joining in any such measures . . . [he] had his leave to set him down for everything wicked."

Within a little more than a year George Washington would of course support both the Revolutionary War and independence. But in 1775 Washington did not know what course the resistance to Britain would take. The War for Independence wrenched American life out of its accustomed patterns. Less violent than many other revolutions, it produced, nonetheless, profound changes in the lives of many Americans. George Washington, a Virginia planter, would become president of a nation that did not even exist in 1775. In contrast, Jonathan Boucher, a Maryland cleric and landholder, would soon become an exile from his American home.

Boucher received a foretaste of this bitter experience a few minutes later when he disembarked at Alexandria. One of the citizens claimed to recognize the minister as a critic of American policy. An angry crowd quickly gathered, and Boucher saved himself only by persuading the mob that the accuser was lying. After this episode he decided never to go to Alexandria again, nor would he venture into any other public place except his own church.

This episode was one of several in which Jonathan Boucher was threatened with violence because of his support of the English government. He was never harmed, but many other, less fortunate opponents of the Revolution, known as Tories or Loyalists, were beaten or tarred and feathered. Moreover, some fifty to one hundred thousand Americans like Boucher were forced to flee the country because of their political beliefs. John Adams estimated that one American in three was in the Loyalist camp at the beginning of the Revolution. Modern historians have revised Adams's figure downward but still conclude that some 25 percent of Americans had the misfortune of opposing the Revolution, the ostensible aim of which was "life, liberty, and the pursuit of happiness" for all men.

The Tories are frequently ignored in accounts of the Revolution, but they deserve our attention. By studying them we can learn about a numerically significant group of men and women, and we can also see the Revolution as a whole with fresh vision. To become a Tory often required more thoughtful deliberation than to become a patriot; sometimes it even required more courage. For two centuries historians have sought to explain the Loyalists. Patriots vilified them as shortsighted opponents of a noble cause. Twentieth-century historians have tried to understand the Tories better by exploring the socioeconomic sources of their attachment to Britain. We now know that the most important Tories were government officials, merchants, and clerics, whose position in the colonies depended on royal support. But these members of the colonial elite were relatively few. A much larger group were members of American religious and ethnic minorities who feared they would be oppressed by other Americans if English control were removed.

We can generalize about Tory characteristics, but allegiance during the Revolution was also affected by one's ideas. Some of the most interesting Tories shared many qualities with their patriot opponents. They were Americans who disagreed with other Americans about the proper character of American society. Jonathan Boucher was such a man.

In some ways Boucher was a typical Tory. A minister of the Church of England, he owed his appointment to the royal governor of Maryland. As a historical figure, he is especially serviceable because his opinions and experiences are unusually accessible: he reveals himself in letters, an autobiography, and a volume of published sermons. In these sources we can explore the events, the personal characteristics, and the intellectual commitments underlying his loyalty. Few men described in so much detail how they became Tories. Yet after studying his writings, one is left wondering whether he did not have much in common with his opponents.

Boucher was born in northern England in the town of Blencogo, Cumberland, on March 12, 1738. His ancestors had lived in this region for many generations and had fought in the border wars with Scotland. War came again seven years after Jonathan's birth when an army marched through Cumberland in an unsuccessful attempt to overthrow King George II. Some of the defeated rebels were executed in nearby Carlisle, their heads hung in display on the city wall.

The short-lived Rebellion of 1745 interrupted an otherwise humdrum existence. Blencogo was a small rural village; its people were poor and worked hard to earn a living. As a youth Boucher had to haul coal, turf, and peat; to drive a plough and work "without intermission" during haying time and harvest. His pleasures were those provided by the rough country environment. Decades later he could still recall places where he had caught a large trout or discovered a bird's nest or fought a "successful battle" against a playmate.

Most of the boys he grew up with would stay in Blencogo and became small farmers. But before Jonathan was twelve he had decided to escape the ceaseless toil of rural life. As a child he had shown an interest in learning. His father taught him to read soon after he learned to talk, and at six he could read and spell almost as well as an adult. Jonathan's parents wanted to encourage him in his studies but were hampered by their own limited means and by the inadequate local schools.

Until he was fourteen Jonathan spent much of his time working for his father. In 1752 he qualified as a teacher in the nearby town of Wigton. During the next few years he taught at several schools while advancing his own education. In 1756 he became assistant to a school-master named John James, a fine scholar and teacher, who took an interest in Jonathan and helped him continue his studies. In 1759 Jonathan heard about a good teaching opportunity in Virginia, and by now he had a fine background as teacher and scholar. His parents protested that he would waste his life — and probably feared he would lose it — in America. But Jonathan wanted to travel, and his parents finally agreed. After a tearful farewell, he began the long journey to the New World.

Jonathan's ship sailed on April 27, 1759. Several times she was caught in violent storms and once was chased by an enemy vessel. Jonathan was at sea for two and a half months before reaching the Rappahannock River on Chesapeake Bay in Virginia. Ironically, his ship sailed into the land of opportunity in company with a ship bearing slaves from Africa.

Disembarking at Port Royal, the young man was immediately impressed with the strangeness of his surroundings: "I was now in every sense of the word in a new world," he writes. "The people, in their persons, manners, pursuits and modes of life were as new and strange to me as their country and climate were." He soon adjusted, however, and felt himself so much at home that he later wondered whether he had not adapted all too well to Port Royal. The social life consisted chiefly of visits and balls, always with plenty of liquor. The people had no literary interests, and so, says he, I "was engaged in many silly frolics with people as silly as myself." Boucher settled into the task of tutoring the four sons of a Virginia planter, but he was dissatisfied with this work and for a while entertained the idea of going into business. But a better opportunity presented itself, one that would pay him well and enable him to pursue his intellectual interests. He was invited to become minister of Hanover, a Church of England parish across the river from Port Royal.

Although he lacked a college education, Boucher's private studies and native intelligence had marked him as a good ministerial prospect. He decided to take the post, but because there were no Anglican bishops in America he had to return to England for his consecration into the Anglican priesthood. He was ordained in London, then traveled by horseback to Blencogo to visit his parents. Now that he was returning to a stable position in America, he realized that he would probably never see his mother and father again. He was twenty-five years old. Many years later he still recalled vividly his last moments with his parents.

Back in Virginia, Jonathan ministered for a time to the congregation at Hanover, then moved to a new position as rector of Saint Mary's Parish a few miles away. Like most other American clerics in the colonial period, Boucher received only a modest salary. To increase his income he purchased cattle, horses, and slaves to establish a plantation, and he also started a boarding school.

Boucher spent seven years at Saint Mary's — years he recalled as "busy and bustling" but not satisfying to a "literary man." The planters were convivial and drank freely, giving little attention to intellectual matters. Naturally inquisitive, Boucher devoted the time he could to solitary studies. For a time he was intrigued by the arguments of contemporary philosophers who questioned the divinity of Christ. He almost became a skeptic himself, but turned to the Scriptures, and having read the Bible in the ancient languages, concluded that the doctrine of the Trinity was a scriptural "fact" that must be taken on faith. His flirtation with heresy persuaded him that complex issues should be fronted with "caution and reverence." He would show the same spirit when he later considered the proper relationship of America to England.

Boucher appears to have been a popular preacher. In other parishes rival denominations, especially Presbyterians and Baptists, were winning Anglicans away from the established church. But Boucher's parish remained orthodox. He advocated treating rival preachers "with well-judged ridicule and contempt, and their followers with gentleness, persuasion and attention." When another minister challenged him to debate the merits of Anglicanism, he refused to dignify the man with a direct reply, sending one of his parishioners, a carpenter with a "voluble tongue," in his stead. Boucher did not oppose religious toleration, but he was convinced that Anglicanism was the one true church and that others fell far short of its excellence.

During his stay at Saint Mary's, Boucher became acquainted with George Washington. The minister's reputation as a schoolmaster was growing, and he was soon boarding thirty pupils. In 1768 Washington wrote asking him to take John Parke ("Jackie") Custis, Martha's son by her first marriage, as a student. Jackie was a somewhat unruly youth who until then had shown no interest in schooling. Washington said that he hoped Boucher could "make him fit for more useful purposes than a horse-racer." Boucher agreed to instruct Jackie, beginning a rather close acquaintance between the minister and the planter. Boucher wrote Washington frequent letters about the boy's progress and made visits to Mount Vernon with his pupil. But Jackie remained an unimpressive student, a fact that Boucher did not try to conceal. He wrote to Washington, "I must confess to you I never did in my life know a youth so exceedingly indolent or so surprisingly voluptuous: one would suppose Nature had intended him [to be] some Asiatic prince." Washington appears to have appreciated Boucher's honesty and left Jackie in the minister's hands for five years.

While Boucher was at Saint Mary's Parish, news of the Stamp Act reached America. This act, placing a tax on newspapers, cards, legal documents, and other paper products, was Britain's first attempt to impose an internal tax on the colonies. In the recent war with France the mother country had acquired a huge national debt and reasoned that the colonists should help pay. The Americans, however, were accustomed to controlling their own internal taxes. They reacted dramatically to the Stamp Act: they drew up petitions, formed mobs, organized a colonywide congress, and imposed a boycott on trade with Britain. A year later, under pressure from English merchants who were injured by the boycott, Parliament repealed the Stamp Act.

This was the first of several conflicts leading to the American Revolution. How did Boucher react? In a letter to his English friend, John James, in December 1765, he indicates that he was strongly on the side of the colonists. He calls the Stamp Act "oppressive, impolitic, and illegal" and argues that the Americans have a traditional right to tax themselves. Even if they had no such right, he says, Parliament is so ignorant of conditions in America that she might as well try to govern "Kamchatka" (part of Russia). He contends that the British agents in America are "too ignorant, or too knavish" to send back the accurate intelligence required for well-informed administration. Why, he says, a British officer recently sent four or five hundred soldiers to be quartered in a town that had only one house! With so little knowledge of America, how can Britain pretend to have a right to tax the colonists?

Knowing Boucher's later loyalism, these are remarkable sentiments, for he criticized not only the Stamp Act but the very idea of Britain trying to make vital decisions about a land it hardly knew. Other future Tories, including Thomas Hutchinson, who became governor of Massachusetts, shared Boucher's view of the Stamp Act. When presented with a choice between imperfect British rule and complete independence, Boucher and other Tories would rally to the royal standard. But they did not favor the complete subjection of the colonies to the mother country. They preferred an equitable balance of power between Britain and America.

Boucher's sympathy for the colonies in their initial struggles with the crown found a counterpart in his consideration for the slaves. During the months when he was complaining about British oppression, Boucher worked to improve the condition of the blacks. Finding that they had been ignored by previous ministers, he baptized almost five hundred of them, half the adult slaves in the parish. Some became regular communicants in his church, and Boucher also encouraged their education.

Although Boucher made a success of his ministry in Virginia — the people would pay him an extra six months' salary when he left Saint Mary's — he wanted to live in a more cosmopolitan city, preferably Annapolis, Maryland, which he named the "genteelest town in North America." For several years friends promised that he would be appointed to the next vacant parish in the town, and in 1770 he was offered Saint Anne's Parish in Annapolis.

The new post delighted Boucher. He claimed there was hardly a town in England as desirable. Soon he met other men who shared his love of animated and intelligent conversation, and with three or four of them he founded "The Homony Club," meeting weekly to hold debates and read compositions. It was so successful that even the governor applied for admission.

The boy from Blencogo had come a long way. He was recognized as one of the brightest people in his province, and his friends included many of the most important men in the South. As yet, though, he had no wife. Several unsuccessful courtships had gone by in Virginia. Now he turned to Eleanor Addison, daughter of a wealthy Virginia planter. Boucher describes her as "handsome, sprightly, and a general toast." She was medium in height and had black hair and eyes with "uncommon animation and lustre." She had been courted unsuccessfully several times before Boucher came along. With no great wealth to offer, Boucher, too, might have failed except that Nelly, as she was called, once dreamed that she married a man who looked like him. When Boucher first appeared on her doorstep with her uncle, she hastened from the room and nearly fainted before she could say to her mother, "Yonder is the man I dreamed of that I was to marry!"

Boucher's marriage to Eleanor Addison is one of the most attractive incidents in his life. Both were in their early thirties and ready to settle down. Shortly after they were married Nelly became pregnant but injured herself and miscarried. For the remaining twelve years of her life she was bedridden three days of four. Nonetheless, a deeply satisfying relationship developed between husband and wife. Both were strong personalities, and they frequently argued; but they prided themselves that they never "went to sleep without kissing and being friends." In his autobiography Boucher describes an incident that suggests the vitality in their marriage. They had been arguing, and to clear the air decided each would list the best and worst features of the other. Their remarks, which Jonathan preserved, are very candid. Nelly stated that her husband's manners were "often awkward, but always interesting." He wrote that she was "artless, blushing, bashful." But their fondness for one another survived their frankness. Years later, after Nelly was dead, Jonathan recalled how she had ended the episode: "And now, my dear *old man*," she said, "prithee end thy catechism; for with all thy romance and eccentricity, all thy foibles and all thy faults, thou art a good and a clever fellow, and I do love thee as much as ever woman loved." Jonathan continues: "And she flung her arms around my neck, finishing the parley in a way of which none but lovers, and I may add, married lovers, can possibly judge."

Boucher remembered the days of courting Nelly as the happiest in his life. In the years after their marriage on June 2, 1772, they would need one another's support. Jonathan was already falling out of favor with the leaders of the patriot movement in Maryland. Although he had taken the "right" side in the Stamp Act crisis, he found himself on the "wrong" side of two popular issues shortly after coming to the new province.

The first had to do with the appointment of Anglican bishops in America. Boucher believed that the church badly needed an American hierarchy, to ordain clergy, to help settle disputes, and to provide order and stability in the church. Against the Presbyterian opponents of the idea he argued quite simply that those who believed in Presbyterian government should be allowed to have their presbyters and those who believed in government by bishops should be allowed to have their bishops. The argument was reasonable, but in the tense atmosphere of pre-Revolutionary political discourse any innovation suggesting the least increase in power for the British government looked like a threat to the colonists. Many opponents of the bishoprics believed that an Anglican hierarchy established in America would oppress other denomi-

Eleanor Adison Boucher, American by birth, she stood beside her husband, Jonathan, as he tried to find his way in the political turmoil of pre-Revolutionary America.

nations. Boucher ridiculed this position — and may well have been correct in doing so — but many Americans disagreed, and no bishops were appointed during the colonial period.

A second conflict questioned payment of salaries to Anglican clergymen in Maryland. Anglicanism was the established faith in the colony. Other religious bodies were tolerated, but the Church of England had the advantage of laws requiring that ministers be paid. Shortly after Boucher's arrival in Maryland, a conflict developed over the proper amount of these payments. Boucher naturally favored the most generous interpretation of the law and published newspaper articles supporting his position. But the opposition appealed to the people's pocketbooks and republicansim. Jonathan realized that the conflict drew on sources deep in Maryland politics. Traditionally one party, which included the Anglican clergymen, had been attached to the governor by royal patronage. The opposition sought to turn "others out that they themselves might come in." Here and elsewhere such conflicts between provincial "ins" and "outs" had acquired new urgency. Any increase in royal prerogatives, such as higher clerical salaries, came to be treated as pieces of a British plot to establish tyrannical control over Americans. Because he was an Anglican clergyman, Jonathan Boucher, who had railed against the injustice of the Stamp Act, became identified with a crown interest.

Boucher's problems were compounded by his unwillingness to shrink from a fight when he thought he was right. He saw critics of the Anglican establishment as ignorant and self-serving, and he treated them with contempt. In defending the church he came to defend the authority on which it rested, the monarchy. Between a populace that appeared turbulent and irrational and a crown that represented tradition and order, he chose the latter.

The commitment that made him an exile in 1775 grew from smaller commitments of the previous five years. He published tracts on bishops and ministerial salaries. He became a confidant of the royal governor, Robert Eden. He refused to join associations and sign resolves against British policy or to honor the fast day proclaimed by the patriots on June 1, 1774, to mark the British closing of the Port of Boston. Above all, he refused to back down from a fight.

The spirit in which he conducted himself rings out in his encounter with a blacksmith who lived on land adjoining his and Nelly's. The man disliked Boucher's political views and also argued with him over property lines. The conflict came to a head when the blacksmith shot and lamed one of Boucher's horses and proclaimed he would deal with the minister in the same way. Boucher realized that his antagonist was much stronger than he, but he knew also that he would weaken his position if he seemed timid. "As I realized we were to come to blows," he writes, "I determined to have the first." One day he took a bare-knuckled swing at the blacksmith and, incredibly, knocked him out with one punch. "No man who has never himself experienced such a state of society as then prevailed in that country," he writes, "can conceive what credit I gained, and I add, what advantage, from this lucky blow." He was now looked up to as a great boxer, which was more advantage to him "than to have been set down as a Newton."

Boucher stood up boldly for his views on many other occasions. One evening while dining in a "large company of men of differing parties and opinions," an acquaintance proposed this toast: "May the Americans all hang together in accord and concord!" Boucher did not really object to this toast, but he tells us he was prompted by an "evil genius" to remark, "In any cord, Doctor, so it be but a strong cord." A stunned silence must have followed this remark, but most of the guests accepted the minister's quip as a harmless joke. One patriot, however, was outraged, and to bait Boucher, he proposed: "Damnation to General Gage, the troops under his command, and all who wish well to them." Boucher and several others refused to drink, at which his antagonist, a man named Sprigg, threatened to fight him. Boucher dared the man to come near, but his reputation as a boxer was well known and the man kept his place. Boucher, relieved that no fight ensued, was confirmed in his belief that "the true way to escape a danger is fairly to meet it."

This was the spirit that carried Boucher through his final years in Maryland. Once, while visiting the governor in the capital, he was summoned by a mob to come before the "Provincial Committee" to face charges of disloyalty to the American cause. The governor and his friends urged Boucher to flee, but he felt it would be safer to face his adversaries. He told the mob that he refused to be forced to go anywhere but that if they would withdraw he would go to the meeting on his own. The men agreed, and Boucher followed them to a crowded room, buoyed up by his initial success. As he entered the room he spotted a tough militiaman, one of the town's meanest characters. To Boucher's surprise, the man whispered to him that if he came through the interrogation well, he had friends in the room who would fight for him. This unexpected support further encouraged Boucher, and he went to the front of the room. There the committee "president" read a list of charges against him. In this tense atmosphere several committeemen argued that a man of Boucher's views should not be allowed to communicate with the public. Then Boucher's turn came. He could not later recall what he said but wrote that "necessity may perhaps be the parent of eloquence." He addressed the crowd rather than the committeemen and, at the end, had many shouting for his acquittal. The "judges," who depended on the people for their positions, went along.

It was a measure of Boucher's unusual strength of personality that he could win popular support even while criticizing the principles the populace now seemed to uphold. But once the war had begun at Lexington and Concord, it grew more difficult to continue preaching. He received so many threats that during spring and summer 1775 each time he preached he would carry two loaded pistols into the pulpit.

The final crisis came in summer 1775. A fast day had been ordered by the Provincial Congress to implore divine help in the confrontation with Britain. Boucher composed a sermon urging his people not to take part in the Revolutionary conflicts. When he arrived at the church, however, he found that his assistant, a man popular with the patriots, was preparing to preach. Soon a large body of armed men — Boucher says two hundred — entered the building. They were led by his old adversary, Sprigg. As in the previous confrontations, Boucher decided it would be best to stand his ground and declared that they would not take him from his church alive.

But as he began to preach, one of his friends grabbed him from behind and told him that twenty men had been instructed to shoot him if he entered the pulpit. Boucher still attempted to deliver his sermon, but supporters and opponents began to throng around him, and Boucher had to conclude that the situation was becoming dangerous. He grabbed Sprigg by the collar and put a loaded pistol to his head, saying that if anyone tried to harm him he would blow out Sprigg's brains. He then walked with his captive through the hostile crowd, mounted his horse, and rode away.

Boucher now faced a distasteful choice. He liked America and thought of the new land as his home. Here were his friends, his wife, and his property. If he left his estate might well be confiscated, but if he stayed he could lose life as well as property. After September 10 there would be no more commerce between the colonies and England. If Boucher was to flee, this was the time.

And so, reluctantly, he decided to return to England. Nelly, who could not bear the thought of separation from her husband, insisted on joining him. Her uncle and cousin also decided to go along. Time was short; they had less than a week to prepare for the journey. The estate would be left in the hands of Nelly's brother-in-law. The Bouchers decided to take only a few possessions, hoping they could soon return. On their last night at home the house was crowded with friends. Boucher had many admirers, even among moderate supporters of the Revolution. He later reflected that all this activity had dispelled his pain "on thus leaving a country where now almost all my attachments were, to go to another now become foreign to me."

On Sunday morning, "amidst the tears and cries" of their slaves, they boarded a small schooner that would carry them to their ship. Exhausted after a night without sleep, they retired to a "miserable cabin," where they lay down with an old sail for a cover and a bag of hominy for a pillow. They spent a day and night on this boat, then reached Quantico, where they boarded the ship that would take them across the Atlantic. Years later Boucher described their departure: "At length the wind came fair, and we sailed with a fine fresh breeze down the Chesapeake; and on the 20th of the month, just about sunset, in a charmingly fine evening, we lost sight of the capes of Virginia, never to see them more."

Thus did Jonathan Boucher leave America, never to return. As he sailed across the Atlantic, George Washington was organizing the Continental army outside Boston. Battles had of course already been fought at Lexington and Concord and Bunker Hill. In less than a year the American colonies would declare themselves an independent nation. By moderating his views Boucher could easily have retained his church and plantation in Maryland as a citizen of the new country, but, ironically, he believed that his freedom would be narrowly circumscribed by joining America's fight for "freedom." To stay, he reflected, would have made "shipwreck of my conscience."

But why? Surely many conscientious men and women favored the Revolution. Boucher had been on their side during the Stamp Act crisis. He certainly had the idealism, independent-mindedness, and courage that Americans like to associate with the Revolution. Imagine the hero he would have been on that fast day in 1775 if he had been a patriot seeking to preach to two hundred armed redcoats. What, then, were the roots of his loyalty? Was it personality or philosophy or cir-cumstances that drove him inexorably into the Loyalist camp?

Boucher's character furnishes one clue. One of his greatest sin-gularities was his yearning after respectability. He had always been drawn to people of wealth and culture. His parents were poor, but to him their background associated them with a more elevated life. Jonathan's grandfather was a gentleman farmer with an estate worth some sixty pounds a year, a respectable sum. The man had married a wealthy girl and doubled his estate with her dowry. But the Bouchers' fortunes were reversed a few years later when Jonathan's grandfather died before his twenty-fifth year, leaving a young widow and three chil-dren, including Jonathan's father, James. The mother married a man who took her and the children to Dublin. Lacking affection for his wife's children, he put them out as apprentices, James to a shoemaker.

James became economically independent by marrying a wealthy young widow and going into business. For a time he prospered, but then the business went bad. He returned to Blencogo where the family lived in "a state of penury and hardship." Foreseeing bankruptcy, he had to sell part of the family estate. Jonathan suggests that his father's personality kept him from success in business: "He was a lively facetious man, sung a good song, and was fond of company, and of course was almost always in company." Jonathan loved his father but could not respect him, and he seems to have sought a father figure in other men, such as John James, his English mentor.

Blencogo too was discouraging. Jonathan called it a "wretched," "obscure," and "unpolished" place. The townspeople respected hard physical work, and Jonathan despised it. An "ill end" was predicted for him.

Jonathan was able to escape the sordid circumstances of his home and village on periodic visits to a wealthy neighbor who befriended him. The lady of the estate, a Mrs. Thomlinson, took an interest in the bright boy. The contrast between the world in which Jonathan was raised and the world to which he aspired was laid out in miniature before each visit when he entered the Thomlinsons' barn to change from his dirty wood clogs into clean shoes to wear into the parlor. The

Thomlinsons' house was Jonathan's introduction to polite society. He recalled that the house made him long for a more genteel life.

As a very young man, then, Jonathan had decided to separate himself from the world in which he lived. For the sake of more wealth, elegance, and culture he would leave Blencogo. In America, too, Boucher was attracted to wealth and culture. As a tutor and a minister he had access to some of the best plantations in Virginia, including George Washington's. He attended balls and dinners with the finest Virginia gentry. He went into debt to be able to make the right appearance on these occasions. "I had not the patience to wait for the slow savings of a humble station," he writes, "and I fancied I could get into a higher, only by my being taken notice of by people of condition; which was not to be done without my making a certain appearance." He borrowed money, purchased fine clothes, and associated with aristocrats.

The pattern was the same in Maryland, where both his intelligence and his appearance won him a place in the governor's circle. The Homony Club, of which he was president, attracted the most socially prominant as well as the most culturally refined people in Maryland. In marriage also Boucher elevated his social station. Although none can doubt that his marriage to Nelly brought about a close personal relationship, it was also socially advantageous. Nelly had a large dowry and helped him purchase the plantation into which they settled after their marriage.

Could it be that Boucher's aristocratic temperament, his attraction to people with wealth and elegance, ultimately led him back to England? Certainly he seems at times to see America as a larger version of Blencogo. There lived the people he mentions who drank too much and had no literary interests, and there we see his bemusement with the people who admired him for his victory over the blacksmith. Even George Washington, one of the wealthiest planters in the South, did not particularly impress Boucher. Washington, he says, had "no quickness of parts, extraordinary penetration, nor an elevated style of thinking."

Set beside Britain, America was backward and raw. Both he and Nelly were impressed with the grandeur of the mother country when they arrived there in 1775. When he took his wife to the cathedral at Canterbury, "whilst the organ was playing and the choristers singing" she was almost overwhelmed by "the magnificence of the building, the venerableness of its history . . . and the solemnity of the worship."

His love of elegance and culture suggests that Boucher was by temperament better suited to England than to America. But this conclusion overlooks the fact that the same attraction was shared by many American patriots. Southern planters and northern merchants mimicked the British in their dress, speech, furniture, architecture, literary tastes, and in other ways. So, too, Jonathan's ambition, his effort to climb above his poverty-darkened background, was matched by that of many patriots. Benjamin Franklin, for one, had many of Boucher's characteristics: independent-mindedness, intellectual curiosity, and personal resilience. Thus, it was not Boucher's temperament that clearly separated him from other Americans.

What, then, of his ideas? Did they differ radically from those of the patriots? The prevailing political ideology among the Whigs was the "libertarian philosophy" that they inherited from John Locke and his eighteenth-century successors. Locke had set forth principles of government in a theoretical model describing how politics had begun. According to Locke, man initially lived in a condition of complete freedom, a "state of nature." This was an inherently good condition, but it involved a crucial problem — some people used their freedom to oppress others. To prevent such abuses men established government. But sometimes governments themselves became oppressive. Revolution was therefore justifiable and could return the government to a condition in which it would defend, not curtail, individual liberty.

The libertarian ideology, emphasizing the government's responsibility to the people, appeared in the colonies in a number of circumstances. Essays by Locke and by such eighteenth-century successors as John Trenchard and Thomas Gordon were read widely. The colonists themselves articulated the libertarian philosophy during scores of conflicts with the royal governors, and they used libertarian philosophical reasoning in opposing the Stamp Act and subsequent oppressive British acts.

Boucher's ideas on government are surprisingly compatible with the libertarian ideology. In fact, he carried belief in the rights of the people further than many patriots. As we have seen, he cared about the welfare of slaves. He proclaimed slavery to be the worst form of tyranny and encouraged the education, Christianization, and fair treatment of blacks. Like many other southern opponents of slavery, he did own Africans — no doubt his desire for status led him to follow colonial practice in acquiring land and servants — but he was thought one of the most humane of masters. A neighbor asked one of his slaves to whom he belonged, and the man answered, "To Parson Boucher, thank God." Boucher's libertarian views came into play also in his opposition to the Stamp Act.

He then agreed with the patriots that governments should respect the rights of individuals, frequently making statements on behalf of these ideas in the 1760's. In the 1770s, however, he began to stress respect for current political institutions. His position as a beleaguered

Anglican minister in a region that had cut ministerial salaries undoubtedly contributed to his sympathy for the status quo. But his posture
was not merely a defensive one. Admitting that some British policies
were bad, he argued that the colonial response was more "wicked" than
the policies themselves.

Boucher believed that the average person is naturally fickle and
can be led away from his allegiance to good government by ambitious
and designing demagogues. He believed that the South was full of
empty-headed orators who loved to sway men's minds for their personal
gratification. Some of them had used the salary question in Maryland
to "train and habituate the people to opposition." He asserted: "King-
doms are shaken and overturned, to gratify these perturbed spirits,
whose natural element is a storm."

The conclusion Boucher drew from such observations was that individuals are more inclined to error than their governments. Political
institutions were initially formed to curtail the activities of "perturbed
spirits" who disturbed the welfare of others. Opposing those who argued
that men are sacred and governments are merely their instruments,
Boucher argued that men are prone to error and that governments, em-
bodying inherited wisdom, should be respected.

During the turbulent days preceding the Revolution, Boucher frequently preached on the idea of "obedience for conscience' sake." At all
levels of society — in relations between parents and children, employ-
ers and employed, and upper class and lower class — the principle of
obedience should prevail. "The manners of a community," he declared,
"may be regarded as one great chain." He admitted that governments
may make errors and stand in need of correction but declared that current notions, such as the idea that "all government is the mere creation
of the people" or that liberty must be protected by a permanent and
systematic opposition to government, could lead only to chaos.

As early as 1773 Boucher asserted that a revolution had already
taken place in America. The opponents of England had aleady gained
effective control of the government. "To public speakers alone," he declared, "is the government of our country now completely committed:
it is cantoned out into new districts, and subjected to the jurisdiction
of these [revolutionary] committees. . . . An empire is thus completely
established within an empire." Boucher believed that in revolutionary
gatherings men's worst tendencies come to the fore: "It matters not that
in our individual capacities we are wise, temperate, and just." He said,
"Collected together in a mob, we inevitably become irrational, violent,
tyrannical." In short, the greatest threat to liberty comes, not from the
state, but from demagogues. The popular orator is especially dangerous
because he obscures the real virtues of a political state and sets before

the people an imaginary creation. The people, he said, are "amused, bewildered, and enflamed, by certain words and sounds of almost magical potency, to attempt the reformation of some imaginary abuses." The most magical and misleading word of the time, he added, was "an undefinable something, which we call *Liberty*."

Boucher thus treated the current idea of liberty as a phantom. No wonder he was out of favor with the Revolutionaries and needed to carry pistols into his pulpit! But even in his apparent conservatism we may wonder whether his ideas were actually so distinct from those of the founding fathers, none of whom advocated a continual state of anarchy. The Declaration of Independence declares that "prudence indeed will dictate that governments long established should not be overthrown for light and transient causes." The Constitution of 1787 was drafted under the influence of men who desired to create an authoritative government that would command the people's respect. During the administrations of the first two presidents political parties were looked upon by many Americans as treasonous, and under the Alien and Sedition Acts of 1798, President Adams sent Americans to prison for criticizing his administration. In such ways the patriots indicated their own respect for stable government.

The difference then between the philosophy of a Jonathan Boucher and that of many Revolutionary leaders was one of degree. Both believed in a blend of freedom and authority. Circumstances, particularly his position as an Anglican clergyman, forced Boucher to look to England for political and cultural standards; other colonists found them in America. He was vilified by the radicals, but we have the perspective of two centuries: his similarity to other Americans is more impressive now than his difference from them.

QUESTIONS

1. What were Jonathan Boucher's main criticisms of America in his early years as a colonialist? What did he like about America?

2. In what ways did Boucher contribute to colonial society and education while he was in America?

3. Like the Patriots, Jonathan Boucher opposed the Stamp Act — why?

4. What was Boucher's position on the questions of bishops and clerical salaries? How did his thinking on these issues influence his relationship to the Revolutionary movement?

5. Why did Jonathan Boucher leave America? How did other people treat him in his final months in the colonies?

6.   In what respects did Jonathan Boucher's temperament appear to separate him from other Americans? What evidence does the author give that other Americans actually shared the same temperament?

7.   What was the Lockean view of government? In what ways did Boucher support it? What was the philosophical basis of his opposition to the Revolution?

8.   What did Jonathan Boucher mean when he argued that liberty is merely a "phantom"?

BIBLIOGRAPHY

BAILYN, BERNARD. *The Ordeal of Thomas Hutchinson* (1974). Fine biography of the best-known American Tory.

BOUCHER, JONATHAN. *Reminiscences of an American Loyalist, 1738-1789* (1925). Boucher's lively and well-written autobiography.

_____ . *A View of the Causes and Consequences of the American Revolution* (1797, 1967). Contains texts of Boucher sermons, mainly on political affairs.

CALHOON, ROBERT M. *The Loyalists in Revolutionary America, 1760-1781* (1973). Extensive survey of Tory history.

NELSON, WILLIAM H. *The American Tory* (1961). Brief, thoughtful survey of Loyalist history.

ROBERTS, KENNETH. *Oliver Wiswell* (1940). Sensitive and beautifully written fictional account of a Loyalist.

ZIMMER, ANNE Y. *Jonathan Boucher: Loyalist in Exile* (1978). Thorough biographical account.

In his first meeting with Gen. George Washington, commander of the Continental army, Lt. Col. James Paterson was unnerved. Paterson, a high-ranking aide of Adm. Lord Howe, had come to meet Washington at Kennedy House, an elegant mansion near the water in New York City. The day was July 20, 1776, and America had been independent sixteen days — or so the Americans claimed. But neither Lord Howe, with more than four hundred ships under his command, nor his brother, General Howe, with an army of 32,000 British and Hessian soldiers at his disposal, took the claim seriously. They regarded Washington as an upstart, a misguided British subject rather than a military commander. Accordingly, they had addressed a letter to him a few days previously as "George Washington, Esq.," omitting his American titles of general and commander in chief. Washington refused to accept any note that did not recognize his official position. To break this impasse Paterson came as an emissary from Admiral Howe, anchored off Staten Island. As he approached Kennedy House, an American honor guard posted at the door stepped smartly aside.

Paterson was greeted by Gen. Henry Knox, one of Washington's most trusted advisers, and was then introduced to the American commander. The British officer was immediately disarmed by the general's appearance. Washington, he knew, was a former Virginia militia officer who had sought unsuccessfully to obtain a commission in the British army. He was a planter in a remote corner of the British Empire and a former representative in an obscure provincial legislature. The royal officer had expected to meet someone who would reflect the mediocrity of this provincial background.

Instead he was greeted by a man who had the bearing and looks of a European monarch. Standing 6 feet 2 inches tall and weighing 210 pounds, Washington was one of the largest men Paterson had ever met. He wore a fine blue coat with wide buff lapels and gold epaulets; his well-tailored buff trousers were tucked neatly into high black riding boots. A wide, light blue ribbon ran diagonally across his broad chest. His solid chin, firm mouth, long, straight nose, and lightly powdered brown hair tied back in a queue at his neck completed his fine appearance.

Washington appeared to melt the smaller man with his massive dignity and direct, penetrating stare. The British officer prefaced every statement with "Your Excellency," and he came cautiously to his main topic, the pardon offered by His Majesty to "rebels" who would lay down their arms and submit to British authority.

The commander bluntly dismissed the subject. "The Americans have not offended," he said, "therefore, they need no pardon." There was nothing more to say. The ruffled Paterson excused himself and hurried back to the familiar world of a British man of war, while

6

THE AMERICAN REVOLUTION

1776:
The Continental Army
in the Year
of Independence

In 1776 the United States declared its independence from Great Britain, becoming the first Euro-American community to attempt to break away from Old World control. The colonists had taken a century and a half to gain the power and confidence to seek independence, but even now success was uncertain. Britain was unwilling to give up the colonies and sent huge armies and navies to suppress the rebellion. The dream of American independence would become a reality only if the United States could create an effective military force. In 1776 hope for independence grew and faded with the Continental army's halting progress.

In his first meeting with Gen. George Washington, commander of the Continental army, Lt. Col. James Paterson was unnerved. Paterson, a high-ranking aide of Adm. Lord Howe, had come to meet Washington at Kennedy House, an elegant mansion near the water in New York City. The day was July 20, 1776, and America had been independent sixteen days — or so the Americans claimed. But neither Lord Howe, with more than four hundred ships under his command, nor his brother, General Howe, with an army of 32,000 British and Hessian soldiers at his disposal, took the claim seriously. They regarded Washington as an upstart, a misguided British subject rather than a military commander. Accordingly, they had addressed a letter to him a few days previously as "George Washington, Esq.," omitting his American titles of general and commander in chief. Washington refused to accept any note that did not recognize his official position. To break this impasse Paterson came as an emissary from Admiral Howe, anchored off Staten Island. As he approached Kennedy House, an American honor guard posted at the door stepped smartly aside.

Paterson was greeted by Gen. Henry Knox, one of Washington's most trusted advisers, and was then introduced to the American commander. The British officer was immediately disarmed by the general's appearance. Washington, he knew, was a former Virginia militia officer who had sought unsuccessfully to obtain a commission in the British army. He was a planter in a remote corner of the British Empire and a former representative in an obscure provincial legislature. The royal officer had expected to meet someone who would reflect the mediocrity of this provincial background.

Instead he was greeted by a man who had the bearing and looks of a European monarch. Standing 6 feet 2 inches tall and weighing 210 pounds, Washington was one of the largest men Paterson had ever met. He wore a fine blue coat with wide buff lapels and gold epaulets; his well-tailored buff trousers were tucked neatly into high black riding boots. A wide, light blue ribbon ran diagonally across his broad chest. His solid chin, firm mouth, long, straight nose, and lightly powdered brown hair tied back in a queue at his neck completed his fine appearance.

Washington appeared to melt the smaller man with his massive dignity and direct, penetrating stare. The British officer prefaced every statement with "Your Excellency," and he came cautiously to his main topic, the pardon offered by His Majesty to "rebels" who would lay down their arms and submit to British authority.

The commander bluntly dismissed the subject. "The Americans have not offended," he said, "therefore, they need no pardon." There was nothing more to say. The ruffled Paterson excused himself and hurried back to the familiar world of a British man of war, while

Washington, Knox, and other members of the commander's official "family" sat down to a lunch of wine, cold meats, cheese, and bread. Knox later wrote to his wife that "Colonel Paterson appeared awestruck. . . . He was before a very great man indeed."

The minor triumph of that day is all but forgotten while the events at Lexington and Concord, Saratoga, and Yorktown live on in legendary splendor. But the winning of American independence was as dependent on matters of ceremony, appearance, and confidence as on larger events. On July 20 Washington had given the appearance of a victorious general and had thus lent substance to the paper pretenses of the Declaration of Independence. Two centuries later Americans would celebrate a single day, July 4, as the anniversary of our national freedom, but in fact independence came through a long series of tribulations rather than in a moment of transformation. To participate in the Revolutionary War in the year of independence was to be at one moment a soldier in a victorious army of well-disciplined soldiers, at another a refugee in a disorderly rout of farmers and artisans. Sometimes independence was as real as the stone walls of New England or the orderly plantations of the South. At other times it was as insubstantial as a dimly remembered dream.

The Continental army was both the symbol and the agent of that dream. The vision of national independence, of an "equal station" in the world, became a reality when the army worked. And "working" involved creating confidence as well as winning battles. It was largely because of his dignified appearance and demeanor — of his ability, that is, to inspire confidence — that George Washington had been chosen commander in chief. When in 1775 the Continental Congress determined that there should be a national army to fight the British, the tall, distinguished southerner was an obvious choice. As an aristocratic planter, his social standing would dignify the Revolution. His Virginia background accentuated the continental character of the Revolution that had begun in Massachusetts. Washington's political moderation made him acceptable to a broad spectrum of political opinion. And his forty-three years gave him the experience to lead the new Revolutionary army and the vigor to stay on the job. Additionally, he impressed his colleagues in the Congress as a man with "an easy soldierlike air." The impression was no doubt encouraged by his garb: he came to the Congress dressed in an ill-fitting uniform he had worn more than two decades before in the Virginia militia. Thus George Washington became commander in chief. He accepted the appointment with characteristic modesty, protesting his limitations and offering to serve without pay. He wrote Martha that he hoped to be home in the autumn, having no way of knowing that the war would drag on for almost a decade or that he would see Mount Vernon only twice in the next eight years.

On June 23 he left Philadelphia, escorted to the city limits with all the pomp the patriots could muster, including a troop of light horse and a military band. Nine days later he rode through a heavy rainstorm to his new headquarters in Cambridge, Massachusetts, and began at once to assume the responsibilities of his command. Conscious of the need to establish his authority, he toured the colonial lines with a ceremonial accompaniment of twenty-one drummers and twenty-one fifers. He found the men in good spirits, encamped in a long line around the besieged town of Boston. They had bloodied the British at Lexington and Concord and then on June 17 had killed and wounded a thousand redcoats in the Battle of Bunker Hill. Although they had lost the hill, they had mauled the enemy, leaving them isolated in Boston.

As Washington toured the lines, however, he did not see a victorious army but an ill-disciplined tangle of men, looking more like the colorful denizens of a county fair than the orderly soldiers of a well-regulated army. Most wore farm clothing or hunting jackets and identified themselves in battle with a slip of paper worn in their caps. They were inadequately quartered in college dormitories, private homes, tents made of boards and sailcloth, or in crude shelters of stone, turf, and brush; and they lacked medicine, blankets, powder, cannon, and food. Worse still, they were unorganized and poorly disciplined. Many militia units elected their own officers and treated them as comrades rather than as superiors. Washington referred to the men rather disdainfully as "a mixed multitude of people."

Under the best of circumstances, organizing the scores of local militia companies outside Boston into a unified command would be difficult. But Washington, a new, untried leader, could not be certain of support even from his fellow officers. Many had fought in recent battles and might question why Washington had received the top position. Israel Putnam, for example, was Washington's senior by fourteen years. Known affectionately as "Old Put," he had already won immortality for his stirring words at Bunker Hill: "Don't fire, boys, until you see the whites of their eyes." Artemas Ward was an experienced soldier, five years older than Washington, and had commanded the Boston siege quite to his own satisfaction before Washington's arrival. Others were British veterans, among them Charles Lee, a proud and eccentric officer who paraded about with a large retinue of dogs.

If Washington was untested and the army disorganized, there were, at least, many good soldiers in his army. Nathanael Greene, a Quaker's son who left his church to fight for the colonies, commanded an orderly, well-supplied group of Rhode Island volunteers. John Glover of Marblehead, Massachusetts, led a colorful regiment of seamen-soldiers, smartly dressed in cocked hats, blue sailcloth jackets, and loose white navy trousers. During the siege of Boston they captured twenty-three enemy vessels, including the brig *Nancy* with 2,000 muskets and a huge 2,700-pound brass mortar that Old Put, rum bottle in hand, christened with the name "Congress." Glover's oarsmen would later prove indispensable when Washington's army had to retreat over the East River and attack across the Delaware.

Equally colorful were the new Continental recruits from the middle colonies. During the summer the first regiments of riflemen began to arrive from Virginia and Pennsylvania. The most famous were Daniel Morgan's ninety-six frontiersmen, who marched six hundred miles from Virginia in twenty-one days with the loss of only one man. The frontiersmen were crack shots and loved to show off by shooting boards from one another's hands. Unfortunately, their boisterous enthusiasm was combined with a dislike of discipline, and they often were the most ungovernable soldiers in an ill-governed army.

Washington's first job was to create a well-disciplined army from the materials of this "mixed multitude." He began by securing supplies; drilling and disciplining the men; and weeding out bad officers, including some who drew pay for absent or nonexistent soldiers. He gave thirty lashes and drummed men out of the army for insulting an officer or punished men absent without leave with extra latrine duty.

Still, an atmosphere of informality and spontaneity continued. Bored by lack of action, soldiers drank heavily. One ill-advised trooper gave a toast to General Gage, commander of the British forces, and was forthwith ridden around the camp in a cart with a rope around his neck. Some soldiers diverted themselves with competitions to catch cannonballs, shot down from Bunker Hill, as they rolled along the ground: several lost their lives in this entertainment. Other men bathed nude in the Charles River at Cambridge and paraded naked on the bridge, much to the chagrin of Washington who remarked that these exhibitionists appeared to "glory in their shame." In a fit of exasperation at these and other misdemeanors he called his men "exceeding dirty and nasty."

But he persevered, and his troops slowly began to look more like an army. He was on the lines every day, ordering, observing, inspecting. The men were drilled twice a day and kept busy digging new trenches. As time passed, the distinctions between officers and men became plainer. Washington wore a light blue ribbon across his chest; his major generals wore a purple sash; and the brigadiers wore pink. Unfortunately, Washington's army dwindled while it improved. As autumn came to Massachusetts and the wind blew cold over sea, forest, and encampment, men began to think of home, and many a soldier on short-term enlistment walked away from the army for the sake of a fire and a warm bed. Washington wanted to replace this "Eight Month Army" with Continentals, recruited for longer terms of service. He was authorized to raise twenty-eight regiments totaling twenty thousand men, officered by leaders appointed from the top down, in conventional military fashion.

But progress was slow. Before long General Washington was complaining of "a dearth of public spirit and a want of virtue" among the citizenry. The recruits signed up at a disappointingly slow rate, many refusing to join because colonial militia units gave better bonuses. Others signed on but drifted away when rain put out their campfires and cold winds blew through their tents. Those who stayed through the first winter demonstrated patriotism both fine and rare. One was Joseph Hodgkins, an Ipswich, Massachusetts, shoemaker who supplemented his meager officer's pay by serving as army cobbler. In late November many of Hodgkins's Ipswich comrades had already left for home. But he wrote his devoted wife that he meant to stay on. "Our all is at stake," he wrote, "and if we do not exert ourselves in this glorious cause our all is gone and we made slaves of forever."

There were too few Joseph Hodgkinses in the encampments around Boston. At the end of the year Washington had raised fewer than ten thousand Continentals. These men, inadequately supported by small contingents of militia, possessed an average of only thirty cartridges apiece. On New Year's Day the siege lines were so ill manned that Washington feared an attack. He wrote a friend despairingly that rather than take command of the Continental army he could wish he had retired in the West to live "in a wigwam."

Fortunately for the Americans, the British were suffering their own kind of discomfort in Boston. Since the disastrous Battle of Bunker Hill the city had been an increasingly unpleasant place; the town nursed scores of horribly wounded soldiers, many of whom died during the summer. The frequent street auctions of the dead men's belongings led one British soldier to write home that Boston was the "slaughter house of America."

The town festered with animosities. British officers disputed among themselves about matters of policy. Tories cursed their supposed deliverers for failing to take decisive action. And Whigs, living awkwardly in a hostile town, suffered persecution from British and Tories alike. As the snows fell, the privation grew worse, with little food and less firewood. Desperate men pulled down fences and houses to burn for warmth. In their frustration the British soldiers sometimes vented their rage on Boston itself. Needing a place to exercise their horses in the crowded town, they stripped the fine wood pews out of Old South Church and turned the gutted edifice into a riding ring.

The fate of the British in Boston was sealed in late February when Henry Knox, a former Boston bookseller, arrived from Fort Ticonderoga with fifty-seven cannon and mortars. His men and oxen had dragged their cargo for many days, crossing the Hudson, where he lost several cannon through the ice, and continuing on crude roads through the steep Berkshires where fascinated countryfolk gathered to touch the precious weapons. On the night of March 4–5 three thousand colonial soldiers worked in the darkness to place these guns on Dorchester Heights above Boston. The ground was so hard they could not dig breastworks, and so they hauled barrels, posts, and bundles of sticks to the hilltop, and next morning the British saw above them a makeshift fort.

They considered attacking the American position, but a great storm swept down from the north, scattering their boats and dampening their ardor. Gen. Sir William Howe, who had replaced Thomas Gage as commander, recognized that their position was untenable and elected to abandon Boston to the patriots. By mutual agreement the British did not destroy the city and the patriots did not molest the British retreat. The vanquished army spiked their cannon and pushed them, along with General Howe's stately coach, into Massachusetts Bay. They embarked, taking with them one thousand Loyalists, the first of almost one hundred thousand such exiles, many of whom would never see their American homes again. On April 17 the British fleet sailed to Nantasket Roads, ten miles away, where they spent ten miserable days at anchor under mist, rain, and a perpetual cloud of cookfire smoke, trying to decide where to go.

It was fitting that the first great American victory should come in Boston, the city whose "Tea Party" had provoked Britain into passing the Coercive Acts, hastening the outbreak of the Revolution. For a decade Boston had been a center of Revolutionary activity: the scene of a bloody "massacre," the birthplace of the Committees of Correspondence, and the victim of economic and political punishment. In its environs the Revolutionary War had begun, and now the last British soldier had been driven from its streets.

But Washington did not celebrate. He entered the city without ceremony, asking only that a Boston minister preach a sermon of thanksgiving. He recognized that the British army in Boston had been a mere fraction of the mother country's strength. Frustrated in Massachusetts by the rebellious colonists, she would certainly strike at some other point. Washington believed that place would be New York City, for several reasons: it was America's largest city and would thus provide ample accommodation for the army; it was surrounded by water, making it easily defensible; it commanded the Hudson River, providing easy access to Canada; and it was centrally located, making it a potential barrier to communication between New England and the other colonies. Recognizing the British interest in New York, Washington said, "It is the object worthy their attention; and it is the place that we must use every endeavor to keep them from."

To do so would put his army to a test. The Continental army in Boston was primarily the creature of local circumstances, drawn in large measure from men who had come out to help their neighbors at Lexington and Concord. In colonial times the provincial armies had been notoriously reluctant to fight battles beyond their own boundaries, and it was not yet clear whether local troops would travel farther in the new war. Thus far, the Revolutionary War had been fought mainly by men near their own homes. A notable exception occurred during the previous fall when Richard Montgomery and Benedict Arnold led a two-pronged attack on Canada. But barely two thousand men had been with them, and even this select force had been plagued by desertions.

Now Washington must try to move almost ten times as many men from Boston to New York. Some would follow for pay; some for adventure; some, like Joseph Hodgkins, because they genuinely believed in American rectitude. When he learned that he was going away, the Ipswich shoemaker wrote his wife, "I would not be understood that I should choose to march, but as I am engaged in this glorious cause, I am willing to go where I am called."

Between late March and early April 1776 the bulk of the Continental army, along with many state militia units, made their way south. Washington left five regiments in Boston under the command of Gen. Artemas Ward and went ahead to New York to set up his headquarters. The soldiers marched three abreast through New England, led and followed by mounted dragoons, their movements coordinated across thousands of yards by drum cadences. They camped each night in fields staked out by an advance party.

After twelve days of marching, the men came to Manhattan, a lovely island located at the mouth of the Hudson River. They crossed onto it in the north and marched through woods, fields, and pastures to New York City at the southern tip of the island. Still a village by modern standards, it was by far the largest town most of the young soldiers had ever seen. Before them lay a cosmopolitan city of twenty thousand inhabitants, a place of solid brick houses, proud spired churches, and row upon row of shops and warehouses.

When George Washington arrived in New York, he occupied an old mansion and supplied it with a new feather bed, pillows, crockery, and glasses; to complete this comfortable lodging he persuaded Martha to join him. In less style, but with considerable enthusiasm, the men adapted to the new environment, soon discovering the "Holy Ground," a seedy but alluring cluster of whorehouses, where many contracted venereal disease and a few were murdered. Others entertained themselves by stealing melons or digging for oysters.

There were other activities that soon consumed their energy. They would have to defend Manhattan against an enemy that could easily command the surrounding waters. With shovel and pick they fortified Brooklyn Heights and both banks of the Hudson. They sank a row of boats to form a blockade across the Hudson halfway up the island and farther north stretched a chain across the river. They did not always build wisely. Some of the earthen walls contained fragments of rock and glass that became secondary missiles when struck with British shells; others, especially those on Long Island, were poorly designed and offered scant protection against a well-planned attack.

Nonetheless, American morale was high in early summer 1776. Washington had at his disposal twenty thousand confident troops. He had even turned an attempt on his life into an American triumph. New York was a stronghold of loyalism, and after Washington's arrival a network of Tories plotted against him. The conspirators bragged of their plans so openly that the plot was easily discovered. Among the conspirators was Thomas Hickey, one time British soldier, now a member of Washington's life guard, who was hanged on June 28 before an appreciative audience of thousands of soldiers and civilians. One witness was Joseph Hodgkins, who wrote to his wife, "I wish twenty more were served the same."

Those who had enjoyed the spectacle of a conspirator at the gallows looked on a less welcome scene next morning. In the lower bay off the tip of Manhattan was a forest of ships' masts flying the British flag. Sir William Howe's fleet had arrived with more than 130 ships. A few days later Howe's brother, Adm. Richard Howe, arrived with an additional 150 ships. Together their fleets constituted 45 percent of the British navy and carried 42,000 soldiers and sailors, the largest military force ever assembled in America. As a land base they chose Staten Island off the southwestern tip of Manhatttan, occupying it without opposition.

Perhaps more disconcerting than the fleet was the casual, even contemptuous manner in which the ships treated the American fortifications. When a shore battery fired, they responded with a short bombardment of the city, as if to suggest they could destroy it at will. In mid-July two British ships, the *Phoenix* and the *Rose*, easily sailed past the blockade and fortifications on the Hudson River and came to anchor forty miles to the north. With little difficulty they beat off an attack by American fireships and, after several days in the interior, sailed unharmed back to the fleet.

By such gestures the British demonstrated their intent to rule the American colonies. But the Americans had simultaneously formalized their claim to independence. On July 9 by the order of the Continental Congress officers read a new document, entitled the Declaration of Independence, to the soldiers at New York. In 1775 many Americans, including George Washington, had anticipated that the Revolutionary War would result in a new status for the colonies within the British Empire. But the past year had shown that Americans could erect governments, pass legislation, and wage war without British help. Thomas Paine's pamphlet, *Common Sense*, urging American independence, had impressed many moderates, including Washington, that independence was the logical goal of the Revolution. The patriots were cheered by the news of the Declaration and celebrated in New York by putting ropes around a statue of George III, pulling it from its pedestal, and melting the four-thousand-pound statue to make bullets and cannonballs.

The hostile armies spent the midsummer of 1776 preparing for battle. Still low on men, Washington sent out an urgent request to neighboring states for help. By now a pattern of recruitment had been established that would last through the war. Each state was called upon to raise a quota of men, determined by the Congress, to serve in the Continental army as state units or "lines." In addition, each state had its own militia units that would supplement the Continental forces if fighting took place in their area. It was always difficult to raise troops. Although bounties of land and money were offered to volunteers, potential enlistees held back, reluctant to be shot or desiring to maintain their trade or farm. Although the Congress stipulated that men should be healthy, more than five feet two inches in height, and sixteen years of age or older, exceptions were necessary. The Pennsylvania Continentals included David Hamilton Morris, age eleven, and Jeremiah Levering, age twelve. One Massachusetts soldier stood a full seven inches under the height standard. Many were beyond their physical prime — 10 percent over forty, and a few were well into their fifties.

Young and old, short and tall, Washington did all he could to mold them into a disciplined force. The early months in Massachusetts had strengthened his belief in the value of discipline and work. When men were not busy digging trenches, he put them through drills and parades. Finding that the customary punishment of up to thirty-nine lashes for misdemeanors was not sufficient to deter misbehavior, he increased the limit to one hundred lashes (and would have raised it to five hundred had not the Congress objected).

To compensate for the rigors of camp life and the dangers of battle, the Continental Congress stipulated that the men should be provided with abundant daily rations. Its November 4, 1775, orders read as follows: "*Resolved*, That a ration consist of the following kind and quantity of provisions: 1 lb. beef, or 3/4 lb. pork, or 1 lb. salt fish, per day; 1 lb. bread or flour, per day; 3 pints of peas or beans per week, or vegetables equivalent, at one dollar per bushel for peas or beans; 1 pint of milk per man per day, . . . 1 half pint of rice, or one pint of Indian meal, per man per week; 1 quart of spruce beer or cider per man per day, or nine gallons of molasses, per company of 100 men per week." Such provisions would have more than supplied the needs of men if they had been available, but often there was an aching chasm of hunger between prescription and reality. The men probably spent more time foraging for food than fighting the British. Often what they had was inadequate, like the bread, which one soldier complained was "hard enough to break the teeth of a rat."

Despite such disadvantages, thousands of men joined Washington's forces in New York. Typical in motivation was Pvt. Joseph Plumb Martin, who is remembered today as the author of the finest account of the war by a common soldier. Martin was a Connecticut farmboy who was sixteen years old at the outbreak of the war, barely old enough to remember the Stamp Act crisis. At first he had no inclination to be caught "in the toils of an army," and he played no part in the events around Boston. But as the months of war passed, he grew hostile to the British and wanted "to be called a defender of my country." In spring 1776, watching as friends marched out of town on their way to New York, he could wait no longer and enlisted in the state militia. His family supplied him with arms, clothing, a piece of cake, and a pocket Bible. Thus equipped, he set out for New York.

While Washington was busy with fortifications, drills, and discipline, the Howe brothers planned how to mount an attack. They were already at an advantage but expected additional reinforcements from Adm. Peter Parker, who would soon arrive in New York with armies commanded by Sir Henry Clinton and Lord Charles Cornwallis. The British delay was occasioned in part by the desire to attack the Americans with as much force as possible and to end the war immediately with an overwhelming victory.

Additionally, the Howes attempted a diplomatic mission, having been empowered not only to wage war against the Americans but also to negotiate with them. Their dual role reflected an awkward compromise between British factions led by the colonial secretary, Lord George Germain, who favored the maximum use of force, and others who followed Lord North in favoring a political solution. Germain's influence was evident in the huge British force at New York. North's resulted in the Howes having been empowered to pardon penitent rebels and states.

As we have seen, the attempts at negotiation fell upon an impasse

when the Howes addressed an invitation to parley to "Mr." George
Washington and Washington refused to receive any communication
that failed to address him as "General." There in microcosm was the
whole issue of American independence. The "Mr." implied that the
Continental Congress had no authority; the "General" implied that the
colonies were independent. Neither side would accept the other's view,
and Colonel Paterson's visit failed to establish a basis for negotiation.
The Howes would be warriors rather than diplomats.

On August 22 British troops began to move in barges across the
Narrows between Staten Island and Long Island to occupy unprotected
beaches near the town of Gravesend. In the evening General Howe had
fifteen thousand troops ready to challenge Washington's positions in
Brooklyn. Three days later Hessian mercenaries were rowed across,
standing at attention in the barges in an impressive display of discipline.

Even before the Battle of Long Island began, Washington was at
a disadvantage. His outnumbered army was divided into two forces,
and those in Manhattan would be unable to help their comrades in
Brooklyn. Moreover, an important segment of the Long Island force
was placed in advance of the well-fortified Brooklyn base, an unwise
decision, because it stretched out the force in a thin, indefensible line,
with a road around their right flank covered by only five men. The error
was primarily the result of poor planning by Gen. Israel Putnam; but
Washington also was to blame, having surveyed the positions and left
them unchanged.

The battle began on August 26 when British and Hessian troops
made a frontal assault against thirty-five hundred forward troops under
Gen. John Sullivan and Gen. William Alexander. The Americans were
holding their own when they heard gunfire on their left flank. During
the night Generals Howe and Clinton had marched behind the Americans along the poorly defended road and threatened to encircle the patriots. British and Hessian soldiers plunged into the American ranks,
using their superior training in hand-to-hand fighting to overwhelm
the patriots, most of whom used rifle butts against fixed bayonets.

The Americans fled from the carnage toward their fortifications
on Brooklyn Heights. George Washington, who had rushed over from
Manhattan to be near the battle, tried to rally them, calling out, "Remember what you are contending for." At that moment, however, self-
preservation seemed to most of the men the main object to "contend
for." Private Martin, who watched the approach of these wounded and
dispirited men, found himself "a little daunted" and began thinking
wistfully of home.

A few of the Continentals' lines had fought bravely even after the
collapse of their positions, but most ran. In all, more than one thousand

Americans were killed or captured. Among the prisoners were Generals Sullivan and Alexander. Fortunately, Howe did not pursue the confused Americans into Brooklyn; had he done so, he might have easily crushed them with his superior force. But, rather than attacking Brooklyn Heights and running the risk of another disaster like that at Bunker Hill, he decided to take the safer course of building protective trenches and laying siege to Washington's position.

In the Brooklyn encampment the defeated Americans were confused and discouraged. The first year of the war had been so easy: they had defeated the British at Lexington and Concord, killed them by the hundreds at Bunker Hill, fortified Dorchester Heights, and forced them out of Boston. Now, in their first major battle since the Declaration of Independence, they had broken and run. No jaunty sounds of fifes and drums, no talk about invincibility circulated in camp; ominous doubts gripped the soldiers. Joseph Hodgkins realized that the ability of America to win her independence was in doubt. "The day is come . . . ," he wrote to his wife, "on which depends the salvation of this country."

There was no question of defeating the British on Long Island, only of keeping the hope of future victory alive through the difficult maneuver of evacuating the army from Brooklyn Heights across the East River to Manhattan. On the night of August 29-30 a cold wind blew from the northeast. Rain fell on the solid wood decks of the British men of war anchored off the tip of Manhattan and ran down the sides of canvas tents and along the muddy paths in the Brooklyn encampment. It sent thousands of British seamen and soldiers scurrying for the cover of ships' cabins and army tents. It left Washington's army free to attempt an audacious maneuver in the wet, blackened world.

Throughout the night a fleet of flat-bottomed boats under the command of Marblehead's John Glover ferried men across the river. Hour after hour the fishermen-sailors worked at muffled oars; Washington stood on the shore supervising the loading. Only after ten thousand men with their arms, horses, and supplies had made their escape did the commander allow himself to be rowed to safety. When the fog cleared in the morning, the British occupied an empty fort.

The evacuation boosted American morale. On Long Island an Anglican parson's daughter, Lydia Minturn Post, began a secret diary she would keep for her husband, an officer in the Revolutionary army. Although Washington's retreat left her in enemy territory, she regarded the escape as a commendable achievement. "What a skillful movement was that of George Washington," she wrote, "a wonderful retreat! — the enemy so near that the sound of their pickaxes and shovels could be heard! It is new proof of his cool forethought and judgment."

On Manhattan, however, the Americans had little time to congratulate themselves. The fall of New York was now inevitable owing to the superiority of the British fleet and their command of Brooklyn Heights, from which they could fire at the American positions in the city. Some of Washington's advisers wisely suggested burning the city to reduce its usefulness to the invader. But the Congress was unwilling to approve such a stern measure, and Washington was unwilling to conduct a hasty retreat. He badly needed to defeat the British, even if only in a skirmish, to bolster American morale. He stationed his main force behind fortifications on Harlem Heights in the northern part of the island but left five thousand men in the city under General Putnam.

The Howes were in no hurry to pursue the war. Anticipating that Washington's recent defeat might make the Americans more willing to negotiate, they dispatched a message to the Continental Congress requesting a parley. A few days later the Congress sent John Adams, Benjamin Franklin, and Edward Rutledge to meet with the Howes aboard the British flagship off Staten Island. The conference was a civil affair accompanied with good wine and a pleasant meal. But there was no real chance for a settlement. The Americans demanded recognition of independence as the basis for negotiation, and the Howes declared that they could merely pardon those who denounced the rebellion. Admiral Howe professed to regret the necessity for the war, saying that if America should be defeated he would "lament it like the loss of a brother." Never at a loss for words, Franklin answered wryly, "My Lord, we will do our utmost endeavors to save your lordship that mortification."

The conference ended where it had begun, and the rival forces continued to prepare for the next battle. The two weeks following the defeat on Long Island had done nothing to restore the shattered American morale. Food and blankets continued to run short, and militiamen, sensing defeat, deserted by the thousands. Still there were many who stayed, watching anxiously for some indication of the enemy's next move. One of the faithful was the young Connecticut militiaman, Pvt. Joseph Plumb Martin, who was one of the soldiers assigned to guard Manhattan's east shore.

On September 14 four British warships sailed up the East River and anchored opposite Martin's position. They were so close that when the sentries standing watch along the blackened shore shouted the watchword "All is well," a voice from one of the ships boomed out, "We will alter your tune before tomorrow night." And indeed they did.

The next morning Private Martin saw the British ship, *Phoenix*, anchored so close to shore that he could read her name as if he "had been directly under her stern." The large ship and her companions were ominous enough, but now a more threatening sight appeared. Scores of small boats packed with British and Hessian soldiers began to make their way toward the Manhattan shore. Soon there were so many that they "appeared like a large clover field in full bloom." The ships opened fire, and "there came such a peal of thunder from the British shipping," says Martin, "that I thought my head would go with the sound." He jumped into a ditch and began to wonder "which part of my carcass was to go first."

Martin's fellow militiamen and their officers were equally impressed and withdrew from the exposed position. When the British landed at Kip's Bay on Manhattan they found a quiet farmhouse and a pleasant field but no Americans. Panic had struck the patriots all across the island. The most endangered were five thousand men in New York who might easily be cut off from Washington's main force on Harlem Heights if Howe had swept across the island. They and the other troops along the East River swelled the country roads leading north from the city.

Soon after leaving their positions at Kip's Bay the men in Martin's regiment were scattered by British grapeshot. Martin found himself alone with two other militiamen as frightened as himself. Hoping to fortify their spirits, they stopped at a house and asked for a drink. The residents, two women and several children, were in tears, frightened by the proximity of battle, but one managed to place a bottle of rum and some glasses on the table for the soldiers, who refreshed themselves and left.

The highways, fields, and woods of Manhattan were alive with movement. Martin came upon men he thought were friends only to find that they were Hessians. He barely escaped and overtook a party of militiamen just as a British force opened fire. The patriots fled in abject confusion, littering the ground with their arms and knapsacks, coats and hats. Martin admitted that he and others were dreadfully afraid. "Every man that I saw," he writes, "was endeavoring by all sober means to escape from death or captivity."

No man suffered more on that day than George Washington. He realized that he could not hold New York but wanted to maintain order in retreat. When he heard the guns on the morning of September 15, he hurried toward Kip's Bay, discovering to his "surprise and mortification" that his sometime army had been reduced to a pathetic mob. Again and again he tried to rally the troops who surged past him. Finally Washington came upon two brigades, less terrified than the others, and stationed them behind a stone wall to oppose a British advance. But as soon as a handful of the enemy appeared, these also fled. Now Washington completely lost control of himself. Throwing his hat on the ground and lashing out with his riding crop at men and officers, he cursed and declaimed: "Are these the men with whom I am to defend America? Good God! Have I got such troops as these?"

But the men continued to run, and Washington slumped in his saddle, exhausted from anger and despair. His aides stayed by their chief, watching anxiously as the last of the soldiers made their escape. Across the field, some fifty British soldiers came toward the paralyzed leader. Washington was too hurt to care what happened. Finally, the aides, realizing that they must act, took his bridle and led their dazed commander to safety. It was the saddest moment in Washington's military career — and it was nearly the last.

The day was as glorious for the British as it was tragic for the Americans. With their men spread across Manhattan, General Howe and his subordinates, Generals Clinton and Cornwallis, stopped for an afternoon respite at Murray Hill, a fine country estate overlooking Kip's Bay. While the pathetic Americans struggled northward through the hot, humid afternoon, the British officers sipped madeira and ate cakes. New York was theirs. Soon, it seemed, Washington must be theirs, and with his fall the little American rebellion would be ended.

A few miles away the remnants of the American army spent a miserable night at Harlem Heights. Their hasty retreat had prevented Howe from dividing the army and cutting off Putnam in New York. But valuable stores and arms had been abandoned to the foe, and there was not enough food to feed the bedraggled refugees. Militiamen by the hundreds were again deserting the apparently doomed army. Worse still, men and officers bore the shame of having fled without testing the enemy.

The soldiers found some solace next day in an engagement near Harlem Heights when two small parties of American and British soldiers ran into each other in no-man's-land between the two armies. As the Americans retreated, a British bugler insulted them with a disparaging air, the signal to end a fox hunt. But the Americans were not finished. Washington sent more men down from the Heights into the engagement and forced the British to abandon their advance position.

This minor triumph afforded some comfort, but the commander in chief could not ignore the dismal state of his army. In the last month of fighting he had lost men, supplies, territory, and pride. It was bad enough to lose the battles, but it was worse to watch the progressive deterioration of the army. For every man killed or captured, four or five soldiers had deserted and gone home, reckoning the Revolutionary War was over.

Washington wondered if it was not over for him also. In a letter to his cousin, Lund Washington, he declared that "the bitterest curse to an enemy" would be to occupy his place. There appeared to be no way to win the war, and yet his associates insisted that he must not quit his position. None of the apparent alternatives was satisfactory. "In confidence," he wrote, "I tell you that I never was in such an unhappy, divided state since I was born."

What most troubled Washington was the volatile condition of his army. Most soldiers were short-term militiamen who retreated and deserted with disturbing regularity in times of trial. Their influence upset the Continentals, who themselves enlisted for only one year at a time. Washington tried to persuade the Continental Congress to provide for an army of soldiers bound to the cause by long-term enlistments. But the Congress balked: such a force would be expensive and might become too independent for the welfare of the young republic. America had revolted against a strong military power and did not want to become overly centralized herself. For the moment, Washington would have to make do with what he had.

British and American forces in New York were now in tenuous balance. Washington occupied the northern part of Manhattan, and Howe occupied the southern. The British could easily land their troops above Washington in Westchester County, thus isolating him in Manhattan, but for the time being they appeared content to occupy themselves with establishing their headquarters in New York City. Their potential comfort was greatly diminished on September 21 when a great fire of undetermined origin destroyed three hundred buildings. Washington, who had wanted to destroy the city himself, concluded that "Providence, or some good honest fellow," had done the job. But even after the burning of New York City the British forces were well housed and supplied. Not so the Americans, who continued to have problems in providing themselves with blankets, clothing, and food. Pvt. Joseph Plumb Martin says he was so hungry that he liked to go on patrols because it improved the chance of finding food. He considered himself fortunate when he could steal a few turnips or beg a sheep's head from the officers' mess. Despite such hardships, hunger was only a "secondary matter" in comparison with exposure to the elements. It was now autumn, but Martin and many of his comrades had only summer clothes and no blankets. They had to spend the night "freezing and thawing" alternate sides of their bodies. "I have often while on guard," Martin writes, "lain on one side until the upper side smarted with cold, then turned that side down to the place warmed by my body and let the other take its turn at smarting, while the one on the ground warmed." On some mornings he awoke to find the ground "as white as snow with hoar frost."

The most memorable event in days of cold, hunger, and desertion was a single act of heroism that became one of the great mythic legacies of the Revolution. After losing Brooklyn and New York, Washington needed good intelligence reports on British movements and commissioned a young captain named Nathan Hale to enter New York as a spy. Clothed in a brown broadcloth suit and a wide-brimmed hat and pretending to be a schoolmaster, Hale wandered unmolested through the British lines gathering intelligence. He was waiting for a boat to carry him back to safety when he was apprehended, searched, and proved a spy. In short order he was condemned to be hanged. At the gallows on September 22 he uttered words that would recall the spirit of American resistance to British tyranny long after the disgrace at Kip's Bay was forgotten. "I only regret," he said, "that I have but one life to lose for my country." Hale's heroic death typified the stoic patriotism of the New York campaign. Denied victories, the expression of American resourcefulness was limited to orderly retreat, uncomplaining privation, and resolute self-sacrifice.

On October 12 the Howes sought to outflank Washington by landing four thousand men at Throgs Neck, a peninsula north of his Harlem Heights headquarters. As they approached a bridge to the mainland, they encountered stiff rifle fire from behind a well-designed fortification. Not realizing that the position was held by only twenty-five Americans, the attackers withdrew and sailed on a few miles to New Rochelle where they made a second landing. Here, on October 18, they overcame spirited resistance from four battalions of Massachusetts troops, well protected behind stone walls.

In the meantime, Washington had realized that his Manhattan position was untenable and began retreating to the north, leaving five thousand men under Gen. Nathaneal Greene divided between Fort Washington on the Manhattan side of the Hudson and Fort Lee in New Jersey on the opposite shore. Washington fortified himself on high ground near White Plains, where Howe attacked him on October 28. Howe managed to take one of the hills on Washington's right flank, forcing the American commander to supervise another night retreat. Washington reassembled his army five miles away at North Castle, and Howe, seeing that could not lure Washington into an engagement, turned south toward Fort Washington. Washington was now forced to make one of the most difficult and, as it turned out, unfortunate decisions of his career.

Fort Washington, the last American stronghold on Manhattan, was on a high cliff over the Hudson, surrounded on all but the river side by the British. Washington believed that the position was not capable of being defended but was persuaded by his subordinate, Nathanael Greene, that it could be held. On November 16 he watched in despair from the opposite shore as his fears were realized. The outer-works of the fort were too extensive to be held by the twenty-eight hundred men left in Manhattan. They were easily overwhelmed, and men retreated into the fort itself. But it was small and impossibly crowded, and at the day's end the situation was hopeless, and the garrison surrendered. It was the worst defeat of Washington's career. In addition to losing almost three thousand men, he lost guns, cannon, munitions, and supplies.

Two days later Cornwallis crossed the Hudson and moved toward Fort Lee. Joseph Hodgkins, then garrisoned at Fort Lee, had built himself a comfortable log cabin and hoped to spend the winter. But in the face of the British advance the Americans had to make a hasty retreat, leaving behind tents, cannon, ammunition — and Hodgkins's homey cabin. After losing New York the disheartened Washington must have hoped for some respite, having retreated from Brooklyn to New York, to Harlem Heights, to White Plains, to North Castle, to Fort Lee. But now he must abandon Fort Lee and cross New Jersey, hoping to station his army between Howe and Philadelphia.

As he and his men fell back through New Jersey his situation grew worse. They lacked food, clothing, and shelter; and the New Jersey militiamen who were expected to muster with his arrival did not materialize. Howe, moving slowly after Washington, offered to pardon those who renounced the Revolution and found thousands of lukewarm patriots willing to accept the offer. Washington's humiliation was completed by disaffection among his officers. General Lee, still commanding seven thousand troops at North Castle, refused to come to Washington's aid and plotted to increase his own power. After the fall of the two Hudson River forts, he wrote to a friend in the Continental Congress, saying, "Had I the powers, I could do you much good." Washington's adjutant general, Joseph Reed, wrote to Lee encouraging him to supplant the discouraged chief.

The trials of autumn 1776 extended well beyond Washington's camp. To the north the Continental army had been pushed out of Canada and barely held on to Fort Ticonderoga. Thousands of Americans in the environs of New York City experienced the hardships of British occupation. The end of America's first year of self-styled independence was drawing near, but many Americans professed doubts about the "glorious cause." Some were ardent Tories like the old woman who while selling milk to Pvt. Joseph Plumb Martin lectured him on his opposition to "our good King George" and warned him that "the regulars would make us fly like pigeons." Others were patriots who genuinely desired American independence but doubted that it was attainable.

The conflicting sentiments of patriotism and fear are set out clearly in an account by Lydia Minturn Post, the woman who had been so impressed with Washington's "wonderful retreat" from Brooklyn. The retreat may have saved the Continental army, but it left families like hers to a precarious existence under British occupation. Separated from her husband, a Continental officer, she went with her three children to live with her father in a pleasant Dutch-style house. The location itself hardly suggested a war. The whitewashed house with its low gabled roof was covered with sweetbrier and creeping vines. Her father, a Church of England minister, had planted ivy and sweet clover in the yard.

This fine pastoral scene had become a place of privation and fear. The army requisitioned men, horses, and wagons for work details and billeted Hessian and British soldiers in their houses. Soldiers carted away trees and fences to provide fuel and housing. Lydia Post spoke with contempt of the German mercenaries quartered in the neighborhood, as many as six in a house. These invaders strung up hammocks in the kitchens and spent the days drinking and smoking. British officers could be even more obtrusive. The Posts had to share their home with a wounded British officer and his two servants. A neighbor endured the presence of an officer and his silly mistress, a woman who knocked holes in their walls to mount a collection of stuffed parrots.

Lydia Post recounts many incidents where neighbors were punished for refusing to flatter the British soldiers. One man was killed on the spot by a bully who tried unsuccessfully to make him say "God save the King." Her neighbors were ravaged also by outlaws who used the disorder of war to facilitate their activities. They came at night, forcing their way into houses and stealing whatever valuables they could find.

Thus, life for conquered Americans was a combination of privation, annoyance, fear, and outrage. For those like Lydia Post the price of liberty was high indeed. She watched with pathetic interest the course of the Revolutionary War after Washington's departure from Long Island. Certainly she was a patriot. "We love this our native land," she wrote her husband. "She is over-taxed, oppressed, insulted." But she was also a realist and knew that the war was going badly. After hearing of Washington's loss at White Plains, she wrote, "Who can look without trembling at the failure of this struggle to throw off our yoke?" When she heard of Washington's forlorn retreat through New Jersey, she felt the American cause was hopeless. "The disparity between the two contending parties," she reflected despairingly, "is so immense." In late December she wrote, "The year has closed disastrous, gloomy."

Lydia Post's account serves as a barometer of public sentiment.

Living close to the war, she found that her patriotic feelings had to fight with her personal observations of British power. Her concerns were matched by Washington's own. In mid-December he found himself on the Pennsylvania side of the Delaware River, having been forced out of New Jersey as well as New York in less than two months. The proud soldier who had faced down General Howe's adjutant in New York a few months before had lost confidence in himself and his cause. He contemplated going south to Virginia and crossing the Appalachian Mountains into the interior to escape the British army. Independence seemed an empty hope. "I think the game is pretty near up," he wrote. "I am wearied to death."

Thousands of Americans shared Washington's discouragement, but it was an Englishman recently migrated to Philadelphia who coined an immortal phrase to describe the feeling in those dark days. A year earlier Thomas Paine had caught the American imagination with his plea for independence in *Common Sense*; now in an essay called "The American Crisis" he called for renewed dedication to the cause. "These are the times that try men's souls," he wrote. "The summer soldier and the sunshine patriot will in this crisis shrink from the service of his country: but he that stands it now, deserves the love and thanks of man and woman." The essay made popular reading in Washington's camp. The commander had seen an army of "summer soldiers" evaporate after the debacle in Brooklyn and Manhattan. But the men who were still with him had "stood," having resisted the temptation to desert.

Still, it would take more than patriotism to keep the army together and win the war. For that there must be victories. Across the Delaware there were British encampments in nearby Trenton, Princeton, and Brunswick. If Washington could cross the river and take them by surprise, he could capture several thousand enemy soldiers along with their valuable stores. But the risk was great; if discovered, the war might be ended in a single battle. It was a desperate gamble but one made necessary by the disasters of the previous months. The Americans had not won a significant victory since declaring their independence.

On the night of December 25 Washington began to embark twenty-four hundred men for the crossing of the Delaware. He had assembled a fleet of long, shallow-draft Durham boats, normally used as trading vessels. These were manned by Col. John Glover's Marbleheaders. During the night the temperature dropped and the wind came howling down the valley. Snow fell on the small transports as they made the three-hundred-yard trip across the cold water between hard blocks of ice. But in the early morning of December 26 the army was across and marched over frozen roads to Trenton.

There they surprised the Hessian garrison, sleeping off a Christmas celebration. The enemy tried without success to organize themselves to fend off Washington's attack, but they surrendered after forty-five minutes. It was a stunning victory. Washington captured a thousand enemy troops and their supplies at the cost of only twelve casualties.

Fearing a British counterattack, Washington took his men and their prisoners back acoss the Delaware. In a few days his soldiers would complete their one-year enlistments, but Washington persuaded most to stay another six weeks. On December 30 he recrossed the Delaware. This time the British were prepared. General Cornwallis was in the vicinity with six thousand troops. On the night of January 2 the British general camped his men near Washington's position on Assumpink Creek. Expecting to attack Washington the next day, Cornwallis remarked, "At last we have run down the old fox and will bag him in the morning." But his greedy prediction was wrong, for Washington once more eluded the British with a night march. Leaving a few men behind to tend the campfires, the Americans marched past Cornwallis deep into enemy-held territory. On the morning of January 3 they routed the British at Princeton, and Washington watched the retreat with childlike enthusiasm. Sitting astride his horse, he waved his sword and shouted, "It's a fine fox chase, my boys."

Cornwallis, who had expected the day to be his, had heard gunfire behind his lines. Afraid that Washington would go on to capture the main British supply depot at Brunswick, he hurried his men back to defend his stores, leaving Washington in control of Princeton. The Americans soon marched on to Morristown, where they established winter quarters deep in the heart of British territory.

The victories at Trenton and Princeton gave an enormous boost to American morale. In Europe the New Jersey counterthrust was described by such eminent military experts as Frederick of Prussia as one of the great campaigns of the century. At home in New York, Lydia Minturn Post credited the American success to divine Providence; to "the judgment, skill, and intrepidity" of George Washington; and to the "deep-rooted indignation" of the patriots who would "do and dare for liberty, or death." Even an old English observer had to admit that Washington's successes restored American confidence. "A few days ago," he said, "they had given up their cause for lost. . . . Now they are all liberty mad again."

The ceremonial dignity of the commander in chief, which had so impressed Col. James Paterson during his meeting with Washington six months before, was now reinforced by Washington's imaginative military leadership. But in the interim he had almost failed. The independence that had been declared so confidently in 1776 was in reality an elusive goal. The Washington who would one day accept a British surrender at Yorktown was also the Washington who was "wearied to death" time and again the first year of the struggle. America was able to persevere beyond the year of independence only because of small triumphs salvaged from great disasters: a patriot spy who died well at the gallows; a general whose bearing encouraged respect despite his inexperience; a few thousand soldiers who stayed with Washington when other thousands deserted; an army that avoided annihilation while suffering defeat; an impassioned publicist who understood "the times that try men's souls."

QUESTIONS

1. The author claims that American independence did not become a reality on July 4, 1776. In what ways was America still subordinate to Britain after "Independence Day"?

2. For what reasons did people join and desert the Revolutionary army?

3. What were George Washington's principal accomplishments and weaknesses as a military leader in 1775-76?

4. Why was Washington "wearied to death" in 1776?

5. "Denied victories, the expression of American resourcefulness was limited to orderly retreat, uncomplaining privation, and resolute self-sacrifice." Explain.

6. Describe the contribution of each of these to the Revolutionary War: Nathanael Greene, Joseph Hodgkins, Joseph Plumb Martin, Nathan Hale, Lydia Minturn Post, and Thomas Paine.

BIBLIOGRAPHY

BLIVEN, JR., BRUCE. *Battle for Manhattan* (1955). Excellent history of Washington's loss of Manhattan.

KURTZ, STEPHEN G., AND JAMES H. HUTSON, EDITORS. *Essays on the American Revolution* (1973). Best modern essay collection on the Revolution.

MIDDLEKAUFF, ROBERT. *The Glorious Cause* (1982). Well-integrated account of the political and military aspects of the Revolutionary War.

POST, LYDIA MINTURN. *Personal Recollections of the American Revolution* (1859). Long Island woman's account of British and Hessian occupation.

ROBERTS, KENNETH. *Arundel* (1929 and later editions). Fine historical novel on Arnold's march to Quebec.

ROYSTER, CHARLES. *A Revolutionary People at War* (1979). Sensitive analysis of the relationship between the Revolutionary War and the American character.

SCHEER, GEORGE F., EDITOR. *Private Yankee Doodle* (1962). Diary of Joseph Plumb Martin.

———— AND HUGH F. RANKIN, EDITORS. *Rebels and Redcoats* (1957). Fine anthology of letters and diary accounts of the Revolution.

SMITH, PAGE. *A New Age Now Begins* (2 vols., 1976). Lively narrative survey of the Revolutionary War.

WADE, HERBERT T., AND ROBERT A. LIVELY. *This Glorious Cause* (1958). Story of two officers, Joseph Hodgkins and Nathaniel Wade — includes Hodgkins's letters.

7

TESTING
THE CONSTITUTION

The
Alien and Sedition
Acts

In 1798 the United States had been independent for two decades,
but the nation's character was not yet fully defined. The Constitution, although creating a republican instrument of government,
could not anticipate every historical circumstance. The political
crisis resulting in the Alien and Sedition Acts was one of many
episodes in which Americans were torn between conflicting political values. In 1798 it seemed that they must sacrifice either free
speech or political unity. The Adams administration chose the
latter, provoking a nationwide debate about American institutions
and inadvertently encouraging the growth of free speech and two-
party government.

When the carriage bearing President John Adams came into view on the morning of July 27, 1797, Newark, New Jersey, was alive with a holiday atmosphere. Flags flew above the streets; church bells rang; young men fired a cannon salute; and local dignitaries stood ready to greet the president. Those without official business crowded the taverns, drinking freely.

President Adams was both pleased and vexed with this display of patriotic fervor. The country was ablaze with patriotism because France had recently insulted three American negotiators. For the past four months the president had found himself delightfully and disturbingly popular. The delight lay in the compliment to his ego, one of the largest in the land; the disturbance, however, grew out of his belief that such adoration was fickle. His Puritan reserve led him to distrust, even while he enjoyed, the momentary cheers of the crowd.

He had hoped to travel quietly from Philadelphia, the national capital, to Quincy, Massachusetts, where he and his wife, Abigail, would spend the summer. The business of preparing for war — expanding the army, building new ships, appointing officers — had left him exhausted. Abigail, too, needed rest, having followed every turn of national affairs almost as closely as her husband. She found Philadelphia's summer air so hot and close that "you had as good be in an oven." She missed her friends at home and now wanted to "slide along to them, unnoticed and without parade."

As the carriage entered Newark, then, the good citizens of that place were more pleased to see the president than he was to see them. Undoubtedly he waved and smiled politely, but he did not stop to greet the notables who had hoped to kiss his hand. As he drove past the young men at the cannon, they chanted in unison, "Behold the chief who now commands." The president probably acknowledged their greeting, but his carriage rattled on, leaving the youths to fire a sixteen-gun salute after their departing commander in chief.

At the doorway of John Burnet's tavern a well-liquored crowd watched the coach as it disappeared down the road. The town's moment of glory had ended abruptly, and there remained only the anticlimax of the day ahead. Perhaps to enliven the atmosphere, one of the men remarked, "There goes the President, and they are firing at his ass."

In response another fellow, one Luther Baldwin, who was said to be "a little merry," expressed his political sensibilities in a few pithy words, "I do not care," said he, "if they fire through his ass."

Suddenly the town had a new event at which to marvel. Here in their midst was a traitor, a sayer of forbidden words. Such, at least, was the conclusion of the tavern owner. "This is sedition," he said. A group of Federalists who had gathered around expressed their agreement. Luther Baldwin had broken the law, and he must pay the penalty.

In due course the tavern wit, known to history only for the ten words he spoke that day, was indicted for speaking "seditious words tending to defame the President and government of the United States." He was tried by a court presided over by Associate Justice Bushrod Washington of the U.S. Supreme Court. Found guilty, he was fined 150 dollars and committed to federal prison until the fine was paid.

Luther Baldwin was apparently punished for his querulous wit. But in truth he was less the victim of his tongue than of his times. His remark was sedition only because in 1798 it was regarded as sedition; in other periods it would never have attracted the attention of the law. It is less significant, then, that Baldwin joked about cannonballs, and presidential anatomy than that such behavior was regarded as a crime.

The immediate occasion for Baldwin's trial was the passage in 1798 of the Alien and Sedition Acts, four statutes aimed at discouraging opposition to the government. The acts, in turn, reveal current thinking about freedom of speech, the legitimacy of parties, and dissent in wartime. All these forces were brought to bear on politics in 1798.

In 1798 the Bill of Rights was only seven years old. The First Amendment declared that "Congress shall make no law . . . abridging the freedom of speech, or of the press." But America lacked a tradition of political and judicial experience to draw out the meaning of that clause. It was generally agreed that certain kinds of speech could be so malicious, so crude, or so harmful as to fall outside the scope of legitimate discourse. Even today such speech-related issues as pornography, wartime dissent, and the sanctity of a reporter's sources have eluded definitive boundaries. It should not surprise us to learn that the early republic had not fully defined the First Amendment.

The issue of free speech was complicated in 1798 not only by the newness of the Constitution but also by the hostility of early Americans to political parties. Eventually parties would seem as right, natural, and patriotic as the Constitution itself. But in the 1790s they were viewed as a cancer in the body politic. In a good republic, it was thought, no right-thinking person would need to criticize the government or form an opposition faction. The Constitution did not provide for parties, and eighteenth-century statesmen generally denounced them as destructive — even treasonous — threats to the nation's unity and welfare. When George Washington became president in 1789, Americans did not expect to be troubled with internal dissent. The Constitution provided an apparently stable government, and Washington had been elected by a unanimous vote in the electoral college. Seemingly any right-thinking individual would now support the government and the administration.

Despite such optimism, however, discord soon emerged encouraging the formation of two rival political organizations. Alexander Hamilton, Washington's able and ambitious secretary of the treasury, served as the catalyst for the divisions of the 1790s. Hamilton wanted to attach wealthy Americans to the government by skillful management of the national debt and the tariff, and by creating a national bank. His financial progam aimed to establish a strong central government allied with a progressive business community. No admirer of the people — he once called the public a "great beast" — Hamilton was distrustful of human nature and felt that America was best governed by a political and economic elite.

The Hamiltonian program led to the formation of the first American party system. Opposition to Hamilton's program centered on Secretary of State Thomas Jefferson. Hamilton despised the common man; Jefferson exalted him. Hamilton wanted a strong federal government; Jefferson favored a modest national establishment. Hamilton felt that America's future lay in the factory. Jefferson believed that the real source of national virtue was the farmer.

During the next five years the Hamilton-Jefferson opposition evolved into a system of political parties. At first these consisted of loose divisions within Congress in 1792. In that year no one opposed George Washington as president, but Hamilton's opponents offered George Clinton as a vice-presidential candidate against John Adams and acquired a party organ in Philip Freneau's *National Gazette*.

During Washington's second administration the breach between Hamiltonians and Jeffersonians — soon to be known as Federalists and Republicans — was further widened by divisions on foreign policy. In 1789 when French patriots stormed the Bastille, a symbol of monarchic tyranny, most Americans rejoiced. The American principle of liberty was apparently gaining ground in Europe, and several of the new revolutionary leaders — notably the marquis de Lafayette, who sent Washington the key to the Bastille — had helped America win her own revolution. But each year the French Revolution grew more radical. The king and many of his supporters were guillotined, and revolutionaries began to attack the church. In 1793 France and England went to war. Many Americans favored England because of trade relations and hostility to radicalism. Others supported France in the belief that France represented the libertarian principles of the American Revolution. England's supporters were mainly those who had favored the Hamiltonian economic program, and France's were by and large Hamilton's opponents.

The conflict came to a head in 1795 with the debate over ratification of Jay's Treaty, a document designed to resolve outstanding conflicts between England and America. Jeffersonians believed the treaty conceded too much. The United States accepted Britain's wartime limitations on trade with France, agreed to deny French privateers the use of American ports, promised not to carry French goods as a neutral, and agreed to settle outstanding British claims against American citizens. In return, Britain promised only to withdraw from several western posts on American territory and to pay for American ships confiscated by the British navy. Nothing was said about Britain's unpopular policy of searching American ships and impressing alleged deserters into its navy.

The treaty was so unpopular that John Jay believed he could have made his way across the country at night by the light of burning effigies. But the Federalists wanted to avoid war with England, and Hamilton had even undercut Jay's negotiating position by secretly assuring the British ambassador that America would not go to war against his country.

The treaty debate in the Senate, which resulted in a narrow victory, crystallized the Federalist-Republican division. In the 1796 presidential election the two parties operated as fully developed political organizations with supportive newspapers, local machines, and presidential candidates. The contest between John Adams and Thomas Jefferson was the first electoral race for the presidency, and Adams's narrow margin of victory in the electoral college, 71 to 68, revealed the close division of stength between the two parties.

The rivalry between Federalists and Republicans was surprisingly shrill in a nation that abhorred party discord. But the expectation of unity made the discovery of disagreement all the more alarming. Each side could accuse the other of disloyalty and corruption because it seemed that its own ideas should prevail. Was not each, after all, the spokesman for the ideal nation? In his Farewell Address, George Washington warned against the "baneful effects of the spirit of party" and the "insidious wiles of foreign influence," but to no avail. Party conflict and fears of foreign intrigue marked the presidency of John Adams and had their apotheosis in the Alien and Sedition Acts.

John Adams was inaugurated president on March 4, 1797. He later said he could imagine George Washington saying to him: "Ay, I'm fairly out, and you're fairly in. See which of us will be happiest!" The new president had good reason to be apprehensive. As soon as he moved into the large stone mansion in Philadelphia that served as the Executive Mansion, Adams began to receive discouraging news from abroad. France was angered by America's recent treaty with England. In the past year France had captured or sunk more than three hundred American merchantmen on the ground that they carried contraband to England; refused to receive America's new ambassador, Charles Cotesworth Pinckney; and decreed that any American sailor found aboard a captured British warship would be executed.

These affronts seemed consistent with grisly tales of domestic turmoil in the self-proclaimed land of "Liberty, Equality, and Fraternity." The Reign of Terror against supposed enemies of the Revolution was now in full force. Aristocrats by the hundreds were tied onto barges and drowned; priests were cut to pieces at their altars; and public guillotine executions were common. The French army was occupying neighboring countries, including the republics of Holland and Switzerland. Many Americans regarded the French Revolution as an obscene perversion of republican principles.

On May 15 President Adams addressed a special joint session of Congress, summarizing Gallic affronts and calling on the legislators to "convince France and the world that we are not a degraded people, humiliated under a colonial spirit of fear and a sense of inferiority." He urged Congress to provide for expansion of the army and the navy.

The request was reasonable, for at that time the military establishment consisted of only two thousand soldiers and a few revenue cutters — hardly enough to convince France of anything. But many Americans, especially those associated with Thomas Jefferson, believed that France's naval policy was no more repressive than England's and preferred the republicanism of France, misguided though it might be, to the obdurate monarchism of England. After the May 15 address Adams became, for the first time in his presidency, the object of attack from the Republican press.

Adams was, nonetheless, as eager to avoid war as the Republicans. Although he might prefer England to France, he realized that in her comparatively defenseless condition America was not a match for France. And so while he urged the nation to prepare for war, in summer 1797 he pressed forward with another attempt at negotiation. With the acquiescence of Congress he sent Elbridge Gerry and John Marshall to join Charles Cotesworth Pinckney in Paris as special envoys.

Adams received no word of their progress until March 1798 when secret dispatches from Paris informed him that the negotiators had been rebuffed by the French government. Several emissaries, called X, Y, and Z in the report, had come with the message that French Foreign Minister Talleyrand would be willing to negotiate if he were given a $250,000 bribe and France was granted a $12 million loan. Such demands were not uncommon. America was already paying bribes to the Barbary pirates on the northern coast of Africa to protect American shipping. But in the atmosphere of distrust and hostility between the two nations, Talleyrand's bribe demand seemed cold-blooded and insulting. The envoy's response to this demand was: "No, no. Not a sixpence!"

Adams notified Congress that the mission had failed and called upon the lawmakers to enact defensive measures. In the meantime, he would permit American merchantmen to arm for their own safety. The initial response to his message was lukewarm because Adams had not yet released the text of the dispatches from Paris. Vice-President Thomas Jefferson called the speech an "insane message," and Republican publicists denounced the president. Expecting to prove that he had exaggerated the crisis, they demanded full disclosure of the envoy's communications.

But the dispatches supported Adams's characterization. They described the so-called XYZ Affair and also revealed that Talleyrand expected America to assume France's debts to United States citizens, including those for ships France had confiscated, and wanted President Adams to apologize for remarks he had made about France.

The news swept across the nation, and the envoys' reply to the bribery demand was embellished by a Federalist journalist into a strident and highly quotable phrase. Charles Pinckney supposedly told the insidious French negotiators: "Millions for defense, but not one cent for tribute." The phrase neatly captured America's belief in its own strength and rectitude.

A wave of patriotic fervor swept across the land. A new song, "Adams and Liberty," was set to a tune that later became "The Star-Spangled Banner." Another patriotic song, "Hail Columbia," by Joseph Hopkinson, received thunderous applause at its first performance in a Philadelphia theater: the audience demanded four encores, joined in the choruses, and shouted their approval. Three cavalry units welcomed John Marshall on his return to Philadelphia and escorted him through an immense cheering throng. From all over the country petitions of support came to President Adams. When, finally, a group of drunken patriots gathered outside the Executive Mansion late one night and serenaded the president with "Hail Columbia," he and Abigail may have longed for more settled times. But the national spirit was aflame, and his was the job of accommodating it.

A deep fear of French aggression underlay the enthusiastic nationalism of such displays. The French Revolution had become turbulent and cruel; French armies had overwhelmed neighboring states and were preparing to invade England; the French navy thwarted American commerce. Many Americans feared that France would dominate both Europe and America. Abigail Adams believed that France aimed "not only at our independence and liberty" but sought also "a total annihilation of the Christian religion." The Massachusetts Federalist Fisher Ames characterized France as "an open hell, still ringing with agonies and blasphemies" and speculated that such might be America's "future state." In his July Fourth oration the president of Yale predicted that if Jefferson and the supporters of France prevailed, Americans would "see the Bible cast into a bonfire . . . our wives and daughters the victims of legal prostitution."

Fear of invasion from France was intensified by belief that the enemy had supporters throughout the United States. Talleyrand, himself, had belittled the pretensions of the American negotiators by insisting that he had support of a "French Party" in the United States. During spring 1798, alarms of war circulated through the country. French privateers continued their raids along the American coastline, and one even had the temerity to sail into the harbor at Charleston, South Carolina, and burn a British vessel in American waters. Letters were discovered in Philadelphia revealing a plot to set fire to the city while citizens were attending religious services on May 9, a national day of fasting. A Francophile mob in Philadelphia, wearing French tricolor cockades, attacked a group of Adams supporters. More disturbing still, French supporters in one city talked about forming a separate volunteer army, to be known as the Republican Blues. And always there were the Republican newspapers, sniping at the administration, belittling the French threat, and destroying the American effort to present a united front to the foreign foe.

Among the Republican publicists the foremost was Benjamin Franklin Bache, young editor of the *Philadelphia Aurora*. The grandson of Benjamin Franklin, he was sometimes known as "Lightning Rod, Junior," perhaps as much for his shocking invective as for his prestigious ancestry. He was impetuous, harsh, narrowminded, and totally devoted to the belief that the sins of the mighty must be exposed. His unremitting hostility led him to make fun of Abigail for crying when her husband was honored with the first singing of "Hail Columbia." He accused her husband of nepotism, misuse of public funds, and monarchic ambitions and called him "old, querulous, bald, blind, crippled, toothless Adams." In return, Abigail described him as "that lying wretch of a Bache."

The *Aurora* and other Republican newspapers, such as John Daly Burk's *New York Timepiece* and Thomas Adams's *Boston Independent Chronicle*, continued to attack Federalist foreign policy despite the revelation of the XYZ affair. They demanded that America try again to negotiate a settlement with France and accused the Federalists of using the war scare to gain support for their party.

Such accusations were galling to Adams during these, the most difficult days in his public career. Abigail wrote to her sister that she had never seen him look so tired and pale. Adams wanted to build up the nation's defenses but hoped, through a display of patriotic resolve,

Abigail Adams. Ardent supporter of her husband and herself resourceful, she believed the president should be spared criticism in times of crisis.

to persuade France to adopt a more conciliatory stand. The administration sought to walk the thin line between a declaration of war and humble acceptance of French attacks. The Republican attitude made his position all the more difficult, because he believed the nation could avoid a potentially catastrophic war only if it appeared united. The Republicans were destroying that chance with their criticisms. They were so pigheaded, so unreasonable, and — Adams must sometimes have thought — so treasonous.

Ever vigilant in support of her husband, Abigail Adams came to regard the opposition as plotting to overthrow the government. "French emissaries are in every corner of the union," she wrote on March 20, "sowing and spreading their Sedition. We have *renewed information* that their system is, to calumniate the President, his family, his administration, until they oblige him to resign, and then they will reign triumphant." Other Federalists declared more bluntly that in the current situation dissent equaled treason. One Federalist editor concluded that any American who "opposed the administration is an anarchist, a jacobin, and a traitor."

By the middle of 1798 many Federalists believed that if the country were to avoid foreign domination and civil strife, the shrill denunciations of the opposition press must be put down. Certainly full discussion of important issues was important in a free society. But when power-mad publicists misused that freedom and printed lies to stir up sedition at home and encourage enemies abroad, they could destroy the republic. Again Abigail Adams caught the spirit of this reasoning when she wrote to her sister on May 26: "I wish the Laws of our Country were competent to punish the stirrer up of sedition, the writer and printer of base and unfounded calumny. This would contribute as much to the peace and harmony of our Country as any measure."

The Federalists developed a two-pronged approach to their domestic and foreign problems. First they made plans for military defense. Adams had already decreed that American merchantmen could arm themselves to stave off French attacks. In April he created the Department of the Navy and appointed Benjamin Stoddert of Virginia its first secretary. During the next three months his supporters in Congress passed acts providing for coastal fortifications, military supplies, and expansion of the army and the navy. Three new frigates, the *Constellation,* the *Constitution,* and the *United States* would be made seaworthy along with other vessels. For the first time since the Revolution, the United States would have an active navy.

A new force of ten thousand men and a provisional army of another fifty thousand would stengthen the army. George Washington, nearing the end of his life in retirement in Mount Vernon, reluctantly agreed to serve as nominal commander but insisted that his old military aide, Alexander Hamilton, be appointed second in command of the force and its actual leader.

Adams completed the rupture between the two nations by suspending all commerce with France and declaring that the old treaties of 1778 were void because of French violations. On July 21 he told Congress: "I will never send another minister to France without assurances that he will be received, respected, and honored as the representative of a great, free, powerful, and independent nation." Adams also considered a declaration of war. Many of his more extreme supporters, called "High" or "Ultra" Federalists, favored the commencement of hostilities. Once he had been appointed to lead the army, Hamilton, in particular, grew excited at the prospect of attacking France's ally, Spain, and taking Florida, Louisiana, and Mexico, at that time Spanish territory.

But Adams was reluctant to declare war. He realized that the country was not yet ready to fight a major European power and surmised that the people's mood was exuberant but not warlike. If the nation must bear the burdens of war, he reasoned, let France rather than America be the first to announce hostilities. In the interim the country could prepare her defenses and wage a "quasi-war" against French privateers.

The second level of administrative policy covered the domestic situation and consisted of the four bills known collectively as the Alien and Sedition Acts. The first three, passed in June and July 1798, dealt with aliens residing in the United States. There were several reasons for the Federalist mistrust of recent immigrants. The first was plain, simple nativism — the belief that the only good American was a native-born American — an idea common among the Federalists of that time. Harrison Gray Otis said that "the native American germ" was sufficient to produce such individuals as are "worth cultivation." In 1798 the Massachusetts legislature proposed a constitutional amendment that would allow only citizens born in the United States to hold public office. Some Federalists wanted to go one step further and end all immigration to the United States. Their nativistic prejudices were heightened because many recent immigrants had come from France and Ireland, where anti-British sentiment and revolutionary radicalism were common. Aliens, once naturalized, tended to support the Republican party, another black mark against each group.

The first of the bills, the Naturalization Act, extended the period of probationary residence prior to citizenship from five to fourteen years, delaying the immigrants' entry into the electorate; the second, the Alien Act, allowed the president to expel any alien suspected of dangerous or treasonous acts; the third, the Alien Enemies Act, empowered the president to imprison or expel citizens of enemy states in time of war. The administration never had occasion to use the last two acts, but their existence on the statute books may have frightened some immigrants into exile and dissuaded other Europeans from coming to America.

The idea underlying these three acts was phrased most explicitly in the Alien Act, which spoke of preventing behavior "dangerous to the peace and safety of the United States." The Sedition Act suggested that Americans as well as foreigners could threaten domestic peace through unbridled dissent. The proponents of the Sedition Act regarded speech as a dangerous weapon. Robert Goodloe Harper, South Carolina Federalist and chairman of the House Ways and Means Committee, warned his colleagues that visionary radicals could shake "the foundations of order" by spreading unfounded discontent among the populace. Joseph Hopkinson, the Federalist lawyer who wrote "Hail Columbia," claimed that an "INTERNAL FACTION" was spreading "groundless jealousies" against the government in order to deliver the country to France.

The consistent theme in these and other Federalist discussions of Republican rhetoric was the charge that their opponents criticized the administration with malice, falsehood, and treasonous intent. The administration's critics did not simply disagree about matters that reasonable people might properly debate; they sought rather to destroy the republic itself for their own greedy ends. They lacked the commonality of interest with their fellow citizens upon which free speech must be based, and in misusing speech they were as guilty of misconduct as an assassin who shot his gun at the president's breast.

Reasoning in this fashion, the Federalists concluded that a sedition bill was a proper measure for protecting the national welfare. The Senate sponsor of the bill, James Lloyd of Maryland, expressed the Federalist view frankly when he remarked that the act would muzzle the administration's opponents. He regretted only that it was not reinforced by a declaration of war to make it easier to "lay our hands on traitors." In a letter to a group of Braintree, Massachusetts, supporters, President Adams declared that seditious speech was the instrument "with which our enemies expect to subdue our country." Or as one of the Federalist newspapers summarized the issue, "It is *Patriotism* to write in favor of our government — it is Sedition to write against it." Political dissent and party activity had come to be identified with treason.

The Republicans, recognizing that they would be its principal victims, opposed the Sedition Act. They complained that it was tyrannical and would undermine the Constitution, and they asserted that there was no evidence that sedition even existed. Upon hearing of the proposed bill, Thomas Jefferson declared that if flew "in the teeth of the Constitution." On June 6 Benjamin Bache claimed it was contrary to the First Amendment. Representative Albert Gallatin of Pennsylvania remarked on the obvious political implications of the act — it was "a weapon used by the party now in power in order to perpetuate their authority and preserve their present places."

Lacking control of either branch of the Congress, however, the Republicans were unable to block the sedition bill. It cleared the Senate on July 4, 1798. On that day a group of Federalists in a New York militia company drank a toast to "One and but one party in the United States," thereby expressing the spirit of the act. Republicans were less in evidence that day, but one group in Easton, Pennsylvania, greeted the bill with this toast: "May the friends of the gag-bill sleep in oblivion until the angel Gabriel sounds his last trumpet." Ten days later the bill was law.

The Sedition Act declared it unlawful to "combine or conspire" to impede the operation of the federal government by insurrection, riot, or unlawful assembly. It was now illegal to write, publish, or utter any "false, scandalous, and malicious" statement against the president or Congress or to excite "the hatred of the good people of the United States" against the government.

The act was broad enough to encompass most forms of political dissent, but for its time it was not a particularly restrictive measure; similar limitations on freedom of speech existed throughout the world. The British Treasonable Practices Act of 1795 was harsher than the Sedition Act, and the common law — the body of legal tradition deriving from previous judicial decisions in England and America — was more severe in several respects. Unlike the existing law, the Sedition Act required proof of malice, allowed truth as a defense, required the jury (rather than the judge) to determine whether a libel had been committed, and stated maximum penalties.

The act did, however, publicize limitations on speech and encourage enforcement, and it inaugurated an era that Thomas Jefferson referred to as the American "Reign of Terror." Charges were brought against twenty-five Republicans, twelve of whom were tried and convicted. Luther Baldwin, our tavern wit, was the most obscure. Many were important Republican newspaper editors, and one was a member of the U.S. House of Representatives. Because of his political position, Matthew Lyon, the congressional victim of the act, attracted special interest.

Lyon had come in his youth to America as an indentured servant from Ireland. He worked hard, purchased his freedom, and fought in the American Revolution. After the war he became one of the most successful businessmen in Vermont, founded the town of Fairhaven, and established a sawmill and an ironworks. An outspoken Republican, he campaigned successfully for a congressional seat in 1796.

When he took his House seat in 1797, Federalists immediately ridiculed him because of his republicanism and his Irish background. When John Allen, one of the extreme nativists in the House, disparaged Lyon's ancestry, the new representative eloquently defended his character. This was his country, he said, because he had "no other" and had fought for her during the Revolution; he had earned everything he owned "by means of honest industry."

Lyon's strident self-confidence only further enraged nativist sentiment against him. One Federalist editor compared him to a wild beast and claimed that he was violent but cowardly. On January 30, 1798, Roger Griswold of Connecticut disparaged Lyon's Revolutionary War record, and in response Lyon spat in Griswold's face. A few days later Griswold attacked Lyon on the House floor, beating him with a cane while Lyon fought back with fire tongs. They rolled on the floor in violent combat until other congressmen finally pulled them apart. The Federalists, outraged that an Irishman's spittle should have touched a native New Englander's face, sought to expel Matthew Lyon from the House of Representatives. After fourteen days of debate the congressmen voted 52 to 44 for expulsion, 12 votes short of the necessary two-thirds margin. For the remainder of the session Lyon was one of the most vigorous Republican spokesmen in Congress, opposing the military defense measures and the Alien and Sedition Acts. He told a friend he expected to be one of the Sedition Act's first targets.

When Congress adjourned in July, Lyon went home to plan his reelection campaign. Federalists throughout the nation were seeking his defeat, and Lyon expected a hard campaign. He lashed out at the Federalists in a letter to his constituents, claiming that under their rule public welfare was "swallowed up in a continual grasp for power, in an unbounded thirst for ridiculous pomp, foolish adulation, and selfish avarice." When a leading Federalist paper in Vermont refused to print his ideas, he began a new journal called *The Scourge of Aristocracy and Repository of Important Political Truths.*

The first issue appeared on October 1, 1798. Four days later Matthew Lyon was indicted for treason by a grand jury convened at Rutland, Vermont. He was charged with bringing the government into disrepute in his letter to the voters. On October 8 Lyon was tried before fourteen local jurors with Justice William Paterson of the U.S. Supreme Court presiding. Because no lawyers were available, he elected to plead his own case before a jury that included many of his political enemies. In his defense he claimed that the Sedition Act was unconstitutional, and, in any event, his statements were neither malicious or seditious — they were simply legitimate statements of political opinion. The jury brought in a verdict of guilty after deliberating for only one hour. The next day, October 9, Justice Paterson sentenced Lyon to four months in jail and a $1,000 fine, declaring that he was making an example of Lyon because, he told the prisoner: "as a member of the federal legislature, you must be well acquainted with the mischiefs which flow from an unlicensed abuse of government."

Local officials took Lyon from the courtroom to the neighboring town of Vergennes, not even giving him time to visit his apartment in Rutland to gather his papers, and locked him in a common jail cell. The bright colors and crisp air of a Vermont autumn gave way to the sharp, white cold of winter while Lyon languished in prison. A single window barely lighted the dark cell; the privy consisted of a stinking receptacle in the corner of the chamber; and the cold room had no fire.

Fortunately for Lyon, his constitution was strong and he was invigorated by a sense of outrage. He wrote to fellow Republicans describing his situation, the squalor of the prison, the injustice of the law. "It is quite a new kind of jargon," he said, "to call a Representative of the people an opposer of government because he does not, as a legislator, advocate and acquiesce in every proposition that comes from the executive." In a short time Lyon was regarded as a martyr. He ran a successful reelection campaign from prison and was returned to Congress by a great majority. On February 9 he was released from jail. As he left the building and stood once more among the open hills of Vermont, he found himself surrounded by a welcoming crowd. Embraced by their support, he walked twelve miles to Middlebury. At the head of the parade his supporters carried American flags that waved triumphantly in the free air of Matthew Lyon's adopted homeland.

The Lyon case was especially important because of the victim's political status and the severity of his punishment. But other cases contained the same ingredients: harsh penalties and public sympathy. The accused included Benjamin Franklin Bache, tried under the common law; Thomas Adams, of the *Boston Independent Chronicle;* Thomas Cooper, a lawyer and later president of the University of South Carolina; and David Brown, an itinerant Republican publicist, who offended the Federalists by constructing a liberty pole in Dedham, Massachusetts. The law's critics claimed that these men had merely exercised their American right of free speech. Republican spokesmen took particular delight in chiding the Federalists for the Luther Baldwin case. Was the government so defensive, they asked, that it could not withstand a harmless joke?

In some areas opposition to the Alien and Sedition Acts was so strong that Thomas Jefferson and James Madison were able to persuade two states to adopt bills condemning the acts. The Virginia and Kentucky Resolves of 1798-99 declared that the laws were unconstitutional and advanced the novel claim that individual states could invalidate improper federal legislation. These resolutions furnished precedents later for the southern doctrine of nullification, a theory that states did not have to honor legislation they considered invalid.

Support for Adams remained strong, however, and other states condemned the Virginia and Kentucky Resolves. But on the whole the Alien and Sedition Acts did more to harm than to help the Adams administration. In 1798 most Americans had feared threats to their liberty from France and from a "French Party" in America. In 1799 the war had not materialized, and Americans began to question the legitimacy of bills that protected them by eliminating dissent. Perhaps the Republicans had been right in holding that the administration wanted to establish a monarchic and tyrannical regime.

Such charges hurt Adams, but ironically he was damaged more by his effort to reduce tensions than by his desire to eliminate sedition. Late in 1798 he learned that Talleyrand, wanting to avoid war, hoped to resume negotiations. The High Federalists sought to prevent Adams from sending a negotiator, but Adams threatened to resign and turn his office over to Republican Thomas Jefferson if they blocked his effort to negotiate. Adams sent a peace mission across the Atlantic in 1799, and a few months later America and France signed the Convention of 1800, calling off the undeclared naval war.

If Adams had cared only for his own political future, he might have fought France and ridden a wave of popular support to a second term. Instead, he allowed the patriotism of 1798 to end in a frustrating anticlimax, making the repressive acts passed in the name of national defense seem unjustified. The Republicans castigated Adams as a tyrant, whereas war enthusiasts in his own party regarded him as too mild.

In this situation Thomas Jefferson was elected president in 1800 by a narrow margin. He pardoned the remaining prisoners jailed under the Sedition Act and allowed the offending bills to expire in 1801 and 1802. The reaction against the Alien and Sedition Acts facilitated a more liberal interpretation of free speech. Criticism might be galling to an administration, but Thomas Jefferson, James Madison, Matthew Lyon, and others had argued forcefully that a free government could not exist without diversity of opinion. This liberal view of the right to dissent has endured for almost two centuries despite periodic challenges.

Political invective was especially virulent in the late 1790s because both sides felt there should be just one party and one truth. Thomas Jefferson was probably the last vice-president to accuse his chief executive of "insanity" after hearing a presidential address. Had the Republicans been in control, they might have sponsored their own Alien and Sedition Acts—certainly Jefferson's record with respect to civil liberties is not unblemished. The acts, however, reinforced freedom of speech by creating a backlash of support for the administration's critics. Once it was admitted that the state could contain several legitimate but competing philosophies, an opposition party could criticize the government without accusing it of tyranny, and the administration could resist opposition without characterizing it as sedition. In such a time the merry wit of a Luther Baldwin can find expression without ever coming to the attention of a Federal court.

QUESTIONS

1. What were the principal issues leading to party formation in the 1790s? How did the "expectation of unity" exacerbate party divisions?

2. The political rhetoric of both parties was especially heated in the 1790s. Give examples of extreme statements by Federalists and Republicans.

3. Why were some Americans hostile to France in 1798? Why did other Americans support France?

4. How did Federalists justify the Alien and Sedition Acts, and on what basis did Republicans oppose them?

5. How did these factors influence the passage of the Alien and Sedition Acts: the newness of the Constitution, the lack of a two-party tradition, Federalist opportunism, fear of France, Republican invective, and nativism?

6. Why does freedom of speech tend to be curtailed in wartime? Were the Alien and Sedition Acts needed to stengthen America in the face of war, or were they brought on by hysteria and paranoia?

7. Why was Matthew Lyon singled out as the only Congressman imprisoned under the Alien and Sedition Acts?

8. How did the persecution of Matthew Lyon, Luther Baldwin, and other Republicans ultimately strengthen the American tradition of free speech?

9. "Luther Baldwin was less the victim of his tongue than of his times." Explain.

BIBLIOGRAPHY

AKERS, CHARLES W. *Abigail Adams* (1980). Lively account of John Adams's foremost supporter.

BROWN, RALPH ADAMS. *The Presidency of John Adams* (1975). Detailed account of Adams's troubled presidency.

DECONDE, ALEXANDER. *Quasi-War: Undeclared War with France. 1797-1801* (1966). History of the naval war with France.

HOFSTADTER, RICHARD. *Idea of a Party System* (1969). Describes early American opposition to parties.

LEVY, LEONARD W. *Jefferson and Civil Liberties* (1963). Argues that Jefferson frequently suppressed civil liberties.

_____ . *Legacy of Suppression* (1960). Surveys the free-speech issue from colonial times to the early nineteenth century.

MILLER, JOHN C. *Crisis in Freedom: The Alien and Sedition Acts* (1951). A colorful account of the Alien and Sedition Acts emphasizing the role of public opinion.

SMITH, JAMES M. *Freedom's Fetters* (1956). An extensive account of the Alien and Sedition Acts written during the McCarthy era, when free speech was again threatened by the government.

SMITH, PAGE. *John Adams* (1963). An engaging two-volume narrative of John Adams's life.

WITHEY, LYNNE. *Dearest Friend: A Life of Abigail Adams* (1981). The personal and public life of Abigail Adams.

8

REPUBLICAN
NATIONALISM

The
Lewis and Clark
Expedition

Early in the nineteenth century the possibilities for American growth seemed limitless. The nation's experiment in representative government captured the imagination of other peoples, and Americans watched with approval as Spanish Americans, emulating the Spirit of '76, fought for independence from European control. They congratulated themselves for whipping the British army in 1815 at the Battle of New Orleans and declared their preeminence in the Western Hemisphere with the Monroe Doctrine in 1823. Americans, it seemed, could do anything. The Lewis and Clark Expedition of 1803-6 provided the country with its first western heroes and revealed a land so bounteous and alluring that nature itself appeared to have smiled upon the American republic.

I n 1803, the year of the Louisiana Purchase, the United States was a
strong, confident nation with a population of 6 million and a dozen
colleges. She was building canals, bridges, factories, and highways and
experimenting with steamboats and gaslamps. Along the Atlantic sea-
board the wilderness had long since vanished, and the land was familiar,
lived upon, subdued.

But there was another America, totally unknown to the people of
the East. When Thomas Jefferson was elected president in 1800, tens
of thousands of native Americans living within the boundaries of the
future United States had never seen a white man. In reality, America
was not one country but many. Its nations included Mandans, Sioux,
Shoshone, and Nez Percé, as well as the polyglot population of Europeans and Africans that knew itself as the United States. Few easterners
had traveled among the western Indians or seen the Rockies. The United
States was bordered by a mystery.

The existence of this unknown land fascinated and challenged
President Thomas Jefferson. Although he was best known as a statesman, Jefferson was a deeply contemplative man and an accomplished
astronomer, archaeologist, geologist, and naturalist. As a young man,
he wrote *Notes on Virginia*, a natural history of his native region. While
in Paris in 1786 he encouraged the American adventurer, John Ledyard,
to walk across Siberia and western America to the headwaters of the
Missouri. Ledyard, accompanied by two dogs, actually covered three
thousand miles across Russia before authorities, suspecting that he was
a spy, shipped him back to Poland. In 1792, as secretary of state, Jefferson supported another abortive expedition to the Northwest.

As president, Jefferson was determined to try again. He delivered
a message to Congress on January 18, 1803, advocating a secret expedition to explore the West. Anticipating that his proposal would be accepted if he offered economic reasons for the expedition, he suggested
that contact would lead to "commercial intercourse." The fur trade of
the upper Mississippi Basin was already being siphoned off into Canada,
and for a cost of only $2,500 the United States could open up the region
to Americans. Impressed by his argument, Congress approved the proposal, and Jefferson began to make plans.

In the meantime, history had radically altered the character of
the proposed expedition. The land Jefferson intended to explore was
owned by France, and in 1802 Napoleon contemplated posting a large
military force in the area. But his army in America was decimated in
Hispaniola while fighting a black insurrection led by Toussaint
L'Ouverture. Needing funds, and having lost interest in America,
Napoleon offered to sell all of Louisiana, then reckoned at about nine
hundred thousand square miles, for $15 million. Jeffferson's opponents
doubted the constitutionality of the transaction and characterized the

purchase of these remote, unknown lands as the "wildest chimera of a moonstruck brain." But the measure won congressional approval, and suddenly the expedition to a foreign land became the exploration of American territory.

The spring and summer of 1803 were given over to preparations. Jefferson chose as leader a man named Meriwether Lewis, whom he described as "brave, prudent, habituated to the woods, and familiar with Indian manners and character." Lewis was born on a plantation in 1774 in Albemarle County, Virginia, in a wood frame house near Jefferson's Monticello. His father died while he was a boy, and he went with his mother to live on the Georgia frontier, returning in his teens to manage the Virginia estate. Lewis soon became one of Jefferson's closest friends, often visiting him to talk about natural science and exploration. Both were interested in the West.

In 1794 during the Whiskey Rebellion, Lewis joined the army; he was a captain in 1801, when Jefferson was inaugurated president. Jefferson chose his old friend as his personal secretary, and the two men worked together in developing the proposal for a western expedition. Jefferson was determined that the expedition would not only blaze a trail to the west but would also gather scientific information about the country through which it passed. At that time there were few professional scientists in the United States, and a bright, interested person could become something of an expert in botany, zoology, or anthropology with little training. Undoubtedly, Jefferson, as an amateur scientist, would have liked to accompany the expedition himself. That being impossible, he planned to provide Lewis with a "cram course" in natural history.

At the president's request, Lewis spent April and May 1803 in Philadelphia studying under the direction of several of the nation's leading scientists at the American Philosophical Society and the University of Pennsylvania. His instructors included Dr. Benjamin Rush, the preeminent American physician of the time. At Jefferson's suggestion, Rush prepared a list of questions for Lewis to ask the Indians. He should study their physical history and learn about Indian diseases, longevity, marriage, menstruation, breast feeding, weaning, heartbeat, diet, medicine, and morals. What were their vices? Were suicide and murder common? Did they "employ any substitute for ardent spirits to promote intoxication"? Finally, Lewis should learn about their religion — sacrifices, burial ceremonies, and affinity (if any) to the Jews. The last question grew out of the ancient belief that the ten Lost Tribes of Israel might have mingled with the natives.

Lewis would not be able to explore all these topics. But the list indicates Jefferson's and Rush's desire to learn as much as possible about the unknown land. Underlying the whole expedition was profound curiosity about the American continent. Jefferson anticipated that American farmers would one day settle the West. The expedition would prepare the way for expansion, but it would also compile a record of what the country was like in its own right.

Jefferson and Lewis agreed that it was essential to recruit good men to accompany the expedition because the explorers would depend on one another for survival. They must screen out unstable adventurers who would resist authority or quit at the first obstacle. "Their qualifications," Lewis wrote the president, "should be such as perfectly fit them for the service, otherwise they will rather clog than further the objects of the cause." He wanted good boatmen, hunters, and craftsmen, men who were strong and steady but willing to accept discipline.

Lewis's most important staffing decision was the choice of an old friend, William Clark, to share the leadership of the expedition. Clark was a tall, redheaded Kentuckian who had served with Lewis in the frontier Indian wars of the 1790s. Born on August 1, 1770, in Caroline County, Virginia, he was a younger brother of Revolutionary War hero Gen. George Rogers Clark, who led the American troops fighting in the old Northwest. In 1784 the whole family moved to the lands George Rogers Clark had known as a soldier. With livestock, slaves, and furniture they boarded a flatboat and floated down the Ohio to Louisville, Kentucky, where they settled into a large log plantation house. In the late 1780s and early 1790s William Clark fought under Gen. Anthony Wayne in a rash of local Indian wars.

Clark and Lewis became acquainted in the army, and Lewis believed his old friend was the perfect choice for a shared command. In addition to being daring and resourceful, he was, like Lewis, an amateur naturalist and could draw birds, fish, and animals during the expedition. Lewis's letter of invitation summarized his view of the expedition. The explorers would develop "an early, friendly, and intimate acquaintance" with the western tribes to foster trade and impress them "with the rising importance of the United States." They would study native culture, wildlife, soil, and plants of the new country. "Believe me," he told Clark, "there is no man on earth with whom I should feel equal pleasure in sharing them as with yourself." Clark's response was immediate and enthusiastic. "My friend," he wrote, "I join you with hand and heart." The close and effective cooperation of the two men would be one of the great assets of the expedition.

Lewis spent the early part of the summer choosing equipment. He showed his ability to anticipate problems by his choice of guns. He was impressed with the accuracy of the Kentucky rifle, but he felt it was too frail to hold up on the long journey. And he redesigned the gun, creating the "Harpers Ferry Rifle," which was used on the expedition and became a standard army weapon, the first to be turned out in mass production. Careful planning was also apparent in his provision for ammunition. Because powder could not be replaced in the middle of the wilderness, Lewis stored it in waterproof lead kegs. After each keg was emptied, it could be melted down for bullets. Lewis rounded out his weapons with a new-fangled device, an air rifle.

Materials for science included a microscope, a quadrant, compasses, thermometers, and a two-volume work explaining Linnaeus's system of animal classification. The anticipated negotiations with Indians would be facilitated by gifts including calico shirts, glass beads, handkerchiefs, magnifying glasses, scissors, needles, thread, knives, tobacco, fishhooks, combs, and peace medals bearing the image of Thomas Jefferson.

The men in what would be called the Corps of Discovery were provided with hunting shirts, greatcoats, and blankets and given copper kettles and an iron mill for preparing food. Dr. Rush supervised the accumulation of medical supplies including epsom salts; opium; and his own invention, Rush's constipation pills. The supplies included many items that were surprisingly modern. The explorers carried a forty-foot-long collapsible canoe with an iron frame and phosphorous matches, which proved a convenience to the explorers and a marvel to the Indians. They brought 193 pounds of powdered soup, which the men soon came to hate, but on at least one occasion it sustained them when other food supplies ran out. Finally, there was a simple but useful instrument that was so innovative Lewis did not even have a name for it. He entered it in his list with the following description:

> Instrument for measuring made of tape with feet & inches mark'd on it, confined within a circular lethern box of sufficient thickness to admit the width of the tape which has one of its ends confined to an axis of metal passing through the center of the box, around which and within the box it is readily wound by means of a small crank on the outer side of the box which forms a part of the axis, the tape when necessary is drawn out with the same facility & ease with which it is wound up.

This instrument would soon be known more simply as a tape measure.

The most important item prepared for the expedition was a sturdy barge built in Pittsburgh, nearly sixty feet long with a raised deckhouse at the rear. Depending on the weather and river conditions, it would be propelled by oars, poles, or sail. On July 5, 1803, Lewis left

Washington and went to Pittsburgh, where the boat was being constructed, to assemble supplies and begin the voyage down the Ohio to the Mississippi. Finding that the barge was not ready owing to the builder's frequent drunkenness and quarrels with his men, Lewis decided to stay on the spot and supervise, "alternately persuading and threatening," to keep the work going.

The boat was finally ready on the last day of August at 7:00 A.M. Within three hours Lewis had the craft loaded and was floating downstream on the Ohio, planning to meet Clark in Louisville and take the expedition up the Missouri River for a winter encampment. The large, shallow-draft barge drew only three feet, but at places the river was a mere six inches deep, and it menaced travelers with teacherous gravel bars and snags laid bare by the season's low water. Anticipating these obstacles, Lewis had written Jefferson a month before, saying, "I am determined to proceed though I should not be able to make greater speed than a boat's length per day."

At times he barely made that. The voyage proved a good testing ground for his men. If they had given out on this trip through settled country, they could hardly have persevered through the long months ahead. The boat ran into its first obstacles shortly after leaving Pittsburgh, and in the following days the men spent as much time walking along the river bottom as floating downstream. They often had to lighten the barge by disembarking, and sometimes they had to dig through gravel shoals. The worst obstructions were snags of timber and brush that blocked the river from bank to bank, requiring the men to unload the cargo and haul the all-too-solid barge. When they could no longer budge their craft, they scoured the riverbank to find help. Lewis reported to Jefferson that in such cases "horses or oxen are the last resort: I find them the most efficient sailors in the present state of navigation of this river, although they may be considered somewhat clumsy."

Through it all the men maintained good spirits and quickly learned to like the simple pleasures of the voyage. At Wheeling they had a watermelon feast aboard the barge. Farther downstream they enjoyed passing beneath leafy sycamore trees and watching hordes of squirrels swimming to the southern shore. Lewis's big Newfoundland dog, Shannon, who accompanied the expedition to the Pacific, plunged into the water after the swimmers, caught many, and brought them back to the barge. In the evening the men feasted on fried squirrel.

In Louisville, Clark joined the expedition with some additional men. In these early stages, though the expedition passed through lands that were extensively settled by Americans, Lewis was already beginning his scientific observations. Near Cincinnati he visited Big Bone Lick and sent Jefferson a report on a collection of mammoth bones.

When the boats reached the Mississippi, Lewis visited the Shawnee and Delaware who lived along the shore and made notes on plants and animals, including a 138-pound catfish the voyagers caught for dinner.

When the expedition reached the Mississippi and began to move north toward Saint Louis, the men entered a new world. The French had explored and settled it more than a century before, but it was still a frontier, controlled largely by Indians. Many of the old French-Canadian settlers were half-breeds with Indian squaws. Lewis and Clark encountered one of these rough, lively men, Louis Lorimer, at Cape Girardeau. The commander of the fort, he had come west after the American Revolution. His long hair, worn in a queue, had once extended to the floor, but proving inconvenient at that length, he now wore it at knee length held discreetly to his back by a belt. Lorimer presided over a rough frontier community of a thousand residents, many of whom had migrated from Kentucky and Tennessee. He and his Shawnee wife provided dinner for the explorers and discussed the country.

The expedition reached Saint Louis on December 5. At this time the city was not yet in American hands, and it would be several months before the Louisiana Purchase and American sovereignty would take effect. To avoid offending the regime, the party set up a winter camp on the eastern, or American, side of the Mississippi at Wood River, opposite the confluence of the Missouri. Here they constructed cabins, collected stores, and recruited the last of their party. By the following spring the expedition would consist of twenty-nine permanent members, plus sixteen soldiers and rivermen to assist the expedition in its first season of travel up the Missouri.

Lewis and Clark assembled a remarkable group of men, most of whom would work well together for the next two years. The most important next to the two leaders was George Drouillard; the son of a Shawnee mother and a French-Canadian father, he was an experienced hunter, scout, and interpreter. Another half-breed, Peter Cruzette, was the foremost boatman on the expedition and entertained the Corps of Discovery and fascinated the Indians with his skill as a fiddler. Patrick Gass was the chief carpenter; in lands where wood houses and boats had to be fashioned from the forests, he provided the means of shelter and transportation. Although Gass had had only nineteen days of formal schooling, he wrote a lively journal of the expedition. Other men rounded out the reservoir of skills enjoyed by the corps: William Warner was a fine cook; William Bratton served as gunsmith; Silas Goodrich was an expert fisherman. One of the most remarkable men on the expedition was William Clark's slave, Black York. Tremendously strong and a good dancer, he impressed the Indians, who had never seen a black

man. There was a fine spirit of anticipation among the men; as one of
the soldiers, John Ordway, wrote to his parents, "I am so happy as to
be one of them picked men."

While Clark supervised the preparations at Wood River, Lewis
spent time in Saint Louis gathering information about the Missouri
country they would be visiting. Approximately eight thousand French-
Canadian and American settlers as well as some two thousand black
slaves lived in Upper Louisiana. Because Napoleon had never sent a
French governor, the nominal chief of the region was still Madrid's
agent, Governor Don Carlos Dunhault Delassus. Lewis quickly made
friends with him and other civic leaders and traders. There were no
major settlements north of Saint Louis, but traders had frequently penetrated a thousand miles up the Missouri. With their help Lewis was
able to construct a rough picture of Indian tribes and terrain to the
north. Early in 1804 he sent Thomas Jefferson the first of his samples
of western flora and fauna, including a horned toad and a slip of Osage
plum.

Despite Lewis's friendly manner and his promise that America had
no designs on Spanish territory, the expedition inevitably excited suspicion among white settlers who had already grown accustomed to regarding the West as their own. Many traders on the Missouri were Englishmen associated with the North West Company and had no interest
in seeing the United States establish a rival trade. One English trader
had already sown seeds of mistrust by intercepting and mistranslating
a message from Lewis to the Sauk and Fox tribes. The Spanish, too,
were apprehensive about American penetration into the West. Governor
Don Carlos was friendly enough, but his superiors opposed the expedition. The boundaries between the new American territory and Spanish-
held New Mexico were but vaguely understood, and in Santa Fe there
was some worry lest the American party should find the headwaters of
the Missouri in the mountains just north of their city. In actuality,
Lewis and Clark were never within a thousand miles of Santa Fe, but a
Spanish expedition left New Mexico in 1804 hoping to intercept the
explorers — a well-nigh impossible goal in a region of almost 1 million
square miles. The abortive Spanish expedition was attacked by Indians
and retreated to Santa Fe before the end of 1804.

Unaware of the Spanish plan, Lewis and Clark continued their
preparations in spring 1804. Their supplies now included two thousand
pounds of pork, two thousand pounds of flour, five barrels of whiskey,
and sixteen "Musquitoe nets." After a year of preparation everyone
wanted to start. From the Capital, Jefferson reported with annoyance
that his Federalist opponents were still belittling the expedition
and would rejoice in its failure. "I hope you will take care of your-

self," he wrote Lewis, "and be the living witness of their malice and folly."

On May 14 the expedition was finally ready, and that afternoon Clark ordered the boats to row across the Mississippi and begin the long journey up the Missouri. They reached Saint Charles, a small French-Canadian community a few miles upriver, and waited for Lewis while he completed the expedition's business in Saint Louis. He came to Saint Charles on horseback, accompanied by friends from the town who made a picnic outing of the occasion.

Then with his men he set forth on the Missouri. In ten days the expedition passed La Charette, the last white community on the Missouri, a place where the great eighteenth-century frontiersman, Daniel Boone, now in his seventieth year, still lived. The men soon fell into a routine that would prevail through the next five months of travel to the Mandan country, sixteen hundred miles away. The keelboat *Discovery,* with Pierre Cruzette standing at the bow, led the small fleet up the river. A sergeant standing amidships gave instructions to the oarsmen, and Lewis and Clark took turns overseeing the fleet from the stern. Two small pirogues, or rowboats, one red and one white, followed the barge.

Clark soon proved himself the company's best navigator and geographer and was most often at the helm, compiling a record of the boat's location, the course of the river, and the appearance of tributaries. Cruzette, having traveled on the Missouri many times before, made moment-to-moment decisions in negotiating the more difficult sections of the river. When their course along the wide river lay through deep water and they were aided by a following wind, the fleet could cover twenty miles or more in a day. But the river often challenged their resources.

Shallows caused the men to disembark and pull the barge with towropes; fierce winds swept down the river causing the boats' crews to seek shelter behind islands; low branches could, and once did, break the *Discovery's* mast. The boats were frequently more troubled by the land than the water. The Missouri was a powerful river, often a half mile from shore to shore. Known as the "Big Muddy" because of the dirt swept along in its current, it continually ate into the shores. Once the men had to flee when a riverbank suddenly collapsed into the water; on another occasion they had to evacuate an island as it washed away from under them during the night. They often came upon traveling sandbars that swirled under the boats, threatening to overturn them.

Hidden logjams were common, too, and thick fogs sometimes obscured the route. The men suffered from the ravages of mosquitoes, boils, and intestinal disorders; one was bitten by a poisonous snake and others collapsed from sunstroke. Despite such hardships, however, the men were excited by their journey. They had joined Lewis and Clark because they liked the idea of exploring a new territory. Journals kept by nine of the men reflect the excitement of voyagers seeing a new land. In the early weeks they passed through flat country covered with cotton-wood, oak, hickory, sycamore, walnut, mulberry, and linden trees. As they traveled farther north they entered the Great Plains, one of the largest grasslands in the world, and beheld tall bluestem grasses that undulated like the waves of the sea over rows of gently sloping hills. The grasses were dotted with wild apples, grapes, and plums, exuding a rich, sweet smell. The explorers awoke to fine warm mornings when a light mist hung on the river and great flocks of geese wheeled past overhead; and they enjoyed evenings when the sun, setting over the vast prairie, illuminated the clear sky and wisps of cloud "in the most beautiful manner."

Meriwether Lewis and William Clark recorded their observations of this country. They listed the names of landmarks already seen by French trappers — Turkey Creek, Bear Medicine Island, Cow Island, Reevey's Prairie — and they bestowed new names, which reflected their own perceptions or experience. A creek flowing into the Missouri past a bluff that looked like a cupboard became Cupboard Creek. A rivulet near which they believed a nightingale had sung during the night became Nightingale Creek.

Lewis was particularly active in locating and identifying new plants and animals. He often left the fleet and walked along the river-bank. A somewhat solitary man by nature, Lewis loved being alone on the prairie. He became a great walker, outdistancing the scouts and hunters, getting so far ahead of the fleet that he sometimes spent the night alone deep in the wilderness.

What did Lewis think about during these solitary travels? He was a pensive man, so introspective and melancholy at times that when he died of a gunshot wound a few years later some of his friends, including Jefferson, assumed he had taken his own life. Separated on his walks from the immediate cares of the expedition — moving boats, mending oars, cooking meals — the captain may have reflected on the strange course of history. The land around him was so pristine it seemed it could never change. Here was a vast wilderness, barely touched by man. Its hills stretched endlessly westward; its pure odors alerted the senses; its grasses swayed with a soft rustle in the wind. It had been neither improved nor degraded by white settlers. No surly squatters lived along its banks, ready to overcharge his men for helping them over snags. No toll roads or bridges or cities scarred the landscape. If Lewis thought about history, he must have known that he and his men would change the land simply by visting and describing it.

But if such thoughts crossed his mind, the country's vastness reassured him. It was a large land and his was a small fleet. After a day of walking alone, he could come down from a hill in the evening and hear the sound of axes, the rattle of kettles, and the voices of men, a tiny encampment in a vast and potent wilderness.

At mealtime the men were well served by the land. The expedition's diet was planned around a three-day sequence beginning with hominy and grease, followed by pork and flour, then by pork and cornmeal. Fortunately, this dreary fare was soon varied by the products of forest and plain. The men frequently ate deer, bear, beaver, and, later, buffalo, as well as gooseberries, raspberries, and wild plums and apples. On August 1, Clark's birthday, he could celebrate over venison and beavertail, followed by cherries, plums, raspberries, and grapes.

As the expedition made its way northwest through the present states of Missouri, Kansas, Nebraska, and Iowa, the work of describing the plants and animals became more exacting. Lewis and Clark were the first American explorers to report the mule deer, the white-tailed jackrabbit, the prairie grouse, and the pronghorn — a distant cousin of the antelope. Whenever possible, they obtained a living specimen or the skin of a new animal. In one pursuit they diverted themselves for a whole day by pouring water into a prairie dog hole in an attempt to capture one of these hitherto unknown creatures.

The explorers were equally interested in making contact with the human inhabitants of the region. All the local Indians were nomadic, living in buffalo-hide tents, and traveling across the country. Shortly after the departure from Wood River, Lewis and Clark began to encounter Indian and French-Canadian trading parties, bound for Saint Louis with cargoes of fur. They persuaded one of these traders, a French Canadian named Pierre Dorien, who had lived among the Sioux for twenty years, to accompany them upriver as a translator. Despite this promising start, they pushed on for day after day without meeting Indians. They placed guards around their camps or stayed on islands to avoid surprise by hostile natives, but no Indians, hostile or otherwise, appeared. Finally Drouillard, the hunter and scout, came across a party of Oto and Missouri Indians and persuaded a delegation from each tribe to come and talk with Lewis and Clark. The place they chose was near a prairie that stood high over the Missouri. They called it Council Bluffs.

On August 2 the Indians arrived, announcing their coming by firing their rifles, indicating by their possession of such weapons that even in this remote land the fur trade was already well established. The Indians and whites spent the first evening entertaining each other with a feast, the Americans supplying pork and cornmeal and the natives contributing watermelon. The next morning they met on a beach beside the river beneath an awning fashioned from the barge's sail. Lewis delivered a speech announcing that white men in the region were now under the authority of the "Great Chief of the Seventeen Nations." Without claiming that the seventeen United States owned the Indian lands, he laid down terms for the Indians. They should regard his country as their friend, make peace with one another, and not obstruct American travel on the Missouri. If they behaved properly, they could anticipate a profitable trade with the United States. Lewis and Clark gave the Indians medals, powder, and whiskey and treated them to a demonstration of the air rifle. The groups parted in good humor.

The explorers met delegations from many other tribes during the following weeks. Usually these meetings progressed as smoothly as had the first. Indians occasionally opposed their progress, but Clark was adept at choosing the proper words and addressing them to the right chief to overcome suspicions, and the expedition continued without delivering or receiving hostile blows. In addition to serving a political function, these conferences enabled the explorers to investigate Indian customs and beliefs. They compiled data on language, religion, society, and population. Later Jefferson would take the observations and publish them under the austere title, *A Statistical View of the Indian Nations Inhabiting the Territory of Louisiana and the Countries Adjacent to Its Northern and Western Boundaries.*

In September and October the expedition still pressed northward through the Dakotas. Leaves were turning to yellows and reds; nights were cold; flocks of migrating geese flew overhead. The men wore extra flannel shirts and huddled closer to the campfires at night. On October 17 Clark wrote, "The leaves are falling fast."

It was time to build a winter encampment. In late October the expedition reached Mandan country, in today's North Dakota, where natives stood on the roofs of their conical earthen houses and waved at the explorers as they rowed by. The region was richly forested, promising good shelter for the winter, and the Mandans and their neighbors, the Hidatsa, were friendly. The travelers went to work felling cottonwood trees and building a fort. In a few weeks they fashioned a sturdy stockade of high spiked timbers and eight log huts daubed with mud. Each hut had a large fireplace and tables, shelves, beds, and benches crafted by the skillful carpenters.

They called the place Fort Mandan and spent the winter here, Lewis and Clark sharing one hut, and the rest of the men sleeping in the other seven. Temperatures soon fell far below freezing. On nights when the thermometer dropped to 30 and 40 degrees below zero, the sentries could stand guard only in half-hour shifts. The sharp winter was eerie and fascinating, and one night the sergeant on guard awakened

Route of Lewis and Clark westward to the Pacific.

all the men to show them a new sight, "the beautiful phenomenon called the northern light." They watched, amazed, as the colors played along the horizon in "floating columns sometimes advancing, sometimes retreating and shaping into infinite forms."

The men had never seen or felt a winter like this, but they lived well. They wore thick clothes, and fires blazed day and night in their sturdy cabins. When the temperatures were comparatively mild they could easily shoot enough game to feed themselves. Music and dance broke the monotony of the winter encampment. On Christmas Day they fired their cannon and muskets and then drank a heady concoction of rum and brandy. Pierre Cruzette produced the fiddle that he had carried so carefully up the Missouri and played while the men clapped and danced.

Throughout the winter Lewis and Clark continued to gather information on local Indians and on the route ahead. The four thousand Mandans and Hidatsa were quite willing to help. The only chieftain who could not be won by gift of peace medal or display of air gun, a man known to the French traders as Le Borgne (one eye), finally came to admire the strangers when he met Black York. Clark's slave was always a center of attraction among the Indians, who had seen whites but no blacks. York enjoyed the attention, sometimes pretending to be a tamed beast, sometimes displaying his enormous strength. But it was the color of his skin that most impressed Le Borgne. Suspecting that it was dyed, he tried to remove the black color and was fascinated when it proved to be real. The Indians were further attracted by the skills of John Shields, the company's best blacksmith. They owned metal tools and weapons that needed repair, and Shields spent many hours fixing Indian implements. Lewis and Clark asked the Indians about the lands up the Missouri, and with Indian help they pieced together a reasonably accurate map of the country between Fort Mandan and the Rockies.

In establishing relations with the Indians, Lewis and Clark met with hostility from local French-Canadian and Scottish traders, who regarded the American presence as a threat to their accustomed control of the Mandan fur trade. One of these men represented the British North West Company, an organization whose best-known explorer, Alexander MacKenzie, had anticipated Lewis and Clark by a decade in making the first overland journey to the Pacific in 1793 on a route through present-day Canada. This English trader was alone, however, and could not dissuade the Mandans from befriending the Americans.

At Fort Mandan the Americans found a fine ally in the person of the young Indian woman, Sacajawea. She was a member of the Shoshone Tribe, whose lands lay in the Rockies along the expedition route. Captured as a child by an enemy tribe, she had been brought to the Mandan country where a French-Canadian trapper, Touissant Charbonneau, had purchased her and made her one of his squaws. Lewis and Clark hired Charbonneau as a guide and translator and got Sacajawea in the bargain. At first this did not seem a promising arrangement. On February 11 she gave birth to a son, Baptiste; the expedition would be doubly encumbered by an infant and a woman — or so it seemed — but within a few months Sacajawea would prove to be one of the most useful members of the party.

When spring arrived at Fort Mandan and the Missouri River was clear of ice, the Corps of Discovery made ready to set forth on another season of exploration. Because the barge would be useless in the mountains, Lewis and Clark sent it downriver with a few men and a wide assortment of reports and artifacts, including animal hides; Indian tools and weapons; plants; and two living creatures, a squirrel and a magpie. These artifacts arrived in Washington a few months later. The Capital had no Smithsonian Museum in those days, so that the animals and hides were unpacked in the White House. The magpie and the squirrel took residence in the president's reception hall, and the skins were aired in the cabinet room. Unable to visit the West in person, Jefferson surrounded himself with its exotic fruits.

On April 7 William Clark went upstream with the two pirogues and six new canoes. Meriwether Lewis watched from the shore as the men parted company. On the excuse that he needed exercise, he walked upriver to join the expedition at nightfall. He probably wanted to withdraw from the corps for a moment and contemplate its achievements and goals. He committed some of his thoughts to his journal: "This little fleet, although not quite so respectable as those of Columbus or Captain Cook, were still viewed by us with as much pleasure as those deservedly famed adventurers ever beheld theirs; and I dare say with quite as much anxiety for their safety and preservation." He calculated that two thousand miles of wilderness lay ahead. Unlike the country they had traversed in the previous year, the western land had not been explored. Lewis was uncertain about what dangers lay ahead, but he was proud of the spirit of his party. The men were "zealously attached to the enterprise" and joined together "with the most perfect harmony." All in all, he was pleased with the thought of the journey, which would surely take them to the Pacific. "The picture which now presented itself to me was a most pleasing one," he wrote, "entertaining as I do, the most confident hope of succeeding in a voyage which had formed a darling project of mine for the last ten years, I could but esteem this moment of my departure as among the most happy of my life." Buoyed up with such thoughts, Lewis walked among the trees along the banks of the Missouri and rejoined the fleet at nightfall.

For the next few weeks the expedition passed through rich country where buffalo, deer, bear, and beaver were abundant. On April 26 they passed the Yellowstone River, which flowed into the Missouri through banks shaded by cottonwood, elm, and willow trees. Early in May they came upon their first grizzly bears. They had heard of these giant beasts from Indians and trappers but concluded that descriptions of their awesome size were exaggerated. The first bear tracks they saw were huge and caused some worry, but they managed to kill two grizzlies with relative ease. Apparently, Harpers Ferry Rifles could easily accomplish what bow and arrow could not. On May 11, however, William Bratton shot a grizzly that refused to die; it pursued him for a half mile and required two balls through the head before it succumbed. The men were impressed to discover that Bratton's initial shot had lodged in the bear's lungs.

A few days later six explorers came upon another grizzly. Four shot and hit him, but the bear charged at them. The other two men fired, only enraging the bear more. The men fled behind bushes and trees and into the river, desperately trying to escape and reload. A marksman shot the bear through the head, and it finally collapsed. Eight balls had struck the grizzly before it fell. Lewis summed up the party's new-found respect for this giant of the West: "These bear being so hard to die rather intimidates us all," he wrote. "I must confess that I do not like the gentlemen and had rather fight two Indians than one bear."

The upper Missouri provided other challenges as well. The river was not running clear, but rocks had replaced silt as the prime obstacle. The water flowed swiftly over a stony bed that tore at canoes and feet. On May 14 the boat carrying most of the important scientific equipment and journals was swamped, and only Sacajawea's quick action saved several important records.

On May 26 Lewis caught his first glimpse of the Rocky Mountains. When he was planning the expedition, he and others had hoped that the only thing between the Missouri and the Columbia might be a short span — say, a half day's march — of hilly plain. But Lewis had learned at Fort Mandan that a range of high mountains lay between the two rivers. He now saw clearly both the beauty and the danger of the Rockies. The "mountains were covered with snow, and the sun shone on it in such a manner as to give me the most plain and satisfactory view," he wrote; but "I reflected on the difficulties which this snowy barrier would most probably throw in my way to the Pacific, and the sufferings and hardships of myself and party in them."

With each day the country presented new difficulties. Unlike the voyage on the lower Missouri, this was not a trip along a well-traveled route. Even Sacajawea, who had grown up in the mountainous Shoshone country, had traveled the route only once before, and then as a twelve-year-old girl and a captive. She is sometimes mistakenly credited with having "guided" the expedition, and she was a valuable member of the party, but she knew little more about the route than Lewis or Clark.

A crucial test came on June 2 when the navigators had to choose between two forks in the river. To determine which was the true Missouri, Lewis and Clark spent a day studying the topography of the country and the speed and clarity of the water. They finally concluded correctly that the south branch was the main river.

A few days later the expedition reached Great Falls, in the present Montana, a beautiful and formidable series of five waterfalls, up to ninety feet high. Lewis was again ahead of the corps and enjoyed contemplating the sight, which he described in one of the more rhapsodic entries in his journal: "The water descends in one even and uninterrupted sheet to the bottom where, dashing against the rocky bottom, it rises into foaming billows of great height and rapidly glides away, hissing, flashing, and sparkling as it departs."

The "foaming billows" might be pleasant to contemplate, but they were difficult to ascend. The explorers must make a hard portage across rough ground and ravines, hauling heavy gear in crude carts fashioned from a cottonwood tree and a boat's mast. Already exhausted from the long upriver journey, many fell asleep instantly every time the portage work came to a halt. A bruising hailstorm fell upon the party, cutting the men, and grizzly bears sought to intimidate these invaders of their territory. The party's morale, however, was equal to the difficulties. "No one complains," wrote Lewis, "all go with cheerfulness."

At the head of the falls, Lewis attempted to float his portable canoe, whose heavy iron frame had lain inert in other boats. He assembled the frame and covered it with hides but could not stop leaks where the hides were sewn together. He tried to caulk the seams and save the craft, which could carry eight thousand pounds of cargo. When he launched the canoe he watched hopefully as it floated tentatively on the current, but its hides soon opened up and the boat sank precipitiously to the bottom. The age of the portable canoe had not yet arrived.

On July 25 they came to a confluence where the Missouri divided into three forks, which they named the Jefferson, the Madison, and the Gallatin. They followed the Jefferson because it had the most westerly course. As they traveled westward the explorers entered a rocky land where steep cliffs fell directly into the river. The leaders became increasingly apprehensive with each day's travel. Ahead lay great mountains with sheer stone faces and snow-clad peaks. If they could find Indians, they might hire horses and guides to help them through the barrier. The landscape was familiar to Sacajawea: here she had gathered berries as a child; there the warriors had collected pigment. But these places were now deserted.

On August 13 Lewis came upon three Indian women. Unable to speak their language, he rolled up his sleeves to show that he was a white man. As they were talking, the Shoshone chief, named Cameahwait, rode up with sixty warriors. When they understood that Lewis and his companions were not from a rival tribe, that they were indeed a new kind of man, and that they came in friendship with gifts, the warriors welcomed and embraced them. As Lewis describes the scene, "We were all caressed and besmeared with their grease and paint till I was heartily tired of the national hug."

Lewis and his advance party spent three days with the Indians. He had made a great beginning with the Shoshone, but he wanted them to meet his main party, still working its way upriver, and the Indians grew suspicious. Was Lewis, after all, an enemy, and would he lead them into a trap? With difficulty the captain coaxed the Indians down to the river, giving them his rifles and dressing his own party in Shoshone garb to assure the Indians that no ambush lay ahead.

On August 16 the explorers must have felt that their mission was blessed. As the main party caught sight of the Shoshone, Sacajawea was speechless with joy; she ran and laughed and sucked her fingers in a gesture indicating a close relationship. By a remarkable chance, the Indians were members of her nation and of the very family from which she had been stolen. Moreover, Chief Cameahwait was her brother. The explorers could not have asked for better entrée into the Indians' good graces.

The explorers made camp with the Shoshone and began to contemplate the next stage of their journey. They knew they were near a river that flowed to the Pacific but did not know whether they could travel safely on its waters. Clark set out to reconnoiter the westward-flowing Lemhi and Salmon rivers and found the route impossibly difficult: the rivers bristled with rapids and their banks were too steep to allow portage or even encampment. They must find some other route, and the explorers decided to go by horseback across the Bitterroot Mountains. They purchased horses from the Shoshone, fashioned pack-saddles out of hides, and began their first long overland trek.

They crossed the first range of mountains without difficulty and descended into the Bitterroot Valley where they encountered a party of Flathead Indians and bargained for horses. Because none of Lewis and Clark's party spoke with the Flathead language, business was carried on by means of three translators. Clark spoke English; one of the privates translated into French; Sacajawea translated into Shoshone; and a Shoshone boy who lived with the Flatheads translated into their language. In this circuitous manner the party obtained a few more horses and set out across the mountains again.

The second range was more difficult. The travelers followed a steep route where the land dropped away into deep valleys and ravines. Two horses slipped off the trail to their deaths. The weather grew colder, and one night four inches of snow fell on the camp. Short of food, the explorers had to eat tallow candles and their two colts. Worst of all, they did not know when they would clear the rugged mountains.

Clark went ahead with a scouting party, finally reaching a place where the plains were clearly visible. He descended and found a party of Nez Percé. Suddenly the ordeal was over. They sold him all the food a horse could carry, and Clark sent one of the men back to relieve Lewis and the main party. With this help they made their way out of the mountains. In a few days the men recovered their strength and were able to build new boats from a grove of ponderosa pines along the Clearwater River.

On October 7, leaving their horses in the care of the Nez Percé, the explorers began the trip down the Clearwater. For the first time on the long voyage they were traveling downstream. Because the season was late, they took chances on the rapids, preferring a hasty to a safe route. Canoes were frequently overturned, but never with much damage to men or equipment. As the party followed the Clearwater into the Snake, they left the Rockies and entered a dry, steep brushland where they traded with Indians for horsemeat and dogmeat and shot prairie cocks. At last they reached the Columbia and saw the Cascade Mountains ahead, the last great range before the Pacific Ocean. The ample waters of the Columbia bore them through the Cascades, and they found signs that they were nearing the ocean: Indian trinkets from the Pacific trade, rain and fog coming from the ocean, and white sea gulls flying above. On November 2 they felt the swell of the tide in the river.

On Wednesday, November 6, the Corps of Discovery camped near the mouth of the river. They built large fires to dry their bedding and settled down for the last night of the westward journey. The next morning rain and a thick fog darkened the land. They continued along the river, stopping at a small Indian village where they traded fishhooks for food and took on a native, dressed in a European sailor's jacket, as a guide. In a few miles the river widened, and as the fog lifted, opening out before them they beheld the waters of the Pacific Ocean. That night they spread their mats on the shore of Gray's Bay with the sound of the ocean in their ears. In his journal Clark wrote, "Ocean in view. O, the joy!"

The corps had still to find its way back east, but now that seemed comparatively simple. They built a winter camp called Fort Clatsop at the mouth of the Columbia, explored the countryside, hunted elk, and took notes on the local Indians. Oregon's winter rain and mist were far less trying than the extreme cold of the previous winter at Fort Mandan.

Lewis and Clark had hoped to encounter a ship that might take them back to the eastern United States, but the seaborne trade to the Northwest was still in its infancy, and no vessel appeared. When spring arrived, the explorers retraced their steps to the Missouri, leaving Fort Clatsop on March 23 and arriving in Nez Percé country seven weeks later. The Indians had cared well for their horses and flew an American flag over their encampment. After waiting for the snow to melt on the high passes in the Rockies, Lewis and Clark explored different routes to the Missouri and then regrouped. They left Sacajawea and Charbonneau in the Mandan country and continued downriver, arriving in Saint Louis on September 23. Lewis immediately wrote to the president announcing their return.

The country was excited to learn that the corps had come back safely from the West. Lewis and Clark captured national attention for weeks. Jefferson welcomed Lewis to the White House — Clark, too, could have visited the president but was busy courting Judith Hancock, for whom he had named the Judith River in Montana. Jefferson had little difficulty in persuading Congress to vote a special bonus in land and money to the veterans of the expedition and appointed Lewis governor of the Louisiana Territory.

The Lewis and Clark Expedition is generally regarded as one of the most successful in history. The explorers had covered more than seven thousand miles from Saint Louis to the Pacific and back and lost only one man — from an unknown disease. They were the first men to cross the continent within the boundaries of what became the forty-eight contiguous states, establishing that there is no convenient water route from the Atlantic to the Pacific. The explorers initiated friendly relations with dozens of Indian nations and compiled extensive records on the character of each. They were the first to discover or describe 178 plants, 15 reptiles and amphibians, 44 mammals, 51 birds, and 12 fishes. Among these plants and animals were the ponderosa pine, sagebrush, the prairie rattler, the steelhead trout, the coyote, and the grizzly bear.

Many veterans of the expedition would go west again. John Colter became a famous frontiersman and trapper, and William Clark settled in Saint Louis, serving as an Indian agent and territorial governor. The territory they had explored caught the imagination of other Americans. The West was now perceived as a reality — and an American reality at that. The United States was blessed with an embarrassment of riches. America had the rich lands of her original boundaries and almost as much country again in the West. The land would offer opportunities for trade, settlement, and adventure to millions of Americans yet unborn. Such was the glorious prospect that lay before Jeffersonian America.

Unfortunately, the conquest would have its sordid side, for the land would change as millions of settlers destroyed Indians and killed wild animals. Even the sweet-smelling wild grasses of the prairies would give way to less romantic, if more profitable, wheat crops. But the Corps of Discovery had been able to see the West without subduing it, and in the young republic there appeared to be no limit to America's resources.

QUESTIONS

1. How did the planning and course of the Lewis and Clark Expedition reflect its scientific intent?

2. How did the following nations or groups of people facilitate or react to the Lewis and Clark Expedition? The French, the Spanish, the trappers and traders, and the Americans themselves?

3. Summarize the reception given to Lewis and Clark by various Indian tribes and individuals.

4. The United States was so large in 1803 that it was difficult to imagine

a time when it would be fully settled. How does the experience of Lewis and Clark support this statement?

5. In what ways did the Lewis and Clark Expedition embody the buoyant optimism of the early republic?

BIBLIOGRAPHY

BAKELESS, JOHN. *Lewis and Clark: Partners in Discovery* (1947). Survey of the expedition's history.

CUTRIGHT, PAUL RUSSELL. *Lewis and Clark: Pioneering Naturalists* (1969). Favorable assessment of the expedition's scientific role.

JACKSON, DONALD, EDITOR. *Letters of the Lewis and Clark Expedition* (1962). Fine anthology of letters.

MACAPIA, PAUL, AND MARY E. MACAPIA. *Lewis and Clark's America: A Contemporary Photo Essay* (1976). Modern photographs of Lewis and Clark's route.

RONDA, JAMES. *Lewis and Clark Among the Indians* (1984). Lewis and Clark as diplomats and ethnographers.

SHEEHAN, BERNARD. *Seeds of Extinction: Jeffersonian Philanthropy and the American Indian* (1973). Chronicles the destructive influence of Jeffersonian policy on eastern Indians.

THWAITES, REUBEN G., EDITOR. *Original Journals of the Lewis and Clark Expedition* (8 vols., 1904-5). Extensive collection of expedition journals.

WOODS, WILLIS F., ET. AL. *Lewis and Clark's America: A Voyage of Discovery* (1976). Nineteenth-century paintings and sketches.

9

THE LIMITS OF
JACKSONIAN DEMOCRACY

The Cherokee
Removal

Andrew Jackson's election to the presidency in 1828 symbolized an age of new opportunity for the common man. The first chief executive born in a log cabin, Jackson proved that almost any man could rise to the highest post in America. During his administration he promoted democratic ideals by attacking the Bank of the United States as a privileged monopoly and promoting rotation in office to broaden political participation. While creating new opportunities for some Americans, however, he curtailed the rights of others. His Indian policy satisfied land-hungry whites but victimized the native Americans. The Cherokee, who had lived for hundreds of years in the southern Alleghenies, suffered especially at Jackson's hands. In response to American policy they had adopted many white customs early in the nineteenth century, only to be forced off their land in the 1830s to "protect" their native customs. Opportunity, it appeared, could damage one group while encouraging another.

Maj Gen. Winfield Scott, a great admirer of the Cherokee, arrived at New Echota, Georgia, in 1838 commanding an army of seven thousand regular soldiers and state militiamen. Addressing his troops on May 17, Scott declared, "The Cherokees, by the advances they have made in Christianity and civilization, are by far the most interesting tribe of Indians in the territorial limits of the United States." He urged his soldiers to show the Indians "every possible kindness." These benevolent words might suggest that Scott was the leader of a mission of mercy designed to rescue the Cherokee from an impending calamity, but ironically, the kindly general was himself the agent of calamity. As Scott uttered his considerate phrases, his men were busy constructing large wood pens with sixteen-foot walls. During the next month they would seek out fourteen thousand Cherokee, living in several thousand square miles of Appalachian valleys and mountainsides, and drive them like cattle into these log enclosures, holding them for shipment to a distant land in the west.

Scott's men divided into dozens of parties and spread out across Cherokee lands, finding the Indians, who had already been disarmed by other soldiers, engaged in domestic tasks. Men were in the fields, women at their spinning wheels, children at play, and families at dinner in their neat log or wood frame homes, when soldiers arrived with gruff voices and fixed bayonets to march them off with the clothes on their backs and the few possessions they could carry.

An old man listened stoically as the soldiers told him he must leave his home. Gathering his children and grandchildren around him, he knelt in prayer, then led his family away. A Cherokee woman used her last moments to feed her chickens. As the Indians left their homes, greedy men arrived to purchase their possessions for a pittance or to steal the remaining livestock and household goods.

Thousands of Cherokees were torn thus from their homes and driven from their lands, transformed in a sickening, brief moment from prosperous farmers and artisans into refugees. One night they slept in their own beds; the next they lay on the ground under crude shelters of boards and bark inside stockades. Among the efficient soldiers was a Georgia militiaman, who later served as a Confederate officer. "I fought through the civil war," he later wrote, "and have seen men shot to pieces and slaughtered by thousands, but the Cherokee removal was the cruelest work I ever knew."

If the Cherokee removal had been the work of a totalitarian government in a country where individual or minority rights were lightly regarded and the state deified, we might regard it as an inevitable tragedy, sad but expected — consistent with the bloated authority of a dictatorial regime. But the American ideology, enshrined in the Declaration of Independence more than six decades before the Cherokee removal, rejects the totalitarian view of the state. Britain's threat to take a few pennies a year in tea taxes had provoked the colonists to revolt and establish a government more "likely to effect their safety and happiness." Andrew Jackson, then president of the United States, was a man who seemed particularly well suited to carry on the libertarian ideals of the founding fathers. "Old Hickory" regarded himself as a man of the people and claimed that any person was worthy of holding public office. On inauguration day in 1829 he had opened the White House and entertained a boisterous mob. Surely Jackson's appreciation of the needs, to say nothing of the rights, of the average citizen would lead him to sympathize with the Indians. Yet he and other Americans regarded the Cherokee as a people apart, not entitled to the same rights as other Americans.

To understand the Cherokee situation we need to review the tribe's early history, their adjustment to the white settlers, and their condition on the eve of removal. In their story we can witness both the vitality of the native American cultures and the curiously insensitive Indian policies of the federal government.

Long ago, according to Cherokee legend, there was no earth, only a great body of water, and above it in the crowded Upper World a multitude of animals, crowded together and longing for room. Finally "Beaver's Grandchild," the Water-beetle, offered to go down to the water and investigate. He skimmed over the surface but could find no land. So he swam to the bottom and came up with some soft mud, which began to grow and grow into a great flat plain. The delighted animals sent birds down to seek dry land, but everywhere the earth was still mud. A buzzard flew down and his wings struck the ground, breaking the earth into mountains and valleys. Finally the mud dried, and the animals came down from the Upper World and dwelt on the earth. The land where the buzzard's wings had struck became the Cherokee country.

Modern scholars have presented a more prosaic picture of Cherokee origins but agree that the Cherokee lived in the southern Appalachians for many generations. At some distant time, the Indians must have come from elsewhere, but the details of that prehistoric migration are uncertain. Scholars have traced a wide network of associations between the Cherokee and other peoples. Cherokee artifacts have turned up in burial mounds in Illinois and Indiana. Their language is Iroquoian, suggesting an earlier connection with Indians to the north. Their pottery is similar to that of Caribbean Indians. Their basket-making bears a strong resemblance to the crafts of the Amazon and Orinoco rivers in South America. During the thousands of years that

Indians have lived in America such far-flung contacts were certainly possible.

But by the time the first white men entered Cherokee lands in 1540, the natives had lived in the Appalachians for so many generations that they could imagine no other place as home. At the time some thirty thousand Cherokee lived in loosely confederated villages, a strong, healthy people, nourished by rich soil and abundant wildlife. They planted corn and potatoes; gathered chestnuts and berries; and hunted deer, elk, buffalo, pheasants, and turkey. Cooking over open fires, they ate from earthenware vessels.

The Cherokee were well housed, many owning both summer and winter dwellings in close proximity. Summer houses were wood structures up to seventy feet long and two stories high, some housing several families. Winter dwellings were smaller, with floors three feet beneath the ground and thick circular walls composed of mud and timbers. Wood bedframes covered with finely woven mats and animal skins hugged the walls. A small fire in the middle warmed these tiny, efficient shelters.

Every Cherokee belonged to one of the seven tribal clans — the Bird, Wolf, Deer, Red Paint, Blue, Long Hair, and Wild Potato. The Indians protected themselves from genetic disease and created wide relational networks by requiring that every person marry outside his or her group. The clan was responsible for enforcing the law with the assistance of the town chief and the tribal council. There was no chief or assembly for all the Cherokee, but the cultural identity of the tribe made the Cherokee a single people.

The Cherokee religion taught the people that their land was a gift from the Great Spirit, Asga-Ya-Galun-lati. They did not "own" the land, strictly speaking, for it remained always the property of their god. But they did own the improvements on the land: houses, crops, and livestock.

Cherokee lives were animated by a perpetual sense of the proximity of sacred beings. "Little People" dwelt in nearby caves, and "Immortals" lived among the mountain peaks. The sun, moon, rivers, rocks, birds, animals, and trees — all were animate. The snowy owl was a star that had fallen to the earth to take a new form. The bears were Indians who had adopted animal form. They could talk to you if they wanted to, but perversely — or wisely — they remained silent.

The Cherokee loved to tell stories about the animals, many of which were later adopted by Joel Chandler Harris for his *Uncle Remus* tales and became part of the broader American folklore. The stories told how the deer got his horns and why the mole lived underground. The most famous of all tells how a tortoise set out to race a hare. "I know I cannot beat a hare," said Tortoise, "but I can try."

The Cherokee celebrated their lives and honored their gods with periodic ceremonies, following the cycle of seasons in a land where nature announced the birth and death of the year with splendid impressions: the sweet scent of azaleas and other species of rhododendron in the spring and the bright colors of maple, oak, and cottonwood trees in the fall. The Indians observed the greatest of the celebrations, the Corn Ceremony, with prayers of thanks for good crops, a feast, music, dancing, and games. In such ways the people celebrated their lives under a Cherokee sky in a place that seemed ineffably their land.

The rhythms of Cherokee life were not affected by the arrival in the Caribbean in 1492 of three Spanish ships. Cortés conquered the Aztecs, and Pizarro overwhelmed the Incas before Europeans even entered the Cherokee lands. The first visitor was Hernando de Soto, who made his way along the Winding Stair Trail through the Appalachians in 1640. His appearance must have impressed the Cherokee, who had never before seen men with horses, guns, and shining armor. But de Soto passed quickly onward, seeking treasures to rival those of the conquistadores. The comparative modesty of Cherokee holdings proved an asset in years ahead when the Spanish established their dominion in Florida. Having no incentive to loot the Cherokee, the Europeans left them alone. Only an occasional visitor moved among the natives, including a Jesuit priest who reported that the Cherokee were "sedate and thoughtful, dwelling in peace in their native mountains."

During the seventeenth century the Cherokee developed a taste for European goods and occasionally raided the Spanish for horses and guns. But they were slow to establish a stable trade with the whites. It was not until 1673 that the first Englishmen, James Needham and Gabriel Arthur, visited the Cherokee. They were such a curiosity that the Indians placed them on a platform for all the people to see. The visitors made a trade ageement with the Cherokee, and Gabriel Arthur returned to Virginia with a party of Indians to collect a store of goods. On their way back Arthur quarreled with one of the natives, a man remembered only as "Indian John," and in a moment Arthur lay dead on the ground, a bullet through his head. Indian John then did a curious and ominous thing: he drew his knife and cut out Arthur's heart. Holding it in his hand and turning east toward the English plantations, he said that "he valued not all the English." The words may be apocryphal, but they represent succinctly the Cherokee sense of independence.

Indian John nearly succeeded in having Needham killed as well, but a Cherokee chief came to the white man's defense, and during the next year Needham adopted Cherokee dress and accompanied the Indians on raids across the Southeast from the Ohio River to Florida. He returned safely to Virginia in 1674, but the English made no more attempts to establish trade with the Cherokee for the next two decades.

Early in the eighteenth century, however, an extensive trade did grow up between the two regions. In Charleston and other southern cities, large trains of packhorses were loaded with widely assorted trade goods: cloth, blankets, hoes, axes, beads, looking glasses, ribbons, guns, knives, hatchets, bullets, powder, flints, kettles, tobacco, pipes, and rum. They wound their way along the steep narrow trails through the Appalachians into the Cherokee towns, where the traders exchanged their wares for pelts, beeswax, and bear oil. In 1708 alone, fifty thousand deerskins and other hides crossed the mountains.

Slowly the contacts with the whites began to change Cherokee society. Not only did the Indians come to depend on English goods, but they also became familiar with English culture. White traders settled in many Indian towns, frequently building the largest houses in the neighborhood, marrying Indian women, raising half-breed families, and advising the natives on European ways. Among the resident traders were intelligent, sensitive men like Eleazar Wiggam and James Adair, who learned the Cherokee language and wrote descriptions of the people.

The Indian villages, which had always consisted of substantial dwellings, acquired the signs of white influence, and by the middle of the eighteenth century many Cherokee lived in log cabins like those of white frontiersmen. On cold winter nights, however, they sought the warmth of the tiny circular "hot houses" they had always known.

In 1735 there were sixty-four Cherokee villages with an approximate population of sixteen thousand. Each village consisted of between twenty and sixty houses, surrounded by gardens, orchards, and hog-pens. The largest building in each town was a council house, capable of holding several hundred people for government councils or religious ceremonies. A sacred fire burned on an earthen mound in the middle of each council house.

The men frequently went away on war parties against the Creek, the Iroquois, the Tuscarora, and other neighboring tribes. In fact, warfare was so common among the Cherokee that they acquired a reputation with the English for being particularly fierce and regarding battle as a kind of pastime. Cherokee women were active participants in every aspect of life, including the military arts. They sat on war councils and even went on campaigns. They raised their children as warriors, forcing them to endure pain and hunger as preparation for warfare.

A softer side of Cherokee life was apparent, however, to most travelers. Eighteenth-century accounts of the Cherokee are filled with admiration. Hungry travelers who fed on Indian bread, corncakes, and hominy mush grew to admire Cherokee cooking. The Indians engaged in many crafts, including making baskets, mats, pottery, bows, clubs, and canoes. Observers commented on the natives' fine bearing and physiques. John Bartram, the naturalist, wrote: "They are tall, slender, erect and of a delicate frame; their features formed with perfect symmetry, their countenance cheerful and friendly, and they move with a becoming grace and dignity."

Having established trading relations with the Cherokee, the English wanted to secure them as allies in wars with other Indian tribes and with the French. In 1730 Sir Alexander Cummings persuaded the Cherokee to inaugurate one of their chiefs as an "emperor" of all the towns and to send representatives to England to negotiate a treaty. On May 4, 1730, he sailed to England with seven principal men of the tribe, including Attakullakulla, a short man known to his people as "The Little Carpenter," but distinguished as a statesman and orator.

In London these leading tribesmen were carefully coached in court etiquette and on June 18 were presented to the king at Windsor Castle. Everywhere they went in London — to the Tower, the Mermaid Tavern, the theater, St. James's Park, the Houses of Parliament — they were observed with wonder as beings from an unimaginably remote region. They negotiated an agreement to become England's allies in war, to trade only with the English, and to return runaway slaves. The English promised, in turn, to punish anyone who injured the Cherokee. During the next half century, the two nations were closely allied, with the exception of a short period of warfare in 1760-61, when English Capt. James Grant destroyed fifteen Cherokee towns, impressing upon the Indians the value of friendly relations with the English.

In the years preceding the American Revolution, Cherokee-English relations were further improved by two able representatives of royal authority. One of the agents, John MacDonald, settled among the Cherokee at Chickamonga Creek and married Anne Shorey, the daughter of a white interpreter and an Indian woman. Their grandson, John Ross, would become one of the principal Cherokee leaders in the early nineteenth century.

Unfortunately, the friendship between Cherokees and English served the Indians poorly during the Revolutionary War. The Cherokee elected to remain faithful to their alliance but received little help from the English. In 1776-77 American armies from Georgia, South Carolina, and North Carolina invaded the Cherokee lands and destroyed more than fifty villages, forcing the Indians to accept the Carolina cession, whereby they lost large portions of territory.

Cherokee resistance to the new American government continued sporadically through the Revolutionary period and into the early years

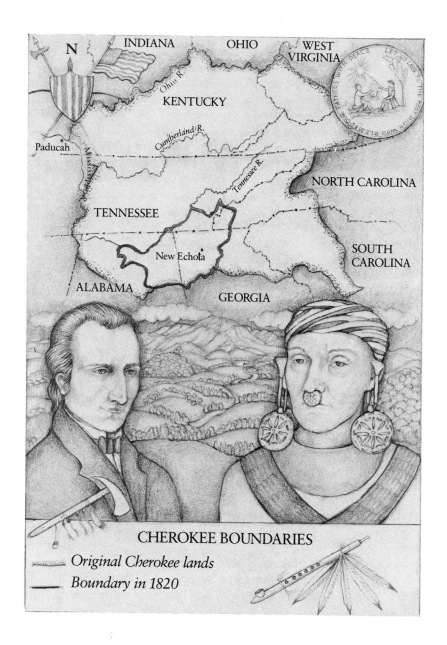

CHEROKEE BOUNDARIES

Original Cherokee lands
Boundary in 1820

of the new nation, but by 1790 most of the Indians realized they would have to make peace with the whites. The Treaty of Holston in 1791 ended hostilities and provided for introduction of the Indians to all the advantages of white society. Its Article 14 called for the Indians to advance their abilities in home industry and agriculture and guaranteed American tools and training to bring the Cherokee "to a greater degree of civilization."

During the next forty years, the Indians, who had already been greatly influenced by European culture, adopted many customs and industries from their white neighbors. The change, known as the Cherokee Renaissance, was facilitated by white settlers. For several generations, traders of predominantly Scotch, Irish, or Scotch-Irish background had been living among the Cherokee, establishing their permanent homes in the Indian lands and marrying native women. As a matter of course, they brought with them some knowledge of literature and crafts.

The Cherokee were especially fortunate in the government's choice of Indian agents in the early nineteenth century. Benjamin Hawkins, who served in this capacity from 1796 until 1801, wanted to devote his life to the Indians and was particularly interested in seeing that the altruistic promise of Article 14 was implemented. Travelers in 1800 noticed signs of progress toward white standards of civilization: women at work at looms and men tending cattle in the fields.

Hawkins was followed by Return Jonathan Meigs, a Revolutionary War veteran and Ohio frontiersman, who began work as the Cherokee Indian agent in 1801 at age sixty and continued energetically in the post for twenty-two years. Under Meigs's direction, the provisions of the Treaty of Holston calling for American aid and training were carried out. The United States distributed plows, hoes, axes, and other tools. White blacksmiths, wheelwrights, carpenters, and other artisans settled in the Cherokee country and taught Indian apprentices their skills. Meigs also assisted the Indians by arguing their positions at treaty conferences and encouraging them to establish a unified tribal government, and he sought to expel whites who threatened the Indians' welfare — unscrupulous traders, fugitives, and squatters.

Meigs knew and liked the Cherokees well, lived among them, and won their respect. In times of famine or disease, he saw that the Indians received assistance quickly and attempted to persuade Washington that they should not be charged for such aid. His last act of kindness to a Cherokee symbolized his long consideration. In 1823 at age eighty-two he turned over his house to an elderly Cherokee chief on a cold night and slept in a tent. But the sacrifice proved too much for his aged body — he contracted pneumonia and died.

Meigs's dedication to the Cherokee was matched by that of many other men, notably among a growing number of Christian missionaries. Early in the nineteenth century, Moravians, Presbyterians, Baptists, and Methodists established missions in the Cherokee lands, where they preached and conducted the first schools in the region. Many learned the Cherokee tongue, and Samuel Austin Worcester translated hymns into Cherokee.

Men like Hawkins, Meigs, and Worcester represented well the spirit of Article 14. They believed that the greatest benefit they could confer upon the Indians was to give them the knowledge and the tools to live as their white neighbors did. In the American government, however, there was a faction that espoused a different progam for the Indians. From the earliest days of colonization many whites had regarded Indian lands as vacant lands, waiting to be properly settled by people of European descent. In the regions surrounding the Cherokee thousands of whites were beginning to feel the need for more land. The Cherokee territory was lightly settled: why not open it to whites?

The Indians were reluctant to part with any of their lands, but the federal government offered them many enticements. In exchange for vacant land the government would give the Indians money that could be used to improve the lands they occupied. If an Indian were displaced when land was ceded to the federal government, he would be paid for his improvements and given land in the West. If he owned no land or improvements, the government would still give him a rifle, a blanket, and a beaver trap so that he could make a start in the West. If he preferred to stay on his land, he could keep a 640-acre homestead, or "reservation," on ceded territory.

With such inducements the Cherokee made several land cessions in the early nineteenth century. By 1817 two thousand Cherokee, slightly more than 10 percent of the tribal population, had moved to a region beyond the Mississippi that became known as Cherokee West. But many Indians were worried about the loss of their native lands. They were confused by government policies that encouraged them to take up the plow and the loom and become "civilized" like the whites but that also enticed them to go west with trap and rifle to live the traditional life of the Indian hunter. One missionary reported the Indian reaction to the two-sided American policies:

> The Indians say they don't know how to understand their Father the President. A few years ago he sent them a plough and a hoe — said it was not good for his red children to hunt — they must cultivate the earth. Now he tells them there is good hunting at the Arkansas; if they go there he will give them rifles.

In 1820 most Cherokees were committed to the first option. Their hunting lands were depleted anyway, and they recognized the need for raising cattle and growing more crops. Their loyalty to the United States was tested by the Creek War in 1814. The Creek, a southern tribe, urged the Cherokee to join them in expelling whites from their native lands. But the Cherokee chose to side with the whites, sending eight hundred warriors against the southern tribe and helping Andrew Jackson win the decisive Battle of Horseshoe Bend.

The degree to which the Cherokee had assimilated white civilization was apparent to any person who journeyed through their lands. The Indian dwellings were log cabins or larger framed houses, usually surrounded by fields, orchards, and fenced pastures. Some of the more prosperous Cherokees owned black slaves and lived as gentlemen planters. Joseph Vann, one the wealthiest men in the region, owned a fine two-story brick house featuring a veranda and imposing white columns.

In 1826 a Presbyterian church report surveyed the diverse holdings of the Cherokee people and arrived at these statistics: 7,600 houses, 22,000 cattle, 46,000 pigs, 2,500 sheep, 2,948 plows, 1,488 spinning wheels, 762 looms, 62 blacksmith shops, 31 gristmills, 10 sawmills, and 18 schools. These figures indicate the degree to which the Cherokee had assimilated white material culture. Another index is provided by the Indian claims filed after removal. Among the household items listed were dishes, cutlery, coffee pots, irons, churns, washtubs, chairs, tables, feather beds, and silk dresses. In addition, many Cherokee owned books written in English, and some even subscribed to English-language periodicals.

In government, too, the Cherokee were influenced by white practices. Although they retained their village chiefs, the Indians formed a central administration with a frame of government modeled on the United States Constitution. The Cherokee republic had a chief executive, a two-house legislature, and a supreme court. The Cherokee established New Echota in their Georgia lands as capital; and it soon boasted a council house, a courthouse, a printing office, stores, and several frame houses.

The Cherokee preserved many tribal customs amid these signs of white influence. Although the leaders frequently dressed in suits, the standard dress for men was fringed buckskin shirts worn over cloth or buckskin trousers and possibly a calico turban and earrings. The traditional sports and ceremonies such as ball play, archery, and the Great Corn Dance endured.

No person better exemplified the Cherokee impulses to adopt white inventions and institutions and preserve native culture than Sequoya, who was born in 1775 the son of a Cherokee woman and a white trader. His relatives included great warriors, among them Old Tassel, the foremost Cherokee chief during the Revolutionary War. Sequoya grew up a solitary, energetic, and enigmatic young man, mastering the skills of silversmith, blacksmith, and trader. Interested in painting but unable to obtain store-bought supplies, he made brushes from horsehair and paints from earth and plant pigments.

Early in the nineteenth century, Sequoya became obsessed with the idea of creating an alphabet to represent the Cherokee language. Although other Indian languages had been put into print, the Cherokee sound patterns were so complicated that no one had been able to represent them with written characters. Sequoya was determined to try, but he disliked white influence and withdrew to a remote region of the Cherokee tribes. He preferred hunting and trapping to farming and even moved away from his family into a small hut in order to pursue his study of the Cherokee tongue. His behavior was so strange that many Indians turned against him, considering him a witch. His detractors even burned his hut with all his linguistics notes.

In 1821 after twelve years of work Sequoya completed a phonetic alphabet. Using the English alphabet, supplemented by other characters, he represented 86 distinctive Cherokee syllables, or sounds, thus arriving at a phonetic alphabet.

When other Indians heard about his accomplishment, they were incredulous but gave him the opportunity to demonstrate his system to the National Council. Because the characters were perfectly phonetic — unlike English — it was possible to learn to read quickly, and within a few hours he proved that he could teach children to sound out words. The rapidity with which the Cherokee people seized on the new method proved both their desire to learn and their attachment to their language. Some Indians learned to read Sequoya's writings in only a few days, and soon, thousands of Cherokee could read the printed words of their language. The National Council ordered the Cherokee's laws printed in the native language and established a printing press in New Echota. The missionary, Samuel Austin Worcester, carried the word of Sequoya's achievements to Philadelphia and Boston, raising large sums of money to buy a printing press and have Sequoya's alphabet cast in lead type. In 1828 the press in New Echota began to print a newspaper, the *Cherokee Phoenix,* in English and in Cherokee under the editorship of Elias Boudinot, a full-blooded Indian.

No achievement of the Cherokee Renaissance contributed more to tribal pride than Sequoya's alphabet. But Sequoya was still not comfortable with life on the fringes of white society, and in 1821, the year he introduced his invention to the National Council, he left his eastern homeland forever and moved to Cherokee West. Despite Sequoya's

Sequoya and his alphabet. Sequoya created a Cherokee alphabet enabling his people to publish a newspaper and write documents in their own tongue.

disaffection, however, the prospect of Cherokee life in the East was bright in the 1820s. While preserving tribal dress, law, and language, the Cherokee had successfully adopted many features of white civilization. They raised cattle and corn, built frame houses, sang hymns, and drafted legislation.

Despite their faithful adherence to the spirit of the Treaty of Holston, however, they would soon be torn from their tribal lands in a government program that made a mockery of the American policy of civilization and conciliation. With each year the white pressure on their borders increased, and the southern states, sensitive to their local "rights," began to demand control of tribal lands within their own boundaries. Andrew Jackson, who became president in 1829, was sensitive to their ambitions. As a westerner, he understood the frontiersman's desire for land; as a nationalist, he opposed the existence of autonomous enclaves within the United States. Having fought with and against Indians, he maintained a sentimental regard for the natives but believed that both they and his white countrymen suffered from too close an association. He was glad enough to let the Indians live their own lives, as long as those lives were far removed from his own country.

Jackson set forth his Indian policy in his first annual message to Congress, on December 8, 1829, stating unequivocally that there could be no independent Indian nations within the United States. Sympathizing with Georgia opposition to the Cherokee republic, he asked whether Maine would permit its Indians, the Penobscot, to form an independent country within the state's boundaries.

Despite his firm opposition to Indian autonomy within the states, Jackson recognized that previous Indian policy had been ambiguous. He believed that the natives could not preserve their integrity as tribes within the United States, even if the states granted their autonomy. Contact with whites inevitably doomed them to "weakness and decay." In the West, however, on a new land guaranteed to them for all time, they could develop at their own pace, absorbing white culture as they chose and eventually create "an interesting commonwealth, destined to perpetuate the race."

Jackson did not favor forced removal. "It would be as cruel as unjust," he said, "to compel the aborigines to abandon the graves of their fathers and seek a home in a distant land." Those who wished to remain could do so. But they must be subject to state law, and they could retain only the lands they had improved. They could not retain vacant tribal lands "merely because they have seen them from the mountain or passed them in the chase." Jackson anticipated that those who chose to remain on homesteads in the eastern states would receive, "like other citizens, protection in their persons and property . . . [and] ere long become merged in the mass of our population."

This was a complex statement. Our knowledge of subsequent history may incline us to simplify Jackson's address into a demand for forced removal. But Jackson distinguished between the tribe and the individual Indian. The natives who fully accepted American laws and American concepts of landownership should be allowed to remain on their present land. But the Indian nation within the nation, with its vast tribal lands and independent government, could not be allowed to continue. In short, the Indians must either accept white society in toto or go west and develop whatever blend of native and white society seemed appropriate.

Jackson's opposition to tribal autonomy seemed to invite the states to take over Indian lands. Georgia had already declared that whites living on Cherokee lands were subject to state law; soon after Jackson's message, that state declared Cherokee laws void and decreed Cherokee lands to be part of the state of Georgia. Because most of the Cherokee territory was in Georgia, this action threatened to destroy tribal autonomy. The state sent troops to take possession of goldfields recently discovered by the Indians, thereafter allowing whites, but not Indians, to mine the ore. In reprisal, Cherokee warriors attacked and killed several whites, furnishing a pretext for further action by Georgia against the tribe.

In the meantime, an Indian removal bill was introduced in the U.S. House on February 24, 1830, by Representative Wilson Lumpkin of Georgia. The bill called for exchange of western land for Indian lands east of the Mississippi, compensation for improvements, and assistance in migration. It would apply equally to the five great southeastern tribes: the Choctaw, Chickasaw, Creek, and Seminole, as well as the Cherokee. The debate over the bill provoked a long and angry discussion about the proper character of Indian-white relations. Although many congressmen agreed with Lumpkin and Jackson that removal was necessary, a substantial minority, including Daniel Webster, opposed the measure.

The opposition was dramatically summarized by Senator Theodore Frelinghuysen of New Jersey in an epical six-hour speech. Frelinghuysen began by examining the early history of the natives, pointing out that they had been on their lands long before Great Britain, itself, had a political existence. The Indians, he said, "are men, endowed with kindred faculties and powers with ourselves . . . they have a place in human sympathy, and are justly entitled to a share in the common bounties of a benignant Providence." The white man had no right to take Indian land by force. "Where the Indian always has been," said Frelinghuysen, "he enjoys an absolute right still to be, in the free exercise of thought, government and conduct." The Indian's natural right to the land had been reinforced by a long series of treaties in which the Indian tribes were regarded as sovereign nations.

Historically, Indians had given up much land by treaty and purchase, but they had a right now to hold on to what remained. Frelinghuysen characterized the whites as insatiably greedy: "Like the horse-leech," he said, "our insatiated cupidity cries, give! give!" Frelinghuysen pictured the white expansionist saying to the Indians: "Away! we cannot endure you so near us! These forests and rivers, these groves of your fathers, these firesides and hunting grounds are ours by the right of power, and the force of numbers." Such conduct was entirely inconsistent with the principles of liberty. We were "the wonder and praise of the world," he said, "freedom's hope, and her consolation." But now we were about "to become the oppressors of the feeble, and to cast away our birthright!" He urged his fellow congressmen to "place the White man where the Indian stands." Some years before "a few pence of duty on tea, that invaded no fireside, excited no fears, disturbed no substantial interest whatever" had excited in Americans a fear of unjust authority and precipitated the Revolution. During the years of war with Britain, the founding fathers had "contended for the very rights and privileges that our Indian neighbors now implore us to protect and preserve to them."

Frelinghuysen's eloquent speech won him national acclaim as well as summarizing the key points in the arguments against removal: the priority of Indian claims to the land; the incompatibility of removal and American libertarian ideals; the venality of the usurpers' motives. But he was not sufficiently persuasive to prevent the passage of the removal bill, and opportunism proved stronger than idealism; the bill was enacted into law in May 1830. In the meantime, Georgia had passed more Cherokee legislation, specifying that contracts between Indians and whites were null and void unless witnessed by two whites and that no Indian could testify against a white man in Georgia courts. Apparently, Jackson's demand that eastern Indians live under white laws did not mean under the same laws that governed whites.

Despite these setbacks, the Cherokee, with the help of supporters throughout the United States, were determined to fight for their traditional rights. At a meeting of the Cherokee Legislative Council in July 1830, the Indians begged Jackson to uphold their treaties, telling him, "inclination to remove from this land has no abiding place in our hearts, and when we move, we shall move by the course of nature to sleep under this ground which the Great Spirit gave to our ancestors and which now covers them in undisturbed repose." The Cherokee opposition leader was John Ross, grandson of the British agent John MacDonald and son of the Scotch trader Daniel Ross. Although he was only one-eighth Cherokee blood, Ross had been raised on Indian land and identified completely with the native cause. Since 1817 he had been the elected leader of the Cherokee Nation. A rather small man with dark hair, heavy eyebrows, and blue eyes, during the 1830s he worked unceasingly to prevent the removal.

For several years the Indians were in limbo, hardly able to believe that they might soon be forced to leave their homeland. Ross was a messenger of hope, periodically returning from battles in Washington and riding through Cherokee towns. The people came in from their farms and lined up for the chance to stand before John Ross and take him by the hand as he assured them that they would win.

Many Indians and whites helped Ross in the battle to retain the Cherokee lands. Elias Boudinot wrote stirring editorials against removal in the *Cherokee Phoenix*, exposing the hypocrisy of the removal policy: "Where have we an example in the whole history of man, of a nation or tribe removing in a body, from a land of civil and religious means, to a perfect wilderness, *in order to be civilized.*" Boudinot castigated the United States for failing to uphold its own promises. The Indians were driven off their lands even though "treaties are declared to be binding, and in them ample provisions are made for the protection of the Indians." He asked, "Who would trust his life and fortune to such a faithless nation?" No Cherokee *voluntarily* would. Stripped of its self-righteous rhetoric, the removal bill said to the Indian, "Go and perish."

Boudinot's essays not only helped unify Indian sentiment but also rallied white support and were reprinted across the United States. Influential men in Washington helped Ross find good legal counsel for the tribe. In 1832 the lawyers won a stunning victory before the U.S. Supreme Court in *Worcester v. Georgia,* a case that arose when Samuel Austin Worcester refused to register with the Georgia authorities as preacher in the Indian Territory. He argued that the new state law requiring such registration was unconstitutional because Georgia had no authority in the Indian lands. The Court found in favor of Worcester, and Chief Justice John Marshall declared that the Cherokee Nation was "a distinct community, occupying its own territories, with boundaries accurately described, in which the laws of Georgia can have no force, and which the citizens of Georgia have no right to enter." The Court thus confirmed the Cherokee position. But President Jackson refused to uphold the decision, reputedly saying, "John Marshall has made his decision. Now let him enforce it." Whether or not Jackson ever made this statement, it accurately summarizes his attitude toward the Court's position. Without the president's support, the decision was a dead letter.

Georgia was so unimpressed by the Court's authority that the state held Worcester in prison for almost a year following the decision. Worse, the state began to distribute the Indian lands by lottery. In the next two years whites occupied John Ross's house, the Indian capital at New Echota, a Moravian mission station, and many other Cherokee dwellings. At the mission the Moravian chapel became a courthouse and the mission rectory was turned into a tavern.

In the face of these defeats, some Cherokees, including Elias Boudinot, began to waver. Boudinot admired many features of white civilization, but he was increasingly repelled by white prejudice. In 1826 he had married Harriet Gold, a white woman who lived in Cornwall, Connecticut, where he had attended a mission school. His cousin, John Ridge, also married a woman from Cornwall. The marriages, which must have seemed at first to confirm Boudinot's full acceptance into white society, soon produced the opposite effect. Anti-Indian racism erupted in Cornwall, and the mission school was forced to close. Boudinot, who had believed Indians could achieve equality through education, was bitterly disappointed. During the removal controversy he met with other expressions of racial animosity. Harassed by the Georgia Guard, he poured his anger and humiliation into a despairing question: "Would a white man have been treated as I have been?"

His experience with prejudice finally convinced Boudinot that the

Indians' best chance lay in separating themselves from white civilization. Between two bad choices removal seemed the lesser evil. Assisted by Major Ridge and John Ridge, two of the nation's foremost leaders, he formed a Removal party and argued that because expulsion was inevitable the tribe should negotiate for the best possible terms. The other four nations had already signed removal treaties, so that there appeared to be no alternative. In October 1835 a treaty council convened at Red Clay, Tennessee, the new Cherokee capital. Under Ross's leadership, the Indians overwhelmingly rejected a removal treaty. Even Boudinot and the other proponents of the treaty voted against it, fearing reprisals from the other Cherokees.

Exasperated by Ross's recalcitrance, Georgia authorities decided upon a desperate act. On the night of December 5, 1835, twenty-five members of the Georgia Guard rode across the Tennessee border and surrounded the small cabin that had served as Ross's home since his expulsion from his Georgia farm. They arrested Ross and a visitor, John Howard Payne, and made them ride through a cold rain back across the border to Camp Benton, Georgia, where they threw the two men into a small cabin that served as the jail. Inside the building, one Indian lay in chains and the body of another hung in the rafters.

Ross and his friend might never have escaped from the horror of their cell had the Guard not violated Tennessee territory, angering the authorities there. Their case was helped also by the fact that Ross's companion, John Howard Payne, was known throughout the country as the composer of a popular air, "Home, Sweet Home," and was occupied at the time in writing a history of the Cherokee Nation. His manuscript, written before this incident, referred to the Georgia Guard as "bandits." As he lay in the grotesque prison, Payne may have wondered whether the term was sufficiently strong.

The two men were released after thirteen days, but in the meantime final preparations had been made for the last act in the legal maneuverings over the Cherokee removal. On December 29, Boudinot, the Ridges, and a hundred other proremoval Indians met and signed the Treaty of New Echota, purporting to represent the wishes of the Cherokee Nation. Ross went to Washington to fight the treaty and offered the government a document bearing the names of more than fourteen thousand Indians who opposed the treaty. Despite this evidence of its specious character, the Senate ratified the document by the narrow margin of one vote.

The Cherokee defeat was complete. Ross continued to fight in Washington, and the Indians hoped for reversal of the government policy. The treaty gave them two years to move west. Before the end of that time, soldiers came onto the Cherokee lands and disarmed all the natives. Having no choice in the matter, the Indians submitted peaceably. Some began to drift to Cherokee West, but most remained in their homes, unable to believe that the end was near.

Only the arrival of Gen. Winfield Scott's troops in spring 1838 convinced the remaining fourteen thousand Cherokee that the nightmare was a reality. Within a month most of the natives were imprisoned, suddenly reduced from citizens of a proud nation to a herd of refugees. Removing the Indians took almost a year, and although the federal government had promised to pay the cost and General Scott attempted to provide well for the Cherokee, the migration decimated the tribe. In wagons and on foot the Indians made their way in large parties across Tennessee, Kentucky, Missouri, and Arkansas into the new lands in Oklahoma. They called their route the Trail of Tears.

Many whites saw them pass by on the road — their physical and spiritual suffering a ghastly sight. One traveler reported seeing Cherokee camped by the roadside, "under a severe fall of rain accompanied by heavy wind with their canvas for a shield from the inclemency of the weather, and the cold wet ground for a resting place." As the traveler moved through Kentucky, he came upon other parties of Indians, many of them laboring over "the sometimes frozen ground . . . with no covering for their feet except what nature had given them." At each camp Indians buried ten or a dozen comrades, the victims of cold, disease, and desolation. In all, four thousand Cherokees died on the Trail of Tears, including John Ross's wife, who, according to legend, gave her only blanket to a dying child. Not until spring 1839 did the last of the Indians reach Oklahoma.

Now only a few hundred Cherokees were left in the Appalachians, scattered bands of refugees hiding in caves in North Carolina. One of them was a man named Tsali, who had been wrongly accused of killing a soldier. Tsali struck a bargain with the government whereby he gave himself up in exchange for the promise that his people would be allowed to stay in the region. He was summarily executed, but the several hundred other Cherokees remained in the Appalachians where their descendants live today, keeping alive the memory of the martyred Tsali.

In the West, the Cherokee immigrants attempted to reconstruct their lives in a strange land. Animosity against the proremoval Indians who signed the treaty was so strong that each of its leaders — Major Ridge, John Ridge, and Elias Boudinot — was executed. But in Oklahoma, as in the Carolina mountains, the nation would survive hardships and divisions and preserve its tribal identity into the twentieth century, a goal both John Ross and Elias Boudinot had hoped to achieve.

To assess the Cherokee removal, one must confront the ugly ironies that lay at the heart of white policy. The government demanded that

Indians adopt white standards of civilization; the Indians complied but then were told they must go west in order to preserve their Indian culture. The Indians lived in a nation that proudly considered itself, in Theodore Frelinghuysen's words, "freedom's hope, and her consolation," but were not even allowed the freedom to keep their own farms and remain in their own homeland. They lived in an age that celebrated the rights and abilities of the common man, but they discovered that in Jacksonian America the common man was a white man, and greedy for Indian lands. The president said they could stay in the East if they accepted white laws, but white laws did not accept them as equals. They were told repeatedly that if they made concessions they would be guaranteed their lands forever; they made those concessions but found that "forever" meant at most a decade or a generation.

Often white men were as vehement as Indians in opposing such policies: Meigs at the Cherokee Agency, Frelinghuysen in the U.S. Senate, Worcester on a mission station and in a Georgia prison. In addition to these and many other whites who supported the Cherokee cause, many half-breeds, men like John Ross and Sequoya, devoted their lives to the Cherokee Nation. All these men, as well as full-blooded leaders such as Elias Boudinot wrestled with the complex problem of Indian and white identity. Two incidents in these years symbolize the elusiveness of the red man's identity in Jacksonian America. In 1841 Sequoya, still seeking an ideal native society, became discontented with life in Oklahoma. Somewhere in the Far West, a legend told him, dwelled the Lost Cherokee, a precious remnant of the original tribe, living in the purity and splendor of the nation's past. At age sixty-six Sequoya set out to find that tribe somewhere in the mountains of Mexico. Sequoya's search ended a few years later with his death in the Mexican desert.

His fate finds a counterpart in the poignant effort of Christianized Indians to find consolation in the white man's deity. On June 17, 1838, ten Cherokee men and women stood in a river near Fort Butler, Georgia, with their white and their red ministers. There, in a ceremony described by witnesses as the most impressive they had ever seen, the ten were solemnly baptized. Then, under guard, they and their ministers were returned to the stockade where they were held prisoner with scores of other Cherokee, awaiting removal to Oklahoma.

Like the new immigrants of a half century later, the Cherokee wanted to preserve their ethnic identity while adjusting to white society. But for an Indian in the 1830s — and, indeed, in other periods of American history — that adjustment was made virtually impossible by the painful shifts of policy in a government that first fostered the Cherokee Renaissance and then forced the Cherokee removal.

QUESTIONS

1. Describe the early history and culture of the Cherokee. How did their past tie the tribe to the southern Appalachians?

2. Describe American Cherokee policies early in the nineteenth century. What were the major contradictions in American programs for the Cherokee?

3. Different whites influenced the Cherokee in different ways. Explain the role of these in Cherokee history: English traders, Return Jonathan Meigs, Christian missionaries, Andrew Jackson, Theodore Frelinghuysen, Georgia, the U.S. Supreme Court, Winfield Scott.

4. The Cherokee could not agree among themselves on the proper course for their tribe. Describe how each of these influenced tribal history: Sequoya, John Ross, Elias Boudinot, Tsali.

5. How was it possible for a nation that valued human rights to force the Cherokee from their homes? How did Jackson defend and Frelinghuysen oppose removal?

6. Describe the similarities and differences between John Ross and Elias Boudinot. Why did Boudinot first oppose, than favor removal?

BIBLIOGRAPHY

CARTER III, SAMUEL. *Cherokee Sunset* (1975). Indian experience in the removal period.

FOGELSON, RAYMOND D. *The Cherokees: A Critical Bibliography* (1978). Excellent bibliography in series sponsored by the Newberry Library Center for the History of the American Indian.

HALLIBURTON, JR., R. *Red Over Black: Black Slavery Among the Cherokee Indians* (1977). Describes slavery among the Indians.

HUDSON, CHARLES. *The Southeastern Indians* (1977). Fine survey of the traditional cultures of the Cherokee and other southern tribes.

MALONE, HENRY T. *Cherokees of the Old South* (1956). Focuses on Cherokee Renaissance.

MOONEY, JAMES. *Myths of the Cherokees* (1900 and later editions). Based largely on oral interviews.

MOULTON, GARY E. *John Ross* (1978). Biography of foremost nineteenth-century Cherokee leader.

PERDUE, THEDA, EDITOR. *Cherokee Editor: The Writings of Elias Boudinot* (1983). Fine collection of Boudinot's writings, including his antiremoval essays.

WOODWARD, GRACE STEELE. *The Cherokees* (1963). General introduction to Cherokee history.

10

ABOLITIONISTS AND ANTIABOLITIONISTS

William Lloyd Garrison and the Broadcloth Mob

In the nineteenth century the greatest blemish on America's character as a free society was slavery, which grew ever more entrenched as cotton production expanded. Many Americans favored slavery, but opposition became a major reform impulse by 1835. In the Boston antiabolitionist riot of that year we can see two facets of antislavery history: the ideals of a leading abolitionist and persistent support for slavery, even in the North.

The ladies began to arrive at two o'clock on the bright autumn afternoon on October 21, 1835, for the meeting of the Boston Female Anti-Slavery Society at 46 Washington Street. The building stood near the center of Boston and bore the sign "Anti-Slavery Rooms." In twos and threes the ladies ascended the stairs to the third floor, where a large barnlike hall was divided by wood partitions into a rude auditorium and a small newspaper office. As they took their seats, they could hear loud shouts in the street below, telling them that this would not be an ordinary gathering of their society.

That morning two merchants, Isaac Stevens and Isaac Means, had asked the *Boston Commercial Gazette* to print a handbill about the meeting — something to "wake up the populace," they said. The merchants had watched with approval as the editor, James L. Homer, worked "as fast as a horse can trot" to write a notice declaring that George Thompson, the British abolitionist, was in town and would deliver an address that afternoon. It was hardly a friendly announcement, for it called upon "the friends of the union" to "snake Thompson out" and offered a purse of $100 to "the individual who shall first lay violent hands on Thompson, so that he may be brought to the tar kettle before dark."

By noon Homer had printed five hundred copies of the handbill, and his apprentices ran through Boston's cobbled streets leaving the notice at hotels, reading rooms, offices, stores, and barrooms. Soon the town buzzed with the news. On Chatham Street an oil merchant read the notice and shouted for his men to get "a bucket of green tar" for use on the abolitionist. In the early afternoon hundreds of people from the shops and wharves and insurance offices strode excitedly through the streets, swelling into a crowd that choked Washington and State streets near the antislavery headquarters.

As this hostile throng gathered in the street and jammed into the abolitionist building, a tall dark-haired man, purposeful in movement, pushed into the building and made his way upstairs to the meeting hall. Some of the intruders had gathered in a hostile knot at the rear. "That's Garrison," several persons murmured.

William Lloyd Garrison walked quietly past them to the front of the room, took a seat near the ladies, then seemed to reconsider and walked back to the men who were milling noisily by the door. Affecting an air of friendly concern, he suggested that they must be confused. "This is a meeting of the Boston *female* Anti-Slavery Society," he said. He assumed that they would not be so "indecorous" as to intrude but added disarmingly: "If, *gentlemen,* any of you are *ladies*—in disguise— why, only apprise me of the fact, give me your names, and I will introduce you to the rest of your sex, and you can take your seats among them accordingly."

Garrison was a man of such innocent and sincere expression that this outlandish proposition confused rather than enraged the intruders. For a minute they quieted down, but the tumult resumed with the arrival of more men who shouted and stamped in the hallway outside. Mounting one another's shoulders, they peered over the partition into the meeting room. They seemed uncertain what to do, and opened and slammed the door with aimless violence. The men were looking for Thompson, but he was nowhere to be seen.

The ladies were disturbed but not deterred by the noise. They would go on with their meeting, even though many members, including Mrs. Garrison, would be unable to get through the crowd to the hall. Mary Parker, the society's president, called the meeting to order while the crowd was "howling with rage." She read from Scripture and offered a prayer asking for guidance, calling for the forgiveness of enemies, and thanking God for preserving them from fear. In the hall the men's rage seemed to abate as they listened to her "clear, untremulous" voice. Hearing her, Garrison was deeply moved. "It was," he said, "an awful, sublime, and soul-thrilling scene."

But on the street the mob, now increased to several thousand, shouted for its intended victim, their cry, "Thompson! Thompson!" filling the air. Boston's mayor, Theodore Lyman, came before the crowd. He told them that Thompson was not in the city and that they might as well disperse, but the crowd refused to depart. Lyman entered the abolitionist building with several constables and made his way to the upstairs meeting hall. He was no friend to abolitionism, but neither was he an advocate of violence, and he felt responsible for the safety of the women, whose best hope, he thought, lay in retreat.

He interrupted the meeting. "Ladies," he said, "do you wish to see a scene of bloodshed and confusion? If you do not, go home."

Maria Weston Chapman, the wife of an abolitionist merchant and guiding light of the ladies' society, answered: "Mr. Lyman, your personal friends are the instigators of this mob; have you ever used your personal influence with them?"

The mayor refused to acknowledge his association with the antiabolitionists. "I know no personal friends," he said, "I am merely an official. Indeed, ladies, you must retire. It is dangerous to remain."

Maria Chapman replied fervently, "If this is the last bulwark of freedom, we may as well die here as anywhere."

This prospect did not please the mayor, nor was martyrdom the immediate goal of the society, so that Lyman was able to persuade Mrs. Chapman and her companions to adjourn the meeting. With his assurance that they would be escorted safely through the crowd, the women finally agreed to leave the building. Outside they were startled to see that the crowd extended far down the streets in every direction. But it was not so much the size of the throng as the familiarity of individual faces that alarmed the women. Maria Chapman records: "We saw the faces of those we had, till now, thought friends; men whom we never before met without giving the hand in friendly salutation; men whom till now we should have called upon for condemnation of ruffianism." The remarkable thing was that it was a "broadcloth" mob — named after the fashionable broadcloth coats worn by many of the "gentlemen of property and standing" who filled its turbulent ranks.

When the women realized that the hostile mob was not merely a gathering of malicious thugs but an assortment of presumably responsible citizens like themselves, they must have felt deeply apprehensive: If their proper defenders were members of the mob, who would help them? But they kept up a courageous bearing, carefully arranging themselves so that each black woman in the group was escorted by two white women, and walked through the hostile crowd to the sanctuary of Maria Chapman's house, where they continued their meeting.

In the meantime, thwarted in its attempt to capture Thompson, the mob turned to Garrison. "We must have Garrison!" they shouted as they pressed around the abolitionist headquarters. "Out with him! Lynch him!" A group of men rushed the door and were barely halted by the police. According to an observer, Samuel Sewall, their faces were "transformed with malice and passion."

The existence of such emotions in a town that characterized itself as the Cradle of Liberty demands an explanation. Massachusetts had been the first state to abolish slavery within its own boundaries and was the only state in which blacks enjoyed civil equality with whites. Why should it now be the scene of such hostility to abolitionism?

The answer lies in part in the state's economic history. In 1780 when slavery was ended by the Massachusetts Supreme Court, there had been relatively few blacks in the state; consequently, the cost of emancipation had been minimal. As the nineteenth century progressed, however, economic changes had made Massachusetts an active participant in the slave economy. The institution was not, of course, reestablished in the state, but with cotton production growing in the South, the prosperity of Massachusetts came to depend on the manufacture of textiles, and the mills that provided jobs and built fortunes in the North required southern cotton, a crop planted and harvested by slaves. New England manufacturers also sold goods in the South, and shippers carried cargoes between the two sections. The traders and manufacturers who dealt with the South controlled most of the large banks in the state.

Many northern businesses and their employees could thus be said to have had a stake in slavery, and their desire to protect that stake helps explain their support of human bondage. A second ingredient in their hostility to antislavery was a cultural phenomenon, a conservative mood that pervaded American society in the mid-1830s. On the one hand, the period brought change and reform, new churches and religious communities, and new ideas about disadvantaged Americans — prisoners, the insane, and women, as well as slaves. But it was also a time when many Americans cherished what they considered the traditional character of their society. In the North as in the South prejudice against blacks, slave or free, was common. Blacks were generally not allowed to vote, were required to ride in segregated railway cars, and were given the worst jobs. Few northerners were willing to risk disruption of the Union for the benefit of the despised race, and many took to the streets in violent defense of traditional order. Such riots were especially frequent in 1835, and an antislavery convention was broken up in Utica, New York, on the same day as the Boston riot. The decade of the 1830s saw the mob lynching of Elijah Lovejoy, an abolitionist newspaper editor in Alton, Illinois, and the burning of an antislavery hall in Philadelphia. President Andrew Jackson characterized the abolitionists as fanatics; his postmaster, Amos Kendall, restricted their use of the mails; and after 1835 Congress adopted a "gag resolution" to table all antislavery petitions. Antiabolitionism was in fashion.

Boston had already taken a stand against the abolitionists in a meeting on August 21 attended by many of the city's leading citizens. For months southern newspapers and statesmen had been warning the North that unless the abolitionists were suppressed they would destroy the Union; the meeting, held in Faneuil Hall, was intended to demonstrate northern support for the Union and the South.

When he had learned of the planned gathering in a building that sixty years before had been the scene of patriot gatherings, Garrison had denounced it in his newspaper, the *Liberator*. "The old cradle of liberty," he said, "it seems, is to be desecrated by a meeting of the friends of slavery and slaveholders! . . . No fiction, no sophistry, can hide the fact from the intelligence of an impartial posterity, that the contemplated meeting is a meeting to take sides with the *slaveholder*, and against his *victim*!"

Despite Garrison's protest, the meeting had been well attended. Mayor Theodore Lyman served as chairman and, with other speakers, used the occasion to chastise the abolitionists and praise the Union. The most vehement speaker, Peleg Sprague, a former United States senator, gestured toward a portrait of George Washington, a slaveholder who had helped Massachusetts win her freedom from Britain.

Southern newspapers reported the meeting with great satisfaction, the *Richmond Whig* declaring: "The people of the North *must* go to *hang-*

ing these fanatical wretches, if they would not lose the benefit of Southern trade; and they *will* do it. They know too well which side their bread is buttered on." Events would soon bear out this prophecy.

On October 21, as the broadcloth mob gathered around the anti-slavery building, the citizens of Boston were about to accomplish by force what they had advocated by words two months before at Faneuil Hall. They would crush the reformers who threatened the Union, their traditions, and their trade. The first victim of their animosity was a symbol rather than a man, the sign reading "Anti-Slavery Rooms." Several men reached out through windows and detached the sign from its hooks, causing it to fall to the ground.

Mayor Lyman later declared that he had ordered the sign's removal. He feared that it would be pelted with rocks, which then might injure the observers, and he hoped the sign's removal would satisfy the crowd. Garrison, however, claimed that the mayor inadvertently encouraged the mob by condoning this "outrage upon private property." At any rate, the rioters quickly broke up the sign, and snatched up pieces as souvenirs. One long fragment, measuring six feet by three inches, was carried to the *Commercial Gazette* office where James Homer, who had printed the announcement that instigated the riot, later cut it up and distributed it among friends as a momento of the antiabolitionist battle for stability and the Union.

While the world outside was in turmoil, Garrison was closeted with several friends in the abolitionist offices. Little in his appearance suggested that this man could have had won the opprobrium of so many of his fellow citizens. Slightly under six feet tall, he had an erect bearing and a contemplative appearance: a receding hairline, a long, pensive forehead, heavy brows, and alert, quizzical eyes. He wore wire frame glasses, stern black clothes, and on his face, an expression of calm rectitude.

Contemporaries and historians a century later castigated him as a narrowminded fanatic, incapable of compromise, humorless, obsessed. His unrelenting hatred of slavery encouraged such characterizations, but he was also a warm human being, a devoted husband, a dedicated advocate of his cause, and a propagandist who genuinely cared about the slave. The English traveler, Harriet Martineau, described his face as "wholly expressive of purity, animation, and gentleness."

His brief lifetime — he was not yet thirty years old — had prepared him well for the martyr's role he seemed about to assume. William Lloyd Garrison was born in Newburyport, Massachusetts, in 1805. His father, an erratic and intemperate sea captain, deserted his family before the boy was three. He was raised by his hardworking mother, Frances Maria Lloyd Garrison, who, he declared, "loved me so intensely that no language can describe the yearning of her soul." Husbandless, diligent, and devoted, she served her son as a model of self-sacrifice.

William received little formal education, and in 1818 he was apprenticed for seven years to the editor of the *Newburyport Herald*. Like Benjamin Franklin, who had begun his career in a similar position a century before, Garrison practiced writing by composing anonymous pieces for the paper. When he was nineteen he became editor of the *Newburyport Free Press*; then worked as a printer in Boston; and in 1828 became coeditor of the *National Philanthropist,* a reform paper. In its pages he attacked a broad spectrum of social evils, including intemperance, war, gambling, and Sabbath breaking.

While in Boston he met Benjamin Lundy, who is credited with having turned his attention to antislavery. Lundy was a Quaker, whose humble existence showed Garrison that social reform was hardly a profitable enterprise: he walked from town to town and printed his small newspaper, *Genius of Universal Emancipation*, in any available printing office. But Lundy's infectious dedication easily attracted Garrison.

Under Lundy's influence Garrison delivered his first antislavery lecture at Park Street Church on Boston Common in 1829, and that summer he visited Baltimore to help Lundy edit the *Genius*. His visit to Maryland convinced him that he should exercise his influence in New England, where he "found contempt more bitter, opposition more active, detraction more relentless, prejudice more stubborn, and apathy more frozen, than among slave-owners themselves." He founded a new paper, the *Liberator*, in Boston "within sight of Bunker Hill." The first issue, January 1, 1831, contained a ringing declaration of principles. Garrison had once approved of gradual emancipation but now demanded an immediate change. "I seize this opportunity," he said, "to make a full and unequivocal recantation, and thus publicly to ask pardon of my God, of my country, and of my brethren the poor slaves, for having uttered a sentiment so full of timidity, injustice, and absurdity."

Reporting that he had already been criticized for vehemence, he justified his radical abolitionism. "Is there not cause for severity?" he said. "On this subject, I do not wish to think, or speak, or write with moderation. No! No! Tell a man whose house is on fire to give a moderate alarm; tell him to moderately rescue his wife from the hands of the ravisher; tell the mother to gradually extricate her babe from the fire into which it has fallen; — but urge me not to use moderation in a cause like the present." He continued with a ringing phrase: "I am in earnest — I will not equivocate — I will not excuse — I will not retreat a single inch — AND I WILL BE HEARD."

In his blunt assertion that slavery must be ended without delay, Garrison took issue with northern gradualists as well as southern slaveholders. The movement against American slavery was already more than a century old in 1831, but its dominant tone early in the nineteenth century was moderate and conciliatory. During the Revolution slavery had been abolished in the northern states, and even in the South the Revolution's emphasis on freedom had borne fruit. Washington, Jefferson, and other patriots regretted its existence, and the southern states passed laws legalizing manumission — the voluntary freeing of slaves by their master — thereby facilitating gradual emancipation.

In the nineteenth century the new cotton gin had increased the importance of slavery by making black production more profitable, but as late as 1827 more than half of the country's many abolitionist societies were in the South. Most antislavery organizations favored gradual emancipation, compensation for the slaveholders, and the return of free blacks to Africa. Within a few years, however, abolitionism in the North became more strident, and antislavery sentiment in the South all but vanished.

A single event, Nat Turner's Revolt, ended the southern antislavery movement. In that Virginia slave rebellion of 1831, fifty-seven whites lost their lives. The revolt was easily crushed, but the fear that had always been present was heightened and spread throughout the South. What had happened in Virginia could happen elsewhere; anyone who suggested that slavery was evil might well cause the next conflagration. In this spirit of dread, slavery proponents sought to drive the abolitionists from the South, prevented antislavery literature from entering the region, and posted rewards for the capture or execution of northern abolitionists such as Garrison. By 1837 there were no longer any abolitionist societies in the southern states.

This tough southern attitude led some northern abolitionists to become more strident in their hostility to the institution. Garrison was such a leader: he was not interested in preserving either the Union or the sensibilities of the slaveholder. The house was on fire, he said, and this was no time for moderation.

Garrison published his views in the *Liberator* and joined with others to form new societies dedicated to the immediate eradication of slavery. In 1831 he helped form the New England Anti-Slavery Society and in 1833 joined in creating a national organization, the American Anti-Slavery Association. These bodies cooperated with scores of local groups such as the Boston Female Anti-Slavery Society and the Massachusetts Anti-Slavery Society. The abolitionists believed that history was on their side when in 1833 they learned that in England, Parliament had abolished slavery in the British West Indies. The man primarily responsible for that act was George Thompson, who spent 1835 touring the United States, and was the object of the crowd's attention in Boston.

Garrison's vociferous opposition to slavery and his stinging denunciation of moderation left him a natural target that October afternoon when the broadcloth mob couldn't locate Thompson. In a sense, his whole abolitionist career had led him to this moment, and he appears to have positively delighted in the attention of the mob. Their focus on him confirmed the force of his own personality and principles.

There was, nonetheless, the problem of what to do. No one would blame him for attempting to escape in hopes of living to fight another day. Garrison's abolitionist friends counseled him that discretion was wiser than vain heroics. With the mob howling in the hallway and the street outside, Garrison decided to depart through the back window, not an easy task for a man more adept at propaganda than gymnastics. When Garrison jumped from the third-story window onto a shed roof below, he landed hard and nearly pitched forward off the roof onto his head. But, catching himself, he found his way into a carpenter's shop behind the abolitionist headquarters. The owners obligingly hid him in an upstairs room while one of the local sheriffs pretended to search the building and then told the mob Garrison had escaped.

Unfortunately, some of the crowd had seen Garrison disappear into the shop. They searched and found the abolitionist hiding beneath a pile of boards. Accounts vary about how Garrison behaved when discovered. One newspaper claimed that he fell to his knees and begged for mercy. But Garrison claimed that he preserved his composure while the men shook him and tore at his clothes. "It is needless to make such extra efforts of violence," he recalled saying, "I shall go down to the mob unresistingly." His words may not have been so deliberate, but it is likely that he was calm: others would later testify that he was. And this was, after all, his great moment.

His captors took Garrison to the window. Several wanted to hurl him to the ground, but another exclaimed, "Don't let's kill him outright!" This view prevailed. A ladder was raised to the window, and after bowing awkwardly to the crowd, Garrison descended with a rope coiled around his waist. He was now in the midst of a mob pressing in from every side, "as if eager to devour him," according to one abolitionist.

It was not yet clear what would occur next. Some rioters hoped to tar and feather the abolitionist and dye his face and hands black with indelible ink; others wanted to hang him or to club him to death. The antiabolitionists were united in their desire to attack abolitionism but divided about what to do with their captive. Suddenly a man tried to strike Garrison with a club, and two others defended him. The protectors were Aaron and Daniel Cooley, brothers who ran a transportation firm and were known for their antiabolitionist sentiments. For unknown reasons they grabbed Garrison by the shoulders and hustled him through the crowd, crying "He shan't be hurt! You shan't hurt him! He's an American!" It was a curious cry, but others in the street took it up. Apparently Garrison had one asset in the eyes of the mob that the Britisher George Thompson lacked. He might be a radical, but at least he was not a foreign radical. In 1835 that mattered. The Cooley brothers' muscles and rhetoric combined to soften the crowd around Garrison, and they were able to carry him toward the city hall, although the throng still pressed around.

Garrison had found temporary safety, but by now the center of Boston was in a state of total confusion. A few men, motivated by a sense of fair play rather than by any love of abolitionism, were attempting to save Garrison. A much larger group surged through the steets calling for his punishment. To onlookers, it was not clear who was in control.

Mayor Lyman had been at the front of the abolitionist building when Garrison was detected. As the men surged away from the building after Garrison, Lyman hurried toward city hall. Along the way a dozen people urged him to save Garrison. "They're going to hang him," said one, "for God's sake, save him!" As the mayor approached Garrison, he could hear people shouting, "To the frog pond with him!" Here was another possible punishment — a brutal dunking on Boston Common.

Garrison allowed himself to be carried along by the crowd. In the scuffle his hat and coat were lost, and his pants were ripped. Having removed his spectacles to protect them, he was nearly blind, yet maintained his composure. Charles Sprague, a banker and a poet, watched Garrison pass down Wilson's Lane. "I saw an exasperated mob dragging a man along without his hat and with a rope about him," he said. "The man walked with head erect, calm countenance, flashing eyes, like a martyr going to the stake, full of faith and manly hope."

As the crowd turned down State Street toward city hall, Henry Ingersoll Bowditch, a prominent physician, watched with a sense of outrage. He urged an acquaintance to help him oppose the rioters and was further outraged when the man refused, saying the authorities were on the side of the mob. "I was completely disgusted," Bowditch later wrote, "and I vowed in my heart as I left him with utter loathing, 'I am an abolitionist from this very moment.' "

Finally the crowd approached the city hall and stood on the pavement where the Boston Massacre occurred sixty-five years before. Garrison saw the irony in his being made an object of "derision and scorn" on this "consecrated spot." As the Cooleys rushed him to the south door of city hall, the mayor arrived with supporters who covered Garrison's retreat into the building.

But Garrison was still not safe. The mob crushed around the building and poured into the north entrance. While Garrison was taken upstairs to the mayor's and aldermen's headquarters, Theodore Lyman addressed the crowd in the hall, saying that if necessary he would die to maintain law and order. Standing on a balcony over the south door, he repeated his speech to the swell of angry people outside. They listened but did not disperse. In the mayor's office a coterie of city officials considered what to do and decided that Garrison would be better off in the Leverett Street Jail. Garrison later claimed that the mayor was more interested in safeguarding the building than in protecting its inmate, but he agreed to go along with the plan on the understanding that he would not have to pay for his stay in jail.

Sherrif Parkman wrote out a writ for Garrison's arrest on the basis that he had disturbed the peace, perhaps to justify imprisoning him. When Garrison later learned that he, the victim of rioters, had been charged with instigating their actions, he was outraged. Nonetheless, the writ reflected public thinking about the abolitionists: their inflammatory rhetoric had created an atmosphere conducive to mob violence. Lyman may have approved of the writ of arrest on the theory that it would serve him well politically.

Now began a journey that Garrison himself described as "incredibly perilous." Because the crowd was still howling outside, the mayor created a diversion by sending a coach and guards to the south entrance while he took Garrison out the north. But he was seen, and Garrison had barely entered the carriage before it was surrounded by a crowd that reminded him of "the ocean, lashed into fury by the spirit of the storm."

Some pulled at the doors and wheels trying to get at him, and others placed a rope around the coach to tip it over. In the midst of this fray Garrison told an incredulous city official that he could win the crowd over if he could have just five minutes to speak to them. No one seemed eager to test his theory. Just as the coach was about to be pushed over, the driver lashed the horses and drew away. Rioters raced after the coach and clung to its sides while policemen pushed at them and the driver ran close to parked carriages to brush them away.

At Leverett Street Jail, police officers forced their way through a small group and escorted the prisoner to safety. Inside they locked him in a cell — "safe," as he said, "from my persecutors, accompanied by two delightful associates, a good conscience and a cheerful mind." During the evening, he had several visitors, including Isaac Knapp, publisher of the *Liberator*; Amos Bronson Alcott, essayist and educator; and John Greenleaf Whittier, poet. Whittier, one of the abolitionist's oldest friends, had published his first poems a decade before Garrison's *Newburyport Free Press*. Whittier especially smypathized with his friend, having himself been the victim of an antiabolitionist attack a few weeks before when he had attempted to speak in Concord, New Hampshire, with George Thompson. Garrison seemed in good spirits and jokingly regretted that his cell was too small to accommodate his friends for the night. Although the abolitionists were greatly outnumbered in Boston in 1835, there were enough of them at least to enjoy a sense of shared participation in a great cause. After his friends left, Garrison fell quickly asleep in his small cell.

The next morning he ate "an excellent breakfast" and sought to immortalize his stay in the Leverett Street Jail with an inscription on the wall. It began: "William Lloyd Garrison was put into this cell on Wednesday afternoon, October 21, 1835, to save him from the violence of a 'respectable and influential mob,' who sought to destroy him for preaching the abominable and dangerous doctrine, that 'all men are created equal,' and that all oppression is odious in the sight of God."

That afternoon Garrison received a judicial hearing, conducted in the jail to ensure his protection. His indictment read: he "did disturb and break the peace of the Commonwealth, and a riot did cause and make, to the terror of the good people of the Commonwealth." The city did not press charges but required Garrison to leave Boston for a time to calm the public. Garrison agreed to do so, and that afternoon he was secretly conducted to the town of Canton, where with his wife Helen he boarded a train for Providence, Rhode Island. So ended Boston's great antiabolitionist riot.

Although the affair lasted only a few hours and caused little damage, it precipitated a debate in the New England press that has continued, in a fashion, to this day. The problem is that of fully understanding the character and motivation of each side in the conflict. As we have seen, the antiabolitionists were moved by economic self-interest — a knowledge of "which side their bread is buttered on," the cynical phrase of the *Richmond Whig* — and by hostility to social and racial tinkering.

Like the previous meeting at Faneuil Hall, the Garrison riot testified to Boston's support of the Union and stability. The mob was composed mostly of merchants, bankers, shipowners, and their employees. Maria Chapman might be disturbed that many "gentlemen" were in the crowd, but so many members of Boston's ruling classes participated that no one had to apologize. Common wisdom in downtown Boston held that it was the right thing to do. Such was the view of the press, the business community, and many public officials.

Yet there was no unanimity of purpose among the antiabolitionists. They had varied in their opinions about how Garrison should be punished — some wanting him killed, others happy enough to tear down the abolitionist sign and give Garrison a scare. The Cooley brothers, who carried Garrison to city hall, had been antiabolitionists but risked their own skins to save Garrison. There were even some who were won over to abolitionism by the enormity of the riot.

In the constellation of actions and responses that made up the riot, the position of Mayor Theodore Lyman is especially interesting. Lyman, we should recall, was an ardent antiabolitionist and had chaired the antiabolitionist meeting at Faneuil Hall. He refused to disperse the crowd or to press charges against individual rioters after the mob violence, even though he recognized many of the participants. But he neither encouraged the rioters nor watched idly as they did their work. He intervened personally to calm the multitude and protect Garrison, urging the abolitionist women to seek safety and encouraging Garrison to escape through a rear window in the antislavery building. He stood by Garrison on the steps of city hall and called upon the rioters to disperse. Having devised the plan to carry Garrison to Leverett Street Jail, he accompanied him to the coach in which he made the journey. In spite of Lyman's opposition to the abolitionist movement and his fear of offending the voters, he extended himself considerably for Garrison.

Clearly, opposition to abolition included many level-headed individuals. They believed that the antislavery movement was impractical, and they favored maintaining the social order. Some may have acted like thugs on the afternoon of October 21, 1835. But others with cooler heads — Mayor Lyman and the Cooley brothers among them — prevented William Lloyd Garrison from suffering great harm. What of Garrison's part in the day's events and his character as a political activist? When he reviewed the riot, Garrison was especially critical of the mayor for having allowed the destruction of the antislavery sign and for not using force against the rioters or pressing charges against those he recognized. Garrison was at his most ungenerous and dogmatic when he criticized Lyman, for his judgment focused on all the mayor's faults without recognizing his efforts on Garrison's behalf.

In such episodes the Garrison appears who struck his contemporaries as so fanatical and narrow. Further evidence for such a view might be taken from Garrison's behavior during the riot. If there ever was a man who appeared to welcome martyrdom, it was Garrison that day. Many observers mentioned his calm, saintly composure. Soon after the affair he wrote his brother-in-law and fellow abolitionist George W. Benson, "imminent as I felt the peril to be, my mind was placid and undisturbed throughout the trying scene; . . . I reposed as calmly in my prison-cell as if no uproar had happened." In his personal account of the riot he said, "I felt perfectly calm, nay, very happy."

Garrison took pleasure in the thought of persecution and remarked that other abolitionists felt the same. A month before the Boston uproar, his friend, Samuel May, had been mobbed in Haverhill, Massachusetts. May's letter describing the event was so buoyant that Garrison told a friend, "By the tone of it you would suppose he had done something better than making a fortune." Garrison said of Whittier's experience in New Hampshire: "His soul, being intangible, laughed at the salutation." Less than a month before the tumult in Boston, Garrison had learned that a price had been placed on his head in the South. Reporting the news to a friend, he said, "My mind is full of peace — I know what it is to rejoice in tribulation."

All this evidence suggests that two of the most serious charges against the abolitionists may be true; that is, that they were psychologically disturbed fanatics, less interested in the well-being of the slaves than in their own righteousness, and that they helped cause the Civil War by inflaming the public mind. According to this thesis the abolitionists were not involved in antislavery because they knew that slavery was wrong, but rather they cared about the slaves because, being misfits and malcontents, the abolitionists could not adjust to white society.

William Lloyd Garrison's character, however, belies the notion that the radical reformer must be driven by a maladjusted personality. His own behavior during the days after the broadcloth riot demonstrate the stability of his personality and suggest the source of his abolitionism. After the events of October 11 he left Boston and traveled with his wife to Brooklyn, Connecticut, to stay with her father. Garrison's relationship with his wife furnishes clues to his character. Helen Benson Garrison was the daughter of George Benson, a retired merchant from Providence, Rhode Island, and an early opponent of slavery. Most of his six sons and two daughters were ardent supporters of the antislavery movement. But Garrison claimed that he was attracted to Helen for familial rather than civic reasons. In 1835, on their first anniversary, he wrote her brother George: "I did not marry her expecting that she would assume a prominent station in the anti-slavery cause, but for domestic quietude and happiness." He continued: she "enables me to find exquisite delight in the family circle, as an offset to public adversity." Although he was a lion in public disputation, he claimed that in Helen's presence he was "as timid, and gentle, and submissive, as a dove." Thus, recognizing his own tendency to become obsessed with the slavery issue, he counted on Helen to provide a humane ballast to the vessel of his ideals.

His experience in marriage intensified his loathing of slavery. On September 4, 1835, he wrote to his brother-in-law, George Benson, telling him how much he rejoiced in his relationship to Helen. His pleasure in their attachment led him to contrast his own fortune with that of the slaves. "What faithful husband," he asked, "can think, for one moment, of having the object of his love torn from his arms by the might of oppression, and not feel indignation and horror swelling like a swift inundation in his bosom? What affectionate wife can imagine the sale of her beloved partner at auction, as a beast is sold, without shuddering as if smitten by the icy hand of death?. . . In this mirror, my dear George, how is the terrific image of the monster Slavery reflected! Should we not hate him with a perfect hatred! Can we be too earnest for his destruction?"

Garrison's love for Helen may also have contributed to his self-awareness and given him a perspective on himself, a sense of humor, a willingness to bend with the wind when necessary. When attacks on antislavery became common in the late summer of 1835, Garrison had written a friend that the violence worried Helen. He suggested that while the atmosphere was heated, the abolitionists should be moderate and limit their discussions to ending slavery in the District of Columbia. But he was not personally bothered by threats. When he learned in September that a gallows had been placed in his front yard with an inscription from "Judge Lynch," he was unworried and simply asked his friends to try to secure it for the abolitionist museum.

William Lloyd Garrison was able to balance his antislavery with a sense of timing. He did not take the mobs too seriously; he could regard the mock gallows as a fine museum artifact and glory in the attention. But his opponents did force him to exercise discretion. He was a husband now and would soon be a father. It was decided that Helen should stay with her family in Brooklyn, Connecticut, while he returned to Boston to remove their furniture.

Garrison arrived back in Boston about three weeks after the riot that had forced him to leave. He rode north from Providence, Rhode Island, in an open railway car, exposed to wind and soot in order to save 50 cents — "no trifling sum" he wrote his wife, "in these days of penury and persecution." At the station he took a coach to a friend's

Helen Benson Garrison. Born into a family of abolitionists, she married a leader in the fight against slavery.

house where he had supper. Then Joseph Tillson, a young helper in the antislavery office, guided him to the home of Joseph Southwick, president of the Massachusetts Anti-Slavery Society. There Garrison was delighted to find another refugee, his friend George Thompson, whose presence in Boston was a well-kept secret.

In a few minutes an abolitionist reunion was in progress. Garrison's brother-in-law, Henry Benson, arrived. Then came Mary Parker, the woman whose "clear, untremulous" voice had so moved Garrison on the day of the riot. She brought with her two antislavery friends,

Anna Grew and Catherine Sullivan. Garrison found his reception "so kind and sympathetic and joyful, that one might almost covet to be mobbed, to obtain such a return." As his friends were talking, Garrison excused himself for a few minutes to go upstairs and write his wife a letter for the evening mail. Hearing his boisterous friends in the room below, he wrote, "What a collection of raving fanatics and dangerous incendiaries! A happy meeting this!"

Later that evening Garrison went to his own house with several friends. In another letter to Helen he described the return to "the house that we fondly expected to call our home, in which we have spent so many happy hours, but which can be our home no longer." He had married Helen to make with her a domestic shelter from the turmoil of his work. The house embodied that ideal of repose. Everything, he said, "seems dearer to me than ever." The carpets, tables, chairs, looking glasses — all seemed "almost to have found a tongue, to welcome my return, and to congratulate me upon my escape out of the jaws of the lion." He continued, "The clock ticks an emphatical and sonorous welcome. As for puss, she finds it a difficult matter, even with all her purring and playing, to express her joy."

The return to the house at 23 Brighton Street in Boston was one of the most poignant and serene evenings in Garrison's life. Here was fulfillment in the midst of privation — the warmth of friendship to balance the fury of the mob, the comfort of domestic bliss transcending the knowledge of imminent removal. That night Garrison slept with deep satisfaction. "As you were absent," he wrote Helen, "I permitted puss to occupy the *outside* of the bed, as a substitute. We reposed very lovingly until morning, without any alarm from mobs without, or disturbance from rats within."

Garrison was cautious during the next few days, not wishing by his presence to become the object of another riot. At his first visit to the antislavery office he saw evidence of the city's continuing animosity to abolitionism. He heard a noise outside, and from a window he watched a procession moving through the street behind a band. The marchers carried a large board with drawings of George Thompson and a black woman. Above Thompson's head were the words, "The Foreign Emissary." The black woman was saying, "When are we going to have another meeting, brother Thompson?" Unaware that Garrison was in the building, the marchers continued on through the city streets, giddy with pleasure at their infantile joke.

The opponents of abolition were still active, it was clear, but the riot had created a backlash of sympathy for abolitionism. Garrison received an anonymous contribution of $45; new subscribers ordered the *Liberator*; and his name was placed in nomination for the state legislature. He belittled the danger of life in Boston, writing facetiously in one letter that his cat was outside and might have "fallen into the hands of Judge Lynch."

But Boston was no place for his pregnant wife, and wanting to be near her, he made arrangements with friends to run the *Liberator* in his absence, packed his and Helen's belongings, and boarded a train for Brooklyn. On the train he sat near two ladies, "one a fat dowager-looking female — the other younger and less corpulent — probably mother and daughter." In Canton a gentleman jokingly expressed his surprise that these ladies should be on the train rather than attending a local Ladies' Anti-Slavery meeting, then in progress.

" 'Oh,' they said quite emphatically, 'we are not antislavery.' "

They spoke as if they were testifying to something more than their view on the great social question of the day. They were testifying to their own character, indicating that they were stable, sensible, respectable — as if no one of any consequence could possibly be an abolitionist.

The loud rattling of the cars and Garrison's sense of propriety kept him from joining the conversation, but he wanted to draw out the implication of their remarks, and say to them: "What! Not antislavery? Do you mean to say that you are in favor of slavery? Or what do you mean? If you are not antislavery, then you are for concubinage, pollution, robbery, cruelty; then you are for making merchandise of God's image, for setting aside the forms and obligations of marriage, for darkening the human intellect, and debasing the soul." He was pleased that a few miles away in Canton, Massachusetts, there were other women, "high-souled, intellectual, courageous, devout females," who were at that moment meeting to express their hostility to slavery.

Garrison arrived back in Brooklyn at the end of November. His first son, named George Thompson Garrison, was born in February. The family spent most of 1836 in Brooklyn where Garrison wrote frequently for the *Liberator* while leaving its publication to friends in Boston. In September 1836, it appeared safe to return to the city, and the family reestablished themselves in New England's largest metropolis.

In the ensuing years Garrison continued to be the most outspoken figure in the abolitionist movement, advocating not only an end to slavery but also civil rights for blacks and full participation by women in the abolitionist movement. Whereas more conservative abolitionists objected to allowing women like Angelina and Sarah Grimké to address their meetings, Garrison encouraged their participation. In 1840 he refused to take part in the World Anti-Slavery Convention in London because women were not allowed to attend.

His views on politics were even more controversial than his support for women. He believed that political action led to corruption and, consequently, voted only once in his life. The Union itself was sinful, he reasoned, because it allowed slavery to exist. In a dramatic gesture of hostility to the federal government he once burned a copy of the Constitution.

Many abolitionists refused to accept Garrison's views on women and the Union, and when his supporters gained control of the American Anti-Slavery Society in 1840, many withdrew under the leadership of Arthur Tappan and formed the more conservative American and Foreign Anti-Slavery Society. Such divisions were disturbing, but Garrison could take consolation in the fact that the abolitionist movement continued to gain support. In the 1850s, after enactment of the Fugitive Slave Law (1850), which provided for the return of escaped slaves to the South, Boston — the town that had rioted against Garrison two decades before — was the scene of riots in support of runaway slaves.

It was Garrison's good fortune to live to see the fruition of his agitation in the Emancipation Proclamation in 1863. At the end of the Civil War he was one of a group of honored guests at Fort Sumter, South Carolina, at the raising of the American flag. Time had not diminished the vehemence of his rhetoric, nor did the charm of the scene soothe his temper. "I hate slavery as I hate nothing else in the world," he said. "It is not only a crime, but the sum of all criminality."

QUESTIONS

1. Who were the anti-abolitionist rioters? Describe their social background and reasons for supporting slavery.

2. William Lloyd Garrison has sometimes been regarded as a fanatic. What evidence in this chapter supports and what evidence contradicts that accusation?

3. Describe the role of Boston Mayor Theodore Lyman in the broadcloth riot.

4. What part did women play in the abolitionist movement, and what special difficulties did they encounter?

5. Garrison favored active women's participation in the abolitionist movement but married a woman who would stay at home and tend the family. Is this a contradiction? Did he fail to apply his principles to his own life?

6. Were abolitionist spokesmen too strident and inflammatory, or did they make an appropriate response to an unjust institution.

BIBLIOGRAPHY

DUMOND, DWIGHT L. *Anit-Slavery: The Crusade for Freedom in America* (1961). Survey of abolitionism; finds Garrison too fanatical and suggests that other leaders, such as Theodore Weld, did more for the movement.

KRADATOR, AILEEN. *Means and Ends in American Abolitionism* (1968). Sympathetic assessment of supposed fanaticism of Garrison and other radical abolitionists.

MERRILL, WALTER M. *Against Wind and Tide* (1963). Biography of Garrison.

_____ AND LOUIS RUCHAMES, EDITORS. *The Letters of William Lloyd Garrison* (1971-). Well-edited collection with many rich and informative letters.

NYE, RUSSELL B. *William Lloyd Garrison and the Humanitarian Reformers* (1955). A useful, concise biography.

RICHARDS, LEONARD L. *"Gentlemen of Property and Standing": Anti-Abolitionist Mobs in Jacksonian America* (1970). Description and analysis of northern hostility to abolitionists.

THOMAS, JOHN L. *The Liberator* (1963). Biography of Garrison.

TYLER, ALICE FELT. *Freedom's Ferment* (1944). Standard survey of reform movements in the early nineteenth century.

WALTERS, RONALD G. *The Antislavery Appeal* (1976). Discusses the character of the abolitionist supporters.

11

REFORM IN THE EARLY REPUBLIC

The Seneca Falls Convention of 1848

In antebellum America reformers adopted many causes. Besides trying to eradicate slavery, they advocated temperance and favored improving schools, hospitals, and prisons. Women were involved in each of these movements and sometimes discussed their own disadvantaged status while meeting to help other groups. But it was not until 1848 that the first American women's rights convention convened in Seneca Falls, New York. The meeting displayed how law and custom placed women in an inferior position and exposed the inconsistency between the egalitarian ideals of the young republic and the injustice of sexual discrimination. Its resolutions would influence the women's rights movement for more than a century.

Charlotte Woodward, a nineteen-year-old farm girl in upstate New York, read the July 14, 1848 issue of the *Seneca County Courier* with growing excitement. After a tedious day of sewing gloves for a local manufacturer, she was intrigued by a small notice that caught her eye:

> WOMAN'S RIGHTS CONVENTION — A Convention to discuss the social, civil, and religious rights of woman, will be held in the Wesleyan Chapel, Seneca Falls, New York, on Wednesday and Thursday, the 19th and 20th of July, current; commencing at ten o'clock A.M. During the first day the meeting with be held exclusively for women, who are earnestly invited to attend. The public generally are invited to be present the second day, when Lucretia Mott, of Philadelphia, and other ladies and gentlemen will address the meeting.

The young girl hardly knew what the announcement meant, and she had probably never considered seriously the question of the "social, civil, and religious rights of women." She was not accustomed to thinking of her status in terms of large social and political issues, but she clearly felt the sorrow of her condition, and the notion of a women's convention struct a sympathetic chord.

The young men of her age were already embarking on challenging careers — as lawyers, merchants, or bankers; as boatmen on the Erie Canal; or as farmers with land of their own. The nation was growing rapidly, and they were helping it grow. But Charlotte Woodward and other women in early America could hope to play only a subordinate part in the vital world that both encompassed and excluded them.

While the men she knew set out to make their fortunes, Charlotte stayed at home and earned a little money by sewing gloves, each day stitching together the precut panels of leather that were sent her in packages from nearby Gloversville. The tedious job left her mind free to wander — untested, undeveloped, unnourished. She would rather have worked in a printing office, setting type, but her prospect for such a job was as remote as that of becoming a banker or a lawyer. All such work was considered outside "the woman's sphere." Even the money she earned was not legally her own but her father's; and later, after she was married, anything she earned would belong to her husband.

And so the small notice in the *Seneca County Courier* was tantalizing, allowing women like Charlotte Woodward to give their own meaning to the notion of the "rights of women," hinting that she and others might deserve a more promising life. Charlotte was so enthusiastic about the convention that she ran over to a neighbor's to share the news with other girls. They, too, had read the notice, and soon a group of Charlotte's friends decided to go together to the meeting.

On July 19 she and six other women set out for Seneca Falls in a wagon pulled by sturdy farm horses. As they neared the town, they were joined on the main road by other wagons, carriages, and surreys bound, like them, for the meeting at the Wesleyan Chapel. Charlotte was surprised and pleased to see that men as well as women had joined the procession. In town they came upon a large crowd gathered in the churchyard.

None of the people who stood outside the Wesleyan Chapel on that summer morning in Seneca Falls had ever before attended a convention on women. The subject of women's rights had occasionally been discussed in the past half century, and new legislation sometimes affected the position of women, but this was the first time a convention had ever met in the United States to consider the general problem of women's rights. Even those who had called the meeting were not certain what would happen; but among them was a woman named Elizabeth Cady Stanton, who had considered more fully than most the position of women in a democratic nation. She and a few friends had suggested the meeting and drafted a preliminary resolution. Her background illustrates the history of women in early America and helps explain both the large social forces and the personal aspirations that came into play at Seneca Falls.

Elizabeth Cady Stanton, who was the guiding light of the Seneca Falls Convention and was a leading figure in the early movement for women's rights, was born into a conservative, upper-class household in Johnstown, New York, on November 12, 1815. Her father, Daniel Cady, was a lawyer, legislator, and judge; her mother, Margaret Cady, a stern Presbyterian woman who bore six children.

Like Charlotte Woodward and other women whose lives she would influence, Elizabeth Cady was aware from her earliest years that she had been born into a man's world. It was all very well for women like her mother to bear daughters — the biological survival of the race demanded the existence of both sexes, after all. But a woman's greatest achievement was to bear a son. Elizabeth's first memory was a conversation she heard in her fifth year when friends had gathered after the birth of her sister, Katherine. Although everyone was undoubtedly pleased at the good health of mother and child, there was sorrow in the house. The friends commiserated with her parents for not having produced a boy.

From her early childhood Elizabeth grappled with the problem of being a female in a world that favored boys and men. The dichotomy between the two worlds was reflected in the development of her personality. She was a lively, intelligent child with sparkling eyes, a pretty face, and a vibrant sense of humor, but beneath this animated exterior she was introverted and depressed, given to dark thoughts and frightening nightmares. Although well behaved, she believed that she was tainted with evil. This anxiety may have developed in part from her Presbyterian upbringing, with its emphasis on humankind's innate sinfulness, and from the rigorous standards of conduct imposed by her parents.

But her uneasiness must have fed also on her sense of discontent with her sexual role. She was attracted to male activities. As a child, she was a tomboy — a phrase used then and today to describe a young girl who enjoyed generally male sports. As she grew older, she longed for educational and vocational opportunities that were provided only for boys. What was the source of these outlandish longings? Surely they were not a woman's ideas.

It did not initially occur to her that her ambitions might be natural human aspirations, and she feared that their source must be an evil force. As a child, Elizabeth had a recurrent dream in which she had been fathered by Satan, and he wanted to reclaim her. After such dreams she would awaken with horror and with a troubled mind would creep to the top of the staircase where she could listen to the adult voices from the room below. These human sounds calmed her, returning her to her daily world.

If, however, the real world was not as disturbing as her dream world, it did contain disquieting problems for a young girl like Elizabeth. Her yearning after manly opportunities was not merely a grotesque fiction; it was a part of her makeup. She was as bright and resourceful as the boys she knew. She played chess and at school was an able student of Latin, Greek, and mathematics.

When she was not at school, she often visited her father's law offices. Comfortable in that adult, male world, she could read legal cases and listen to his conversations with clients. In 1826 when Elizabeth's only brother, Eleazer, died shortly after graduating from college, her grief-stricken father told her, "Oh, my daughter, I wish you were a boy." The statement is more complex than it sounds. Daniel Cady was a sensitive man and was well aware of his daughter's abilities. He did not simply wish that she had been a completely different person, for she already had the energy and ability he would have wanted in a son. If she had been a boy, however, she could fill the worldly role for which her character and intellect so well prepared her. He wanted that — for her sake as well as for his.

But Elizabeth was a girl, and early in the nineteenth century this status meant that however strong or smart or energetic she might be, much of life was closed to her. On her visits to the law office, where she saw women shackled to dissolute husbands, unable to free themselves by divorce or even to control their own money or children, she learned a great deal about these limitations. In marriage a woman quite literally lost her legal personality and became in a real sense the property of her husband, who gained complete control of her possessions and ownership of anything she might earn during wedlock. He could even beat her if he so chose, and she had no legal redress. She could not testify in court, because she was considered to have no legal character separate from that of her husband. Realizing that she disliked laws discriminating against her sex, the young men who studied law under Daniel Cady teased her by pointing out many such rules in statute books. One Christmas day they made a point of telling her that a fine coral necklace and bracelets she had just received would some day belong to her husband. More than sixty years later she remembered one of the students saying: "Now if in due time you should be my wife, these ornaments would be mine; I could take them and lock them up, and you could never wear them except with my permission. I could even exchange them for a box of cigars, and you could watch them evaporate in smoke."

The fact of inequality grew even more evident when Elizabeth graduated from the local academy. At school the girls and boys had been able "to study and play together with the greatest freedom and harmony," and she and other girls had competed successfully with boys in all things. But at the end of the academy years, the boys went off to Union College in Schenectady, proud and handsome in their new clothes, while the girls remained behind. When, said Elizabeth, "I learned of the barrier that prevented me from following in their footsteps — 'no girls admitted here' — my vexation and mortification knew no bounds."

Though she could not go to Union, Elizabeth was able to find other opportunities for growth. An academy for young girls had recently opened in Troy, New York, under the direction of Emma Willard. Most women's academies in the nineteenth century were "finishing schools" that taught women to be ladies and wives; but Emma Willard believed that girls should have the same educational challenges as boys and modeled her curriculum after that in men's colleges. Elizabeth attended Emma Willard's school and graduated in 1832.

She received further education in the company of her cousin, Gerrit Smith, whom she frequently visited in Peterboro, New York. A wealthy landowner who devoted much of his time to reform causes, Smith taught Elizabeth about abolitionism and temperance reform. She saw fugitive slaves, whom Smith sheltered and sent to Canada; she attended antislavery meetings; and she associated with people who believed that the world could be changed. Her parents had espoused a static view of reality. There were facts of life that one must simply learn, and the mature person adjusted to the world as it was. But Smith and his friends believed society was changeable, that if the individual and the community were in conflict, the community might be to blame rather than the individual.

Among the reformers who visited Gerrit Smith's house was an abolitionist lecturer and organizer named Henry Brewster Stanton. Ten years Elizabeth's senior, he was widely regarded as the most eloquent antislavery orator of his time. During autumn 1839 he and Elizabeth conversed by her cousin's fireside and traveled together to local reform meetings. One day while they were horseback riding through the bright autumnal woods, Stanton surprised Elizabeth with "one of those charming revelations of human feeling which brave knights have always found eloquent words to utter, and to which fair ladies have always listened with mingled emotions of pleasure and astonishment." The description of Stanton's proposal, written by Elizabeth fifty years after the event, invokes the image of a strong, assertive man and a weak, submissive woman. But if such feelings accompanied the proposal, they hardly characterize the marriage.

In their years together Elizabeth frequently displayed her resourcefulness and initiative, having to contend first with her parents, who opposed the match because of Stanton's abolitionism. Antislavery had not yet become fashionable in the North, and people like Stanton were frequently regarded as deluded fanatics whose utopian schemes endangered the Union. But Elizabeth persisted in her attachment despite their opposition.

On May 10, 1840, the young couple stood before a Scottish clergyman, Hugh Maire, and were joined in marriage. Even the ceremony reflected Elizabeth's independent temperament. With some difficulty, but with her husband's approval, she persuaded the minister to omit the promise to "obey" her husband from the wedding ceremony, because, as she later wrote, "I obstinately refused to obey one with whom I supposed I was entering into an equal relation." Both husband and wife were strong-willed individuals whose personal ambitions would test one another's patience in the years ahead. But after nearly a half century of marriage, Elizabeth Stanton could write that she and Henry Stanton had lived together "without more than the usual matrimonial friction."

After the ceremony the Stantons sailed for England, where Henry was to be a delegate to the World's Anti-Slavery Convention, held in London. In London, Elizabeth Stanton furthered her education through discussions with women delegates to the convention. Many opponents of slavery opposed inclusion of women as participants or speakers in

Henry Stanton. A reformer himself, he usually *supported his wife, Elizabeth Cady Stanton, when she fought for women's rights.*

organizations they regarded as male and the first issue debated at the London convention was the seating of female delegates. Henry Stanton and William Lloyd Garrison, among others, favored including women, but they were outvoted. Garrison was so disgusted that he refused to participate in the meeting, joining the ladies in an observation gallery instead. "After battling so many long years," he said, "for the liberties of African slaves, I can take no part in a convention that strikes down the most sacred rights of all women." Henry Stanton was annoyed but was not sufficiently outraged to boycott the convention.

In London, Elizabeth Stanton met Lucretia C. Mott, a Quaker minister from Philadelphia. Mott and other Quaker women, nourished by the liberal atmosphere of a faith that encouraged women to speak in church, were active in various reform movements. She and Elizabeth Stanton immediately became good friends. Walking arm and arm through the streets of London, they discussed the idea of an American women's rights convention. In Mott's company Elizabeth realized for the first time in her life that her discontent about her place in the world could be transformed from a personal grievance into a program for change.

The proposed convention was delayed for eight years, but when the Stantons returned to the United States, Elizabeth's education in reform movements continued. For two years she and Henry lived in Johnstown, where Daniel Cady received Henry Stanton as a student in his law offices, hoping perhaps that the legal profession would mute the radicalisms of his new son-in-law. In 1843 the Stantons moved to Boston where Henry opened a law office and Elizabeth devoted her attention to rearing her first three children. Her work at home gave her confidence in her own abilities. When she properly diagnosed why her first child cried constantly, she claimed that she had learned "another lesson in self-reliance." While rearing a family she maintained her interest in reform by associating with local abolitionists, including Frederick Douglass, William Lloyd Garrison, Lydia Maria Child, and Maria Weston Chapman. In Boston, as in her cousin's house at Peterboro, she met people who believed that the world could be improved by reform activity.

In 1847 the Stantons left Boston and returned to rural upstate New York where Henry opened a law office in Seneca Falls. The change was discouraging, for here Elizabeth was occupied with a seemingly endless round of trivial household tasks. "My duties were too numerous and varied," she later wrote, "and none sufficiently exhilarating or intellectual to bring into play my higher faculties. I suffered with mental hunger, which, like an empty stomach, is very depressing." As she observed the "wearied, anxious look" of other women, she recognized that they, too, felt weighted down by immediate cares and excluded from the real excitement and challenge of life. She wanted to do something to improve their condition and hers.

During this troubled time she visited Lucretia Mott, who was staying with a friend in nearby Waterloo, New York. Recognizing that she would find a sympathetic audience in Lucretia Mott and three other Quakers, Jane Hunt, Mary Ann McClintock, and Martha C. Wright, Elizabeth poured out her feelings of "long accumulating discontent." They were so moved by her complaints that they decided to hold a meeting on women's rights the following week. That evening they wrote an announcement for the *Seneca County Courier*.

While women like Charlotte Woodward, the glove seamstress, were reading the notice, Elizabeth Stanton and her friends began to plan the meeting, assembling on Sunday at Mary Ann McClintock's house to draft an agenda and proposals. At first they expected this to be an easy task, for their grievances were many. As Stanton later wrote, "They had felt the insults incident to their sex, in many ways, as every proud, thinking woman must, in the laws, religion, and literature of the world." But how could they express their ideas in a plain, forceful resolution? The task seemed overwhelming, and "They felt as helpless and hopeless," wrote Stanton, "as if they had been suddenly asked to construct a steam engine."

They resigned themselves finally to reviewing various "masculine productions," including statements from temperance and antislavery conventions. But these "seemed too tame and pacific for the inauguration of a rebellion such as the world had never before seen." Finally, one of the women read the Declaration of Independence. Here, at last, was a suitable model. Sitting around a mahogany table in the McClintock parlor, the women rewrote the Declaration to emphasize women's grievances. The villain of the piece became "all men" instead of George III, and the specific complaints of the founding fathers gave way to a list of women's grievances culled from statute books, church practices, and social customs. With the completion of this document they were ready to conduct America's first women's rights convention.

On the morning of July 19 Elizabeth Cady Stanton, Lucretia Mott, and three hundred other men and women gathered at the Wesleyan Chapel at Seneca Falls. They found the church door locked — perhaps the local minister had suddenly grown faint of heart at the thought of this extraordinary meeting in his church — but soon a small boy was lifted through a church window, and he unbolted the door. As the large crowd entered the building, the women leaders quickly and somewhat apprehensively reviewed the situation. The number of Quaker reformers, working women, and townspeople greatly exceeded their expectations. The women had initially planned on an all-female meeting for the first day, but they were glad now to discover forty men in the audience. Their declaration called for a revolt against male rule, but several "well disposed men," including Henry Stanton, had helped draft the document; other men, among them James Mott, Frederick Douglass, Ansel Bascom, and Samuel Tillman, had come to the convention. In deference to male familiarity with public meetings, the women appointed Lucretia Mott's husband, James, to moderate. Later generations of reformers might regard this decision as a failure of nerve, a retreat to male domination in the very moment of revolt. But Elizabeth Stanton and other women recognized that one need not be a slave to oppose slavery, or a woman to oppose injustice to women. And so they felt comfortable with support from a "well disposed" male.

The meeting began with speeches. Lucretia Mott summarized the condition of her sex and called for the education and elevation of women. Ansel Bascom, a New York politician, described a bill that had just passed the state legislature giving property rights to married women. And Samuel Tillman, a law student, read objectionable statutes affecting women. Elizabeth Cady Stanton spoke briefly but was so overawed that she felt like "running away" and spoke in a timid voice that could hardly be heard. The next day, however, she redeemed herself.

On the second day the convention began with a reading of the

"Declaration of Sentiments," which provides a concise summary of the laws and attitudes that defined a woman's position in nineteenth-century America. The preamble followed almost exactly the wording of the American Declaration of Independence and thus identified the issue of women's rights with the principles of the founding fathers. It began: "We hold these truths to be self-evident: that all men and women are created equal; that they are endowed by their Creator with certain inalienable rights; that among these are life, liberty, and the pursuit of happiness; that to secure these rights governments are instituted, deriving their just powers from the consent of the governed."

These inalienable rights had been continually abused by men: "The history of mankind," the declaration read, "is a history of repeated injuries and usurpations on the part of man toward woman, having in direct object the establishment of an absolute tyranny over her."

The Declaration of Sentiments continued, like the Jeffersonian original, by listing specific grievances. Some of these were political. The government denies woman "her inalienable right to the elective franchise," taxes her without her own consent, and forces her to submit to laws "in the formation of which she had no voice." Even the most "ignorant and degraded men" received these same rights without question.

Woman's disabilities were even more pronounced in her status in marriage. Wedlock was a repressive institution in which men had the right to rule as absolute monarchs. By law, a married woman was "civilly dead" — without rights to property, even to her own wages. She was not even considered morally responsible, because if she committed a crime in the presence of her husband he was considered culpable on the presumption that he was her master. Moreover, men were free to beat their wives, and in a divorce the law favored male claims to guardianship of the children.

The woman's position was further weakened by laws and customs that denied her an equal place in society. She could not receive "a thorough education, all colleges being closed against her," and she was barred from the professions; even the path to the ministry was closed on the claim of "Apostolic authority." She received "but a scanty remuneration" for the humble jobs she was allowed to perform. Even the moral code was easier on men, among whom such activities as drunkenness and fornication were regarded as minor peccadilloes.

In all these ways men attempted to destroy woman's "confidence in her own powers, to lessen her self-respect, and to make her willing to lead a dependent and abject life." Elizabeth Cady Stanton had not suffered from many of the worst outgrowths of woman's subordination. Her husband did not beat her or misuse his legal control of her property,

Lucretia Mott. Taught self-reliance by the Quakers. she in turn encouraged Elizabeth Cady Stanton to take up the fight for women's rights.

nor was she one of those women whose husbands sold their jewels for money to spend in the local saloon. But since her early childhood she had felt humiliated by the knowledge that she occupied an inferior position in society. She had seen men with less intelligence than hers leaving for a college she could not attend, voting when she could not vote, and working where she could not work. She knew the many ways in which her society undermined women's confidence and self-respect. Her solution, expressed in the declaration, was simple and direct: women must have "immediate admission to all the rights and privileges which belong to them as citizens of the United States."

To reach this goal the Declaration of Sentiments called for supporters to educate the American people about the wrongs women suffered. Toward that end the delegates passed resolutions for specific reforms. They condemned all laws that conflicted with "the true and substantial happiness of women" and prevented a woman from "occupying such a station in society as her conscience shall dictate." Such laws were contrary to nature, and hence were invalid. The delegates condemned the "double standard" in moral precepts and claimed "the same amount of virtue, delicacy, and refinement of behavior that is required of women in the social state, should also be required of men." The convention resolved that God intended woman to be man's equal.

Accordingly, she should speak out on social issues; participate in "trades, professions, and commerce"; and move beyond the "circumscribed limits" imposed upon her by "corrupt customs," thus entering into "the enlarged sphere which her great Creator has assigned her."

All these proposals passed the convention by unanimous vote. But one other resolution encountered stiff opposition. This was the declaration that "It is the duty of the women of this country to secure to themselves their sacred right to the elective franchise." A substantial portion of the delegates were unwilling to accept the idea of woman suffrage. Some were Quakers who opposed it because they did not favor political activity by men or women; others believed that the measure was too radical. Henry Stanton, who had favored other reform proposals, refused to attend when woman suffrage was discussed. Apparently many of those who favored equality for women in education, the professions, and marriage wanted to preserve some vestige of male supremacy.

But Elizabeth Cady Stanton and her supporters felt that the right to vote furnished the key to all other rights, because men passed the laws that circumscribed women's rights. In defense of the famous ninth resolution — the first woman suffrage proposal to be voted on in an American convention — she delivered an eloquent address, urging the importance of the measure. She received impressive support from Frederick Douglass, who had come to the convention from his home in nearby Rochester. Douglass, the great black abolitionist, was fully occupied with writing and speaking for the antislavery cause. Having suffered beatings, hunger, and other trials in his youth as a slave, he might easily have thought little of the oppression of women. But he was a highly principled man and believed that one could not denounce one form of oppression while accepting another. He spoke forcefully in defense of Stanton's suffrage proposal, linking his cause with hers. In the end the measure passed by a close vote.

The convention adjourned late in the evening of the second day. It had been a gathering of men and women who believed that many current laws and customs were unfair to women and that their declaration and resolutions were statements of common sense. But to the nation at large, the events at Seneca Falls seemed either ridiculous or threatening. In 1848 most Americans believed that a woman's "natural" sphere was the home. Her sole obligation to society was to create a comfortable domestic environment for her children and husband. Men should be engaged in worldly activities; they developed new industries, built railroads, designed canals; they settled the West, removing obstacles with ax and rifle; they fought in the Mexican War, acquiring new territory for America. A woman's role in all these manly activities should be dependent and supportive. She must provide an oasis of tranquility for the businessman back from his work, the frontiersman home from the fields, and the soldier returned from the battlefield.

The public reaction to the Seneca Falls Convention reflected the predominantly conservative attitude of the nation as a whole toward the question of women's rights, many newspapers declaring that the gathering had been inappropriate and outlandish. The meeting was dubbed "The Hen Convention," and its participants were described as cranks, amazons, and frustrated spinsters. The women had attended their convention "at the expense of their more appropriate duties."

The demand for women's rights was so startling that many editors had trouble explaining specifically in what ways it was wrong. They tended to fall back on their own version of natural law. No well-balanced woman would demand more rights, they said. "Every true hearted female will instantly feel that this is unwomanly." The demand for women's rights would destroy "things established at the creation of mankind." An editor in Philadelphia declared that in his city women already influenced human affairs through their control over men's souls. "They soar to rule the hearts of their worshippers," he said, "and secure obedience by the sceptre of affection." Continuing his romantic description of female influence, he said, "A woman is nobody. A wife is everything. A pretty girl is equal to ten thousand men, and a mother is, next to God, all powerful." In such ways the idealized power of woman was used as an excuse for making her powerless.

In general, the press also sought to ridicule the Seneca Falls Convention by pointing out seemingly absurd implications of women's rights. If the proposed revolution were to occur, society would have to be "radically remodeled" and its "organic laws" overturned. If women wanted to participate in some traditionally male occupations, they must participate in all and not just "those employments only which require the least exertion and are exempt from danger." Thus, in what one editor regarded as the ultimate absurdity, she would be required ultimately to put on "the panoply of war."

To balance out the intrusion of women into man's sphere, men would have to engage in women's work. One journalist wrote that the Seneca Falls Declaration implied that men must "wash dishes, scour up, be put to the tub, handle the broom, darn stockings, patch breeches, scold the servants, dress in the latest fashion, wear trinkets, look beautiful, and be as fascinating as those blessed morsels of humanity whom God gave to preserve that rough animal man, in something like a reasonable civilization."

Although such criticisms dominated the press, a few newspapers welcomed the women's rights proposals as part of the general "democratic progression" of the age. The editor of the *Rochester Daily*

Advertiser wrote that "nature" did not require women to be confined exclusively to the drudgery of raising children, and superintending the kitchens, and to the performance of the various other household duties which the cruelty of men and the customs of society have so long assigned to them." He welcomed the idea of an exchange or blending of roles. "Can not women fill an office," he said, "or cast a vote, or conduct a campaign, as judiciously and vigorously as men? And, on the other hand, can not men 'nurse' the babies, or preside at the wash-tub, or boil a pot as safely and as well as women?"

Despite such scattered support, however, the signers of the Seneca Falls Declaration and resolutions were generally condemned. Many former participants were surprised and dismayed by the widespread press criticism and sheepishly withdrew their names from the convention documents, concluding, apparently, that personal ridicule was too high a price to pay for their goals. But others were encouraged by the start they had made. Many of the Seneca Falls supporters would remain staunch backers of the women's reform movement in the years ahead. Others heard about the convention in the papers and were encouraged to communicate with Stanton and Mott. One of these new recruits was Susan B. Anthony, who read about the convention and eventually became one of the nation's outstanding women's rights organizers.

A new movement had been launched, and in small ways women could begin to live according to its ideas. Elizabeth Cady Stanton began to see herself in a new way, as something more than the appendage of a man. She could not yet vote or hold office, but she could at least declare her independence by insisting on being called by her own name rather than by her husband's. Her defense of this practice in a letter to a friend, Rebecca R. Eyster, a year before the Seneca Falls Convention, is one of her clearest statements of her quest for personal identity. She wrote: "I have very serious objections, dear Rebecca, to being called Henry. There is a great deal in a name. It often signifies much, and may involve a great principle. Ask our colored brethren if there is nothing in a name. Why are the slaves nameless unless they take that of their master? Simply because they have no independent existence. They are mere chattels, with no civil or social rights. . . . The custom of calling women Mrs. John This and Mrs. Tom That, and colored men Sambo and Zip Coon, is founded on the principle that white men are lords of all. I cannot acknowledge this principle as just; therefore, I cannot bear the name of another."

Elizabeth Cady Stanton lived until 1902. She remained married to Henry Stanton and reared seven children, but the Seneca Falls Convention changed her life. For the next half century she devoted much of her time to speaking and organizing on behalf of women's rights.

She and Susan B. Anthony formed one of the most creative partnerships in the history of American reform movements and laid the foundation for the woman suffrage amendment and many other reforms.

Just as Stanton had startled some of her friends by proposing a suffrage resolution at Seneca Falls, she continued to keep her friends off balance with new proposals. She advocated, for example, easier divorce laws and condemned the church for its subordination of women. "To be eternally politic and polite," she said, "was to do violence to yourself." She was reluctant to allow women to become too complacent about the character of their movement. Women's demands had to be continually reevaluated and restated. With her keen intellect, bright charm, and sparkling humor, she was a leading figure in the women's movement in America for five decades.

The issue articulated at Seneca Falls in 1848 was one of the most complex in the history of American reform. It was a revolt against male domination in which many "well disposed men" participated. It began a women's rights movement that many women were afraid to embrace. It occurred at a time when Americans supported many reforms, and yet it was ahead of its time. In the year of the Seneca Falls meeting the New York legislature did pass a bill granting women more control over personal property in marriage, but few Americans in 1848 were willing to consider the idea of equal employment or suffrage for women.

The Seneca Falls Convention reflected the disposition of Americans in the early republic to question every institution and reevaluate every social convention. But the response revealed the bedrock of conservatism that left many reforms such as emancipation, racial integration, and women's rights to the future. For leaders like Elizabeth Cady Stanton and followers like Charlotte Woodward, however, it was exciting to have taken the first step on the road to equality.

QUESTIONS

1. What disadvantages did people like Charlotte Woodward and Elizabeth Cady Stanton experience as women in the early 1800s?

2. Why do you think Stanton was dissatisfied with her lot as a woman in 1848? Why couldn't she be content to be a wife and a mother?

3. In what ways did Stanton assert her independence prior to the Seneca Falls Convention?

4. Why were Quaker women better prepared to assert themselves in public gatherings than non-Quaker women?

5. In what ways did "well disposed men" support the Seneca Falls Convention?

6. What specific grievances were aired at Seneca Falls, and what solutions were offered?

7. Why were many participants at the convention opposed to the woman suffrage proposal?

8. Describe the press reaction to the convention and explain why it was generally so hostile? How did opponents of women's rights justify their position?

9. What was accomplished at Seneca Falls?

10. Why did leaders of other reform movements lend support to women's rights?

BIBLIOGRAPHY

BANNER, LOIS W. *Elizabeth Cady Stanton* (1880). Fine brief biography.

DU BOIS, ELLEN. *Feminism and Suffrage: The Emergence of an Independent Women's Movement in America, 1848-1869* (1978). Development of women's rights movement after Seneca Falls.

FLEXNER, ELEANOR. *Century of Struggle* (1975). Survey of the women's rights movement.

GRIFFITH, ELIZABETH. *In Her Own Right: The Life of Elizabeth Cady Stanton* (1984). Well-researched and admiring biography.

MELDER, KEITH. *Beginnings of Sisterhood: The American Woman's Rights Movement, 1800-1850* (1977). Women's rights background to Seneca Falls.

STANTON, ELIZABETH CADY. *Eighty Years and More* (1898). Stanton's vivid and suggestive autobiography.

STANTON, ELIZABETH CADY, ET AL. *History of Woman Suffrage* (6 vols., 1899-1922). Useful survey with Seneca Falls documents.

STANTON, THEODORE, AND HARRIOT STANTON BLATCH, EDITORS. *Elizabeth Cady Stanton as Revealed in Her Letters, Diary, and Reminiscences* (1922). Includes many valuable Stanton letters.

TYLER, ALICE FELT. *Freedom's Ferment* (1944). Standard survey of early nineteenth-century reform.

WALTERS, RONALD G. *American Reformers* (1978). Overview of early nineteenth-century reform.

12

MANIFEST DESTINY

Down the Sante Fe Trail with Susan Shelby Magoffin, 1846–1847

In the 1840s American expansionists dreamed of occupying the continent from sea to sea. The Southwest belonged to Mexico and the Northwest was jointly controlled by England and the United States, but supporters of "manifest destiny" argued that God had ordained these lands for exclusive use by the American people as a showcase for liberty and democracy. Through diplomatic negotiations in 1846 the United States was able to gain the Oregon Territory, then a wilderness. The Southwest, however, had been settled for more than two centuries by immigrants from Mexico, and could not be won by peaceful negotiation. In 1845 the United States annexed Texas, which had fought for its independence from Mexico in 1837, and in the next year the United States went to war with Mexico. By 1848 the United States had gained a million square miles of territory, all carved out of Mexico. The moral problem inherent in spreading democracy by the sword was evident in the experience of a trader's wife, Susan Shelby Magoffin, and other American civilians and soldiers who entered New Mexico in 1846 with General Stephen Watts Kearny and the Army of the West.

As the sun sank low over the Kansas plains on the evening of June 12, 1846, Susan Shelby Magoffin, a young bride, busied herself gathering wildflowers. The prairie blossoms were so abundant that she repeatedly filled her arms with flowers, discarded them, and filled her arms again. At last she grew tired of her grasslands ramble and returned home to feed the chickens. As twilight fell over the prairie, she heard the barnyard sounds of dogs, cows, and mules, mingling with men's voices. She finished her work and stepped inside for supper.

These events suggest moments in the ordinary routine of nineteenth-century rural life, linking Susan Magoffin with thousands of other farm wives in the United States. But nothing else in Susan's life on that night in 1846 was the least bit conventional. Her "house" was a tent; her neighbors slept in freight wagons; and the men outside were Mexicans as well as Americans. Susan Magoffin was beginning a trip that no other American woman had made. Her husband, Samuel, was a merchant who made his living by carrying goods overland from Missouri to northern Mexico along the Santa Fe Trail. The trade was twenty-five years old, but Samuel was the first trader ever to bring an American wife along on the rugged journey. That night in the tent Susan revealed the spirit of adventure underlying her journey when she wrote in a notebook: "My journal tells a story tonight different from what it has ever done before. . . . From the city of New York to the plains of Mexico is a stride that I myself can scarcely realize."

Susan Magoffin's journey would have been extraordinary at any time, but in 1846 political events would add to her adventures. In 1844 James Polk had been elected to the presidency on a platform promising to expand America's boundaries westward. He capitalized on a national mood of "manifest destiny" — a belief that American institutions were so inherently righteous that the United States would, with God's blessing, occupy the continent from sea to sea. In 1845 Polk annexed Texas, which had recently won its independence from Mexico. He then opened negotiations with the Mexicans, hoping to persuade them to sell the remainder of the Southwest to the United States. But Mexico was unwilling to give up half its territory, and so Polk used a border skirmish as a pretext for war, which was declared on May 13, 1846. During the next two years American armies would knife into Mexico through Santa Fe, Matamoros, and Vera Cruz. The nationalist dream of 1844 would be a reality in 1848: American flags would flutter over scores of Mexican villages from Texas to California.

What was it like to be in Mexico in the presence of a conquering army? How did the Mexicans feel about the American conquest? Susan Magoffin's experience suggests that during the era when the United States absorbed a large portion of Mexico, Americans were also absorbed by Mexico, acquiring Mexican habits of speach, thought, dress, and diet. Her journal reveals the American capacity for both openness and ethnocentrism.

By the 1840s several hundred men set out each year by wagon and horseback from Missouri carrying merchandise to Santa Fe. Two of the foremost traders were Samuel Magoffin and his brother James. James entered the trade in 1825, the year the United States sent a party to mark the Santa Fe Trail. Three years later Samuel joined his brother in the trade. James traveled as far south as Mexico City, and the brothers established stores in Chihuahua and Saltillo, hundreds of miles south of Santa Fe. They liked the Mexican people. In 1830 James married a well-born woman from Chihuahua, Doña Maria Gertrudes Valdez. Her brother Gabriel Valdez was also a trader, and her cousin Manuel Armijo was a merchant from Albuquerque who would become governor of New Mexico.

The Magoffin brothers exemplify the close relations that American merchants were able to establish with the Mexicans. James was at various times consul to Saltillo and American commercial agent in Chihuahua and Durango. Samuel was trusted to carry the payroll for the Santa Fe garrison. The people of northern Mexico welcomed the goods from the United States, which included books, clothing, drugs, and a printing press. They in turn exported silver and furs to America. The famous 'Missouri mule" was really an import from Mexico, and in parts of Missouri the Mexican peso circulated as freely as the American dollar.

In 1846 Susan and Samuel Magoffin were in Independence, Missouri, making their final preparations for the overland journey. Independence, a town of trim wood-frame houses, stood at the threshold of the American wilderness. Steamboats arrived from St. Louis loaded with traders, gamblers, speculators, Oregon-bound immigrants, Indians, fur trappers, and blacks. At Independence the travelers saw Mexicans in sombreros and French-Canadian mountain men in buckskin. The clang, clang of hammer on iron filled the air as a dozen blacksmiths shoed horses and repaired wagons.

Samuel and Susan left Independence in a carriage, protected from the elements. Their party included Susan's servant Jane, who went in another carriage, and a number of Mexican servants and teamsters, who drove the freight wagons with Samuel's merchandise. Little in Susan Magoffin's background suggests that she would undertake such an arduous trip. Her parents were wealthy Kentuckians, and her grandfather, Isaac Shelby, was the first governor of the state. A photo taken in 1845, when Susan was eighteen, shows her wearing an elegant brocade dress. Long black hair and dark eyebrows accentuate a pretty

oval face, and a look of quiet contentment brightens her eyes. The photo
may have been taken for her fiancé, Samuel Magoffin, whose portrait
was painted on an ivory medallion at roughly the same time. He is
forty-five years old, twenty-seven years older than his wife, and looks
like a respectable judge. A roll of fat above his bow tie gives him a
second chin, sideburns curl from his ears almost to his lips, and a
receding hairline accentuates his thoughtful forehead. He looks pleased
and self-assured: a hard-working man whose life is about to be crowned
with marriage to an attractive and well-born young lady.

The Magoffins were married in Kentucky on November 25, 1845,
and went to New York for their honeymoon. In the ordinary course of
life, Susan would then have settled down in Kentucky or Missouri while
Samuel set off alone to attend to his business interests in Mexico. Susan
does not explain why she decided to accompany her husband, but several
reasons are evident. She had been interested in that remote region since
her schooldays, when she learned about the "table plains" of the
Southwest — we call them mesas. She hoped the prairie air would be
good for her health. And she and Samuel cherished each other's
company. Susan's journal begins with almost fifty pages of love poems.
Her first words of Spanish in the account are *mi alma* (my soul), her
nickname for her husband.

On the first night out the Magoffins stayed in a house ten miles
from Independence. The next day they left the settlements behind.
"Now the prairie life begins!" wrote Susan. Morning brought the noise
of teamsters cracking whips and "whooping and hallowing" over the
mules and oxen. Their fourteen wagons of trade goods were pulled by
twelve oxen each; a baggage wagon was pulled by four oxen; and the
Magoffins' and the maid's carriages were pulled by two mules each.
Two men on mules drove the "loose stock" — another nineteen oxen.
The men were Mexican and American teamsters.

In 1846 the Santa Fe Trail was busier than usual, for the merchants
shared the road with 1,500 soldiers belonging to the United States Army
and to various volunteer companies, all on their way to the Mexican
War. One of the soldiers, John Taylor Hughes of the First Regiment
of Missouri Cavalry, poetically described the army's line of march: "As
far as the vision could penetrate the long files of cavalry, the gay
fluttering banners, and the canvas-covered wagons of the merchant
teams, glistening like banks of snow in the distance, might be seen
winding their tortuous way over the undulating surface of the prairie."

No paved highway led to Santa Fe, but only a vague route across
750 miles of dirt, sand, rocks, and mud. Wagons bogged down in the
mud, and oxen had to be hitched in double or triple teams to move

them at all. One of the Magoffin wagons got stuck so badly that twenty-two oxen were hitched to it, and even they were unable to move it. Finally the teamsters "whiped out" the wagon by beating the oxen with their whip handles, "yelling all the time," wrote Susan, "till one is almost induced to believe their throats will split."

At the creeks and rivers the party found no bridges, only fords through shallow water. The wagons made their way down slippery banks and plunged into the streams, hurrying sometimes to get across before a rainstorm could swell the river. On a good day they covered twenty or twenty-five miles. Often they made only ten, traveling one mile an hour or slower.

During the night the Magoffins stopped at customary resting places. No hotels or shops or taverns graced these spots; only the convenient supply of wood and water distinguished them from the rest of the prairie. They were usually named for a geographic feature or local event. "The Lone Elm" was, naturally, a place with one elm tree. "Council Grove" was the scene of a meeting between Indian and white leaders in 1825. "Big John's Spring" was named for an early pioneer who liked to carve his name on trees with a tomahawk.

Susan traveled comfortably in her carriage, protected from the elements. On cold, rainy days she wrapped herself in a buffalo robe and looked out at the countryside. When the sky cleared, she got out to walk, easily keeping up with the slow-moving wagons. She picked prairie flowers, which she pressed in her diary, and she gathered gooseberries to eat. At night Susan and Samuel slept in their army tent. A table was fastened to the center pole, and above it was a stand holding their mirror and combs. The rug was made of sailcloth, and their chairs were portable stools with seats of carpet. Outside lay their dog, a greyhound named Ring, whom Susan called "a nice watch for our tent door."

When days of heavy rain stalled the wagons, Susan stayed in the tent and knitted, read books, and wrote letters. One rainy afternoon she and her husband sat comfortably in bed as a stream flowed through the tent. Samuel rested his head in Susan's lap and "dozed a little and talked a little." Her contentment shines through the early pages of the journal. "Oh, this is a life I would not exchange for a good deal!" she wrote, "There is such independence, so much free uncontaminated air, which impregnates the mind, the feelings, nay every thought, with purity. I breathe free without that oppression and uneasiness felt in the gossiping circles of a settled home." Camped one evening in a bed of wild roses — with rosebushes at the door and *inside* the tent — she wrote, "It is the life of a wandering princess mine."

Day after day the Magoffins worked their way westward, sometimes alone, sometimes in company with other merchants or soldiers. Parties would split up as one segment fell behind to repair wagons; a few days later the lagging traders might pass their former comrades, now repairing their own wagons. Susan faithfully recorded the changes along the trail. On the Kansas plains the wagons moved through grass so tall "as to conceal a man's waist." One evening Susan walked out on the prairie at sunset. To the west all that she could see was "a waving sea of tall grass." She had never seen "a more imposing sight."

Along the way they came to "tourist attractions." No billboards advertised these sites, and no merchants ran souvenir stands nearby, but word of mouth and descriptions in Josiah Gregg's *Commerce of the Prairies*, the classic account of the Santa Fe trade, told travelers what to expect. Susan particularly enjoyed "Dog City," a community of prairie dog burrows near the Arkansas River. As the wagons passed, "the little folks like people ran to their doors to see the passing crowd. They could be seen all around with their heads poked out, and expressing their opinions I supposed from the loud barking I heard." It was, she thought, "a curiosity well worth seeing." At Pawnee Rock, another "curiosity," Susan celebrated Independence Day and literally made her mark on the trail by carving her name in stone. The rock already bore the names of hundreds of other travelers.

The Santa Fe trail passed through stunning vistas and amusing curiosities, but it also brought peculiar hardships. The heat was the first and most persistent obstacle, parching man and animal alike. Between the watering places even muddy water collected from gullies in the tall grass could seem to Susan "a luxurious draught." The oxen staggered under their burdens, and when released from the yoke some "absolutely crept under the wagons for shade." Sunsets brought some relief, but in the hot tent Susan slept uncomfortably in her slip. "Even that would have been sent off without regret," she wrote, "had not modesty forbid me."

Fear was a constant companion on the prairie, sometimes vaguely felt, sometimes painfully active. A week out of Independence the Magoffins first encountered wolves. Just as Susan was falling asleep in the tent "The delightful music began. . . . It was a mixture of cat, dog, sheep, wolf, and the dear [Lord] knows what else." Ring, the greyhound, rushed out barking fiercely at the wolves, scaring them off. They came back later, however, and Susan wished Samuel, who was accustomed to wolves and slept peacefully at her side, was not "so well engaged."

Indians, too, brought fear. During the past two decades a dozen men had been killed on the trail by the natives — not a large number out of the hundreds who had made the trip, but enough to breed caution. When Susan carved her name in Pawnee Rock, Samuel had watched carefully for signs of hostile Indians — and Susan worked quickly.

Neither wolves nor Indians attacked the Magoffins, but they did suffer other mishaps. One day as their carriage was descending a riverbank, it flipped over, crushing the sides and top. Bruised, Samuel carried his stunned wife to the shade of a tree, rubbed her face and hands, and poured whiskey into her mouth. Slowly she regained consciousness. The wagon was a mess: books, bottles, baskets, and pistols were spilled onto the ground, but neither of the Magoffins was seriously injured.

The worst pest on the trail, was the mosquitoes. They were a common enough annoyance, something to be endured. But one evening they were a positive menace. Susan knew something was wrong when the mules pulling her carriage became restless and ran past the wagons, shaking their tails, desperate to rid themselves of the pests. The Mexican driver struggled to hold them in. "Holà, los animales!" he shouted, "Como estande bravos!" (Ho, animals! How wild you are!) When they stopped for the night at 10:00 the mules were "perfectly frantic" to escape their tormenters. Unable to hold them, the driver let them free to "shift for themselves" for the night. Samuel covered his face and neck with pocket handkerchiefs and directed the men setting up the tent. Meanwhile Susan hid in the carriage with her face smothered in a shawl and "listened to the din without." "Millions" of mosquitoes swarmed against the sides of the wagon. It "reminded me of a hard rain. It was equal to any of the plagues of Egypt. I lay almost in a perfect stupor, the heat and stings made me perfectly sick."

The mosquito attack and the carriage wreck were the most dramatic episodes in Susan's "rite of passage" into the wilderness. In such ways she experienced the great distance between the settled parts of the United States and the new lands in the West. Now she was realizing facts that before had been only images, lessons in school, reports from her husband.

For hundreds of miles the Magoffins saw no hotels, no habitations of any sort. Then in southeastern Colorado a building appeared in the distance that looked like an ancient castle. It was Bent's Fort, a private trading post that carried supplies for mountain men and Santa Fe traders and served as a depot for American soldiers. Constructed in 1833, it was a massive structure, 135 by 180 feet, with walls four feet thick and fifteen feet high. At diagonal corners stood two round watch towers, and over the gateway was a room with windows on all sides and a telescope mounted on a pivot, with which sentries could scan the countryside for hostile Indians. The fort was built in the Mexican style of adobe bricks, made of sun-dried mud and straw. An interior well provided crystal-clear water. Around the courtyard were two dozen rooms — kitchen, dining room, blacksmith shop, barber shop, and billiard room. There was also an ice house that received, according to Susan, "perhaps more customers than any other." Soldiers, trappers, Indians, and traders mingled in the courtyard. After the quiet of the prairie the noise seemed incessant: chickens cackling, mules braying, blacksmiths hammering, children crying, men shouting.

Samuel arranged for lodging and soon the Magoffins were installed in a large room on the second floor, furnished simply with bed, chairs, washbasin, and table. They could look out at the courtyard on one side, the prairie on the other. The ceiling was of timber, but the floor was dirt, and Susan had to throw water on it several times a day to keep down the dust.

The Magoffins stayed in Bent's Fort for two weeks. Samuel was eager to press on, but the traders could not move until the army was ready. Finally Gen. Stephen Watts Kearny arrived with his soldiers. "It seems the whole world was coming with him," wrote Susan. James Magoffin, Samuel's brother, also arrived in Fort Bent on his way to a conference with the governor of Santa Fe.

Within a few days the Magoffins set out again on the Santa Fe Trail. Soon they crossed the Arkansas River, which they regarded as the southern border of the United States. "I am now entirely out of 'The States,' into a new country," wrote Susan. She grew poetic as she contemplated this departure from her "own dear native land." America was "that which I love and honor as truly as any whole-souled son or daughter of the fair and happy America (for the United States are considered to possess that bright name above) ever did." She wondered whether she would ever "behold its bright and sunny landscape, its happy people, my countrymen, again." Patriotism was in the air in 1846, not only in the journals of the eastern cities, but in the hearts of citizens everywhere, and certainly in the thoughts of an eighteen-year-old trader's wife as she crossed the Arkansas River.

No signs or border guards, however, separated the United States and Mexico. Nor were there towns on either side of the border to distinguish the people and cultures of the two regions. Ahead lay more wilderness. The wagons moved through a dry land of sand hills and mirages — the first Susan had seen. At first they traveled quickly, covering eighteen miles in a day. From the plains they worked their way into stony hills, then up into mountains. They passed piñon trees and wild cherry blossoms. One night they found themselves among "stupendous mountains, forming an entire breastwork to our little camp." Susan spotted a snowcapped peak in the distance; she was hardly able to believe she had seen snow in August.

In the mountains they feasted on wild turkeys, prairie chickens, and rabbits. The nights were so cold that they needed to cover themselves with two blankets and a thick quilt. The Raton Pass, which they were now crossing, was the roughest part of the Santa Fe Trail. The men worked the wagons down the pass by locking the brakes and standing six on a side to steady each wagon over the worst places. Inevitably wheels were broken, and sometimes so many were being repaired at once that the trail seemed "like a regular shipyard."

A rider approached the train from the south and told them that James Magoffin had arrived in Santa Fe and was negotiating with the governor of New Mexico. If James was successful, the Mexicans would allow the American army to enter Santa Fe. If not, an army of four thousand Mexicans might, at this moment, be preparing to fight Kearny's force of fifteen hundred.

But for the moment the Magoffins continued south toward Santa Fe. Just beyond Raton Pass they were approached by three Mexican rancheros, selling cheese, bread, and *aguardiente*. a native brandy. These were the first natives they had met since crossing the border, and Susan did not like them. To her they seemed like "huckster-women after a steamboat." Nor did she like their food. The bread was hard, and the cheese was "very tough, mean looking, and to me unpalatable."

In fact, Susan seemed to like nothing at all about the first Mexicans they met. She described the *casa grande*. the biggest house in the village of Mora, as "a little hovel, a fit match for some of the genteel pig sties in the states." The people seemed even stranger than their dwellings. They swarmed around Susan "like bees," and she felt like the prize exhibit in a "monkey show."

Susan felt disdain as she looked from behind her veil at this new world. The children were in "a perfect state of nudity," and their mothers were poorly clad, wearing only petticoats, chemises, and buckskin moccasins. "The women slap about with their arms and necks bare," wrote Susan. Their dresses were too short, barely covering their calves, and worse still, when the women crossed a creek, they would pull the hems "up above their knees and paddle through the water like ducks, sloshing and splattering everything about them."

The Magoffins stopped for a midday meal at Las Vegas, New Mexico. The usual crowd gathered, and much to Susan's disgust they followed her into a dining room, seating themselves on chairs and the floor, enchanted at the presence of this lightskinned American lady. Susan, however, was less than enchanted with her first meal in New Mexico. The men and women chattered and smoked "little cigarritas" — tobacco wrapped in corn husks. Mothers held their babies under their shawls — "I shan't say at what business," reported an embarrassed Susan. Someone brought out a tablecloth, "black with dirt and grease," followed by a half dozen tortillas wrapped in a dirty napkin along with a bowl of meat, green peppers, and onions. No cutlery arrived, and Susan was appalled to learn that she was supposed to dip the tortillas into the meat and eat with her hands. "My heart sickened, to say nothing of my stomach."

Back in the carriage she watched with relief as the village with its motley collection of "men, women, children, and dogs" disappeared around a curve. "Joy beat in my heart," she recalled, "to think that once more I was at liberty to breath the pure air of the prairie, and to sit alone in my little tent, unmolested by the constant stare of those wild looking strangers!"

When Susan Magoffin entered New Mexico in 1846 the United States was on the verge of a new kind of cultural contact. In the past the United States had occupied lands that were previously home to non-Europeans. In many of these the tribes were nomadic or lived in simple bark shelters. They could easily be moved from one section of the country to another ahead of the white settlers. But the Mexicans were different. Many lived in substantial houses of brick and timber and worshipped in large, well-built Catholic churches. The invading Americans could not easily move them, out of sight or out of mind. But would the invaders recognize the Mexicans for who they were: men and women with distinctive customs and beliefs, as aware of their own heritage as the Americans were of theirs? Was manifest destiny a doctrine of conquest merely, or could American expansion accommodate the distinctive qualities of native peoples?

At the very moment when Susan was entering northern New Mexico, her brother-in-law James was in Santa Fe, negotiating with Governor Manuel Armijo. Although the Mexicans greatly outnumbered the Americans, Magoffin persuaded Armijo to disband his army and retire from New Mexico. We cannot be certain why Armijo gave up without a fight. He may have been awed by stories of American military valor; he may have been bribed. But James was able to persuade Armijo to leave. On the trail into Santa Fe he had joked with another trader, a Mexican named Gonzales, about "the thousand advantages to being conquered" by the United States — not the least, he said, were "liberty and equality." James had a gift for mixing humor and persuasion. It was fortunate also for the Americans that James was, through his Mexican wife, a cousin of the New Mexican governor. At any rate, his negotiations with Armijo cleared the way for the American army to enter Santa Fe without bloodshed. Armijo agreed to retire from the capital without a fight.

A few days later General Kearny reached the first Mexican settlements. At the village of Las Vegas he organized a ceremony that he would repeat again and again in other villages: he called together the religious and civil leaders of the town, explained that New Mexico was now American territory, and administered an oath of allegiance. In Las Vegas he stood on one of the flat-roofed adobe buildings with two Mexican army captains and the alcalde, or mayor, and addressed a crowd of 150 villagers. He had come by order of the United States to take possession of New Mexico, he told them. He had a strong force with him, and another American army would soon join the first. The people were absolved of allegiance to Governor Armijo and Mexico and now must give their allegiance to the United States. Kearny emphasized the advantages they would gain with American citizenship. The United States would protect them from Indian raids, which were common throughout New Mexico, and would guarantee their personal and religious liberties. The American government, he declared, would "protect the poor man as well as the rich man." The alcalde and the two captains then swore an oath of allegiance to the United States. Kearny shook their hands and turned to the crowd. "I shake hands with all of you through your alcalde," he said, "and hail you as good citizens of the United States."

Several soldiers in the Army of the West wrote accounts of the public reaction to the ceremony. One said that the people appeared "perfectly friendly," another that they raised "a general shout," and a third said they raised a "faint shout." A soldier named Marcellus Ball Edwards wrote in his journal that the oath was clearly taken under compulsion. "These poor creatures," he wrote, "were evidently compelled to take it for fear of giving offense to our army." Another soldier, Philip Cooke, recorded with irony that "the great boon of American citizenship," was thrust "by the mailed hand" upon the Mexicans.

But Kearny and many of his men regarded themselves as emancipators rather than conquerors. The General was confident that as American citizens the people of New Mexico would enjoy more freedom than under Mexican rule, and he demanded that his men treat the Mexicans as fellow citizens. He issued an order declaring that "humanity as well as policy requires that we should conciliate the inhabitants by kind and courteous treatment." He assured the Mexicans that not even "an onion or a pepper would be taken from them without a full equivalent in cash." When the army camped at Las Vegas he told the men that if any soldier so much as let his horse wander unattended into a Mexican cornfield, that soldier would walk the next day.

Word of Kearny's behavior preceded the army, and as he approached Santa Fe, each village seemed friendlier than the last. The people embraced one another "in token of their joy at the change of government," one soldier reported. An alcalde told Kearny that "God ruled the destinies of men," and because he "had come with a strong army among them to change their form of government, it must be right."

On the afternoon of August 18, 1846 the Army of the West reached the adobe city of Santa Fe. They marched four abreast down the hill to a plaza at the center of town. The streets were cluttered with dogs, but many of the people had fled. One soldier recalled that on side streets, "men, with surly countenances and downcast looks, regarded us with watchfulness, it not terror; and black eyes looked through latticed windows at our column of cavaliers, some gleaming with pleasure, and others filled with tears." Despite Kearny's earlier professions of friendship, the residents of Santa Fe, many of whom had close ties to the government, feared that the soldiers had come to pillage their city. The Mexican men had been told they would be branded on the cheek by the Americans with the letters "U.S."

At the plaza the soldiers stood around a hastily erected flagpole, a bugle sounded, and as the sun dropped behind the mountains, the Americans raised their flag above Santa Fe. Cannons on the hilltop boomed a thirteen-gun salute. Over the din of men and horses the soldiers could hear a "wail of grief " from the houses as "the pent-up emotions of many of the women could be suppressed no longer."

Susan and Samuel Magoffin heard the news from Santa Fe as their wagon train worked its way through little villages beyond Las Vegas. That night they camped alone in a pine forest at the foot of a mountain. The next day Susan's attitude toward the Mexicans suddenly seemed to change from disdain to respect. Perhaps the knowledge that they could pass safely into the capital made this strange land seem less hostile. Perhaps the villages were less squalid as they drew closer to Santa Fe. Perhaps the shift was internal: after a few days in the unfamiliar culture its strangeness had worn off and Susan was ready to accommodate herself to the new land.

She seems to laugh at herself as she describes her change in attitude. The carriage tongue broke by a little creek outside the village of San Miguel, forcing the Magoffins to halt while two army carpenters worked on it. The usual assembly of Mexicans soon crowded around. "I did think the Mexicans were as void of refinement, judgment, etc., as the dumb animals till I heard one of them say *'bonita muchachita'* [pretty girl]." This compliment caught Susan's attention, and you can almost see the twinkle in her eye as she writes: "Now I have reason and certainly a good one for changing my opinion; they are certainly a very *quick and intelligent people!"*

Suddenly the whole business of meeting the Mexicans took a new tone. Many of the *mujeres* (women) came to the carriage to shake hands and talk with Susan. One brought her some tortillas, goat's milk, and stewed goat meat with onions. And Susan actually liked it. "They are decidedly polite, easy in their manners, perfectly free." Suddenly she was viewing the people in a different way — dropping her guard, letting herself experience the Mexican culture.

A few days later the Magoffins came to the top of a hill, and there below them were streets, churches, and houses — the first real city they had seen in almost two months of travel. Night had fallen, and so Susan could not see Santa Fe clearly, but she felt the significance of the moment. "I have entered the city in a year that will always be remembered by my countrymen, and under the 'Star Spangled Banner' too."

Santa Fe was a city of 6,000 people, the largest in New Mexico. The roadways were crooked and narrow. Along the main street were flat-roofed adobe houses, one story high. Some blocks were devoted to cornfields — "fine ornament to a *city,* that," wrote Susan. A mountain stream ran through Santa Fe; irrigation canals carried water from its banks past the houses and into the fields, gardens, and orchards. People washed their clothes in the irrigation ditches in front of their own houses. The markets sold fresh fruits and vegetables, including fine ripe grapes brought in from local vineyards in wicker baskets carried by burros.

The main plaza was a large open square fronted by the government palace, a cathedral, houses, and shops. Roofs hung over the sidewalk: "It makes a fine walk," remarked Susan, "and in rainy weather there is no use for an umbrella." Susan liked Gloriatta, an enclosed park planted with cottonwoods, and the dry mountain air — Santa Fe is situated 6,950 feet above sea level. "One can walk through the deep grass here," wrote Susan, "and his shoes will never show at any time, either late in the evening or at early dawn, the slightest moisture."

The Magoffins moved into a Mexican house opposite a church. Susan described *Nuestra casa* (our house), as "quite a nice little place." The main room was long with a dirt floor, plank ceiling, and white-washed adobe walls. Cushioned benches of adobe along the wall provided seating, and a screen behind protected backs from whitewash. One side of the room was carpeted and served as a parlor, where the Magoffins received their many guests. The other side was bare earth with a table — the dining room. Nearby was *la cocina* (the kitchen). The bedroom was "a nice cool little room" with two windows. It could be darkened at midday, enabling Susan and Samuel to indulge in one

Catholic church in El Paso where Susan Shelby Magoffin, a Protestant, went to worship.

of the most agreeable local customs: "I must say it is truly pleasant to follow after the Mexican style, which is after dinner to close the shutters and take a short siesta."

Susan soon settled into the role of housewife. She began her days by "superintending the general business of housekeepers, such as sweeping, dusting, arranging and re-arranging of furniture, making of beds, ordering dinner." She went shopping and worked on a dress and taught the servants their jobs. In her own house Susan seems almost to have evolved into the nineteenth-century ideal of the good homemaker. "Mine is a quiet little household. The servants are all doing their duty, the great bugbear to most house-keepers; and if I can do my duty so well as to gain one bright smile and sweet kiss from my good, kind husband on his return, my joy will be complete."

In such moments Susan might almost have been in her native Kentucky, but many reminders told that she was in a foreign land and that in 1846 Santa Fe was an occupied city. The church bells, which seemed to be chiming all the time, day and night, mingled with the "everlasting noise" of the army. Soldiers were camped near the Magoffin casa. "From early dawn till late at night they are blowing their trumpets, whooping like Indians, or making some unheard of sounds, quite shocking to my delicate nerves."

The army, however, furnished one of Susan's pleasantest diversions, the society of other Americans. The officers regularly called on the Magoffins, the only American couple in Santa Fe. Their agreeable society was a reminder to Susan of the difference between the Mexican community and the Americans. Their company, she said, was "quite desirable to be sought after in this foreign land where there are so few of our countrymen, and so few manners and customs similar to ours, or in short anything to correspond with our national feelings and fireside friendships."

General Kearny's chief activity during the early months of the American occupation of New Mexico was to secure his position by tact and force. Upon entering Santa Fe he promised the people that he would not change their customs or threaten their religion. He then toured the region, bearing the news of American conquest. One evening after returning from his diplomatic mission, he stopped by to visit the Magoffins and gave them a "graphic account" of his reception in the Mexican towns. On his diplomatic mission he had attended feasts, balls, and Indian "sham battles." In one village he and his officers followed a train of priests, carrying candles "lighting the train of the Virgin Mary." He told Susan he felt as if he was "making a fool of himself." But by this gesture and others he indicated that Americans would respect Mexican customs and beliefs.

The United States hoped to pacify New Mexico through gestures of good will, but General Kearny did not take it for granted that parades and banquets alone would enable him to control the prize that had fallen so easily into American hands. This was apparent one morning when Kearny, riding "a splendid bay charger," came by to take Susan on a tour of the city's defenses. She mounted her horse, and they rode off through the "clogged streets" of Santa Fe. He showed her his artillery, arranged in two rows on the outskirts of town, and guided her past Armijo's army barracks, now occupied by Americans. Then they climbed a steep hill. At the summit men were building a fort out of massive adobe blocks. Susan stood at the edge and looked at the city and the plains and mountains beyond. The fort stood one hundred feet above Santa Fe and only six hundred yards from its center. Its presence guaranteed that Santa Fe would remain in American hands. Susan reported that from the hilltop "every house in the city can be torn by the artillery to atoms."

The Americans did not want to appear as conquerors in New Mexico. They preferred to regard themselves as offering an attractive alternative to government by the distant and sometimes corupt regimes in Mexico City. But tensions were created by the behavior of American soldiers. Kearny instructed them to treat the Mexicans well, but liquor, prejudice, and the fact of occupation made some of the men behave badly. Susan saw some of this in her own house. One day an officer wandered into the parlor, uninvited, and tried to treat Susan like an old friend. He "staggered to a seat where he sat and ran on with foolishness and impudence." Fortunately, Samuel was home and took him off her hands. Another drunken officer "went off into ecstasies about the war." He was "all eagerness for a fight," wrote Susan, "and says he has done all things in his power to provoke one."

Most of the soldiers could communicate with the Mexicans only with simple gestures and a few Spanish words. The awkwardness of the language barrier was apparent when soldiers were billeted with a Mexican family. "My Spanish friends are very courteous," writes William Richardson, a Missouri volunteer, "but there is little to relieve the monotony of our intercourse, as from my ignorance of the language I am unable to converse with them." The frustrated soldiers often changed Spanish words to English for the sake of convenience, finding similar-sounding American words as substitutes. *Frijoles* (beans) became "freeholders," the *Rio Purgatoire* (Purgatory River) became the "Picket Wire," and *aguardiente*, the Mexican brandy, became "the ingrediente."

The Mexican reaction to the Americans took many forms, but naturally the natives were as unsettled as the soldiers by the foreign army suddenly intruding into their midst. New Mexico had traditionally maintained a degree of independence from Mexico City. Only a few years before, in 1837, the people had risen against an appointed governor, Albino Perez, who tried to change the laws, collect taxes, and appoint new government officials. Governor Perez and sixteen of his assistants died in the rebellion. But the American presence inevitably disrupted life in Santa Fe. Rumors flew that Armijo would soon return with an army of five thousand and retake the capital. These tales frightened his former followers, some of whom fled the city fearing a triumphant Armijo would persecute them as traitors. Other Mexicans, remaining in Santa Fe, lamented that they might never again see their departed friends. Hostility to Mexico City did not guarantee enthusiasm for American government, especially when it was not yet clear what sort of government that would be. Kearny's aide-de-camp, Abraham Johnston, recalled a Mexican soldier's remark on seeing the American army marching toward Santa Fe. "My God!" he said, "What is to become of our republic!" Marcellus Gibson thought that some Mexicans welcomed the American presence, but said that they were "far from receiving us generally as deliverers."

Within a few weeks of Kearny's occupation of Santa Fe another two thousand American soldiers arrived, Missouri volunteers and members of a Mormon batallion recruited from immigrants on their way to Utah. Gibson reported that with all the soldiers in Santa Fe, "the grogshops do a thriving business." The Americans made noise, got drunk, and chased after Mexican women. In theory, they were the agents of liberation and progress. In practice the soldiers were often obtrusive and insensitive. A huge cannon was fired off in the center of Santa Fe to welcome newly arrived soldiers. The blast shattered the few precious panes of real glass in the city.

The Americans probably did more damage and made more enemies through carelessness than hostility. One morning Private William Richardson was camped near a Mexican village. Suddenly a group of villagers came into camp "in a great rage about something." It turned out that the captain had broken the bank of the local millpond the night before to ensure that it would not overflow and dampen his tent floor. Richardson reports, "The water of course rushed out with great force, tearing the embankment down, and washing the earth away for a considerable distance, stopping their mill, and leaving many families destitute of water." Richardson was disgusted with the captain's behavior, which he says, "met with little favor from his men, to their honor be it spoken." But when a lieutenant sought volunteers the next day to repair the damage, the men were unwilling to stand in the cold water and work without compensation.

A few months later an English adventurer, George Frederick Ruxton, traveled through New Mexico and found widespread hostility against the Americans. "I found over all New Mexico," he writes, "that the most bitter feeling and most determined hostility existed against the Americans, who certainly in Santa Fe and elsewhere have not been very anxious to conciliate the people, but by their bullying and overbearing demeanor towards them, have in a great measure been the cause of this hatred." He spent one evening on the way to Taos with an Indian family. His hostess fixed him a meal, but seemed reserved until she discovered he was an Englishman.

"Gracias a Dios [Thanks to God]," she exclaimed, "a Christian will sleep with us tonight and not an American!"

Such instances of provocation and hostility were not, however, universal in New Mexico. Among both Americans and Mexicans were many types of people. In the United States there were outspoken war opponents as well as enthusiastic expansionists. Henry David Thoreau and Abraham Lincoln, among others, questioned whether the United States belonged in Mexico. Even among the soldiers there were dissenters. One of the armies sent into Mexico included many Irish Catholics who were so disgusted with camp life that they were persuaded by their fellow Catholics in Mexico to desert and serve in the Mexican army in a "San Patricio Brigade."

Among the Mexicans too were many varieties of opinion. Some Mexicans had enjoyed their contacts with the American merchants during the twenty-five years of the Santa Fe trade and believed that the United States would govern justly. Stephen Cooke visited the padre's house, where he saw curtains decorated with pictures of American presidents. The Mexicans were impressed too by Kearny's respect for the Catholic church and his reappointment of Mexican civil officials in the new government. When Kearny toured northern New Mexico to administer the oath of allegiance, eighty Mexican horsemen rode with him as a sign of support. Along the way hundreds of villagers fell in with the line of march.

In meeting the Mexicans Susan Magoffin had an advantage over most of the soldiers. Ever since leaving Independence, Missouri, she had been in daily contact with Mexicans, and she was soon learning Spanish. In Santa Fe, Spanish words and expressions grew frequent in her diary: *la niña* (the little girl), *muchacha* (girl), *una señora* (a lady), *bastante* (enough), *duraznos* (peaches), *El Señor Vicaro* (the priest). Along with the American traders and soldiers who found their way to the Magoffin palor, Susan and Samuel welcomed many Mexicans to the house. Some were old friends of Samuel's; others were new acquaintances. Shortly after they arrived Doña Juliana called. "She is a woman poor in the goods of this world," wrote Susan, but "a great friend to the Americans and especially to the Magoffins whom she calls a *muy buena familia* [very good family]." Susan was proud that she had carried on a conversation in Spanish for half an hour with Doña Juliana. "Whether correct or not, she insists that I am a good scholar."

Many of Susan's encounters with the people of Santa Fe reflect eagerness on both sides to befriend the other. The Mexicans wanted to know about her "*madre, padre, hermanos, hermanas* [mother, father, brothers, and sisters]." They examined her knitting and sewing, and Susan reported, "in an instant they can tell me how it is done, though perhaps 'tis the first of the kind they have ever seen. What an inquisitive, quick people they are!" she thought.

Susan and Samuel mingled with the people on public occasions. They went to a dress ball given by General Kearny as a gesture of friendship toward the Mexicans. The room was decorated with American flags, and the people were brightly dressed in "the seven rainbow colors." The women wore dresses of silk and satin, fine *rebozos* (shawls), and "showy ornaments, such as huge necklaces, countless rings, combs, [and] bows." A guitar and violin furnished lively music. Men and women circled the floor in a "mazy dance." Others sat along the wall, puffing cigarettes and filling the room with a cloud of smoke. A plump, short priest was there, dressed in bright robes. He was "a man rather short of stature, but that is made up in width." And "Doña Tula" was there, a wealthy and independent woman who ran the most prosperous card rooms in Santa Fe. One of the soldiers jokingly held out a handful of corn husks and a horn of tobacco for Susan to roll a cigarette. The Mexican women were smoking, but Susan's acculturation did not include the seemingly unladylike practice of puffing a cigarette, and she politely refused. Susan's friends from the army danced with the Mexican woman and drank aguardiente. On the wall was a portrait of General Kearny, draped with an American flag that flew during the day from a hundred-foot flagpole in the city plaza. The picture showed Kearny handing a constitution to the Mexican people. Below it was a single word: *Liberdad* — Liberty.

On such occasions the Mexicans and Americans seemed more like cousins at a large family reunion than the peoples of two warring nations. This easy mingling was apparent to Susan a few days later at their first Mexican dinner. She and Samuel were invited to dinner by the Leitendorfers, an American trader and his Mexican wife, along with General Kearny and other guests. The women were seated at one side of the table, the men at the other. They ate *sopa de vermicile* (vermicelli soup), *carne asada* (roasted beef), and other Mexican dishes. For dessert they had a pudding made with boiled milk seasoned with cinnamon and nutmeg, a dish so pleasing to Susan that she decided to get the recipe.

During the meal General Kearny offered an interesting toast. Raising his glass he declared, "The U.S. and Mexico — They are now united; may no one ever think of separating." These words suggest an attraction between two peoples who naturally gravitate together, rather than the triumph of a conquering nation. Forgotten for the moment were the guns of Fort Marcy or the American soldiers camped nearby. Kearny expected that with a little encouragement, such as he had shown in carrying candles in a Mexican procession, the people would be delighted to become Americans. To Kearny and other expansionists of 1846 America was not an aggressive nation imposing its culture on other peoples, it was rather a liberal system of government that made room for men and women of many nations and religions.

On December 15, 1846, President Polk expressed a similar idea when he declared that America was in Mexico due to "a patriotic desire to give the inhabitants the privileges and immunities cherished by the people of our own country." Like Kearny he could think of Mexico as "now united" to a larger America that was still growing, still making its way westward. Kearny and Polk, living in the age of manifest destiny, assumed that other peoples would appreciate being absorbed by the United States. And about some people, like the guests at the Leitensdorfer dinner party, they were correct. The Mexicans at the table were not resentful or lukewarm at Kearny's toast. Instead they greeted his words with enthusiastic shouts of *viva! viva!* ("long live" or "hurrah").

In such moments the joining of the United States and Mexico seemed natural, fraternal. But there were other ingredients in the cup of manifest destiny. Not every Mexican was as eager for union as these friendly guests. Far to the south American and Mexican armies were maneuvering, preparing for battles in a war that was far from over. And in the villages around Santa Fe Mexican patriots were at this moment trying to arouse the populace to rebel against the Yankee invaders. Susan Magoffin's until-now peaceful sojourn in New Mexico would soon be filled with anxiety and with the threat of imprisonment or death.

At the end of September in 1846 the markets in Santa Fe were selling fresh vegetables and "the most delightful" peaches, grapes, and melons. But Susan knew the growing season would soon end, for she could see snow on the mountains nearby. General Kearny saw the snow, and it may have encouraged him to quicken his departure for California. On September 25, just a month after he had entered Santa Fe, he divided his army, leaving some men in New Mexico and taking the rest on a difficult march toward Los Angeles. Another force, under Col. Alexander William Doniphan, would soon march south to El Paso and Chihuahua.

Assured of protection by Doniphan's army, the American merchants resumed their journey into the interior of Mexico, where they would continue their trading. Susan reported in her diary, "Lo, we are camping again!" She had enjoyed her "casa" in Santa Fe, but she relished being back in the one "house" that was her own. "It is quite cool and our little tent is comfortable enough. It is a fine thing." The oxen struggled along the sandy road, which followed the Rio Grande. In the distance Susan could see the flat mountains that she called "the table-planes of Mexico."

The people along the road south of Santa Fe were as eager as their northern cousins to study the Magoffins. The Pueblo Indians, whose villages lined the road, crowded around "as thick as some flocks of sheep and goats" and peered under the tent, calling it *la casa bonita* (the pretty house). "They are certainly the most inquiring, prying, searching people I ever saw." They came with serapes full of *muchas cosas a vender* (many things to sell): eggs, grapes, tortillas, onions, watermelons, and apples. Their "great passion" was bottles. Susan was called *comadre* (godmother) by one old Indian woman simply because she made Samuel, who had jokingly refused, give the woman a bottle.

At times Susan was annoyed by the persistent curiosity of the natives, but more often she was wonderfully open to new people. An old woman came by one day just after the Magoffins had set up their tent. She and Susan sat together for a half hour and talked about "all family concerns from the children down to the dogs." The woman asked about Susan's parents. "I ran off from them just for a husband," she replied. "Pues, es mejor no?" (Well, is it not better?). The old woman laughed heartily.

"El marido es todo del mundo a las mujeres." Susan added, (The husband is the whole world to a woman.)

The old woman laughed again in agreement. "She thinks though I am young, I am old enough," wrote the nineteen-year-old Susan.

Ordinarily Samuel would have led his wagon train straight through El Paso into Chihuahua, about five hundred miles south of Santa Fe. But these were not ordinary times. Word came from the army that the traders should wait until Doniphan could clear the way into El Paso. The Magoffins decided to rent a house in San Gabriel, a tiny village along the trail. Expecting to spend the winter there, Susan planned to familiarize herself with local customs. "I must learn a good many of the New Mexican ways of living, manufacturing serapes, rebozos, [and] making tortillas, chili peppers, and chocolate."

While they were in San Gabriel, Samuel served as the local doctor. The medicines he carried cured some illnesses, and soon he was regarded as a "skillful *médico.*" Samuel charged little or nothing for his work, though some patients gave him gifts of food in return. "It shows a feeling of pure gratitude," Susan remarked, "which I constantly see manifested among these people for any little kindnesses done them." On Saint Gabriel's feast day, the Magoffins' landlord came by the door, telling them to prepare no dinner. Later he brought chili with *carne de carnero* (mutton), stewed chicken with onions, and a dessert made of bread and grapes. The people of the village, Susan observed, had been preparing their dishes for a week. They apparently enjoyed sharing their creations. "The home folks would think me a great favorite if they could see how the good people of the village are sending me tortillas, *quesos* [cheeses], *dulces* [sweets], and the like."

In such encounters the American entry into New Mexico was a meeting of cultures rather than one people subjugating another. But even as the Magoffins lived peacefully in San Gabriel, tensions underlying the American occupation were working their way to the surface. First came news that James was robbed by Apaches who occupied the wild countryside flanking the thin ribbon of Mexican settlement along the Rio Grande. He lost his carriage, mules, clothes, and trade goods.

Then came rumors from the south that a large Mexican army was on the march toward Santa Fe. The main body of traders, stopped thirty miles beyond San Gabriel, were said to have circled their wagons and sunk the wheels to the hubs as a breastwork against the enemy. One trader decided to give up, selling his goods for what he could get and returning to Santa Fe. Others were "crazy to get on" and make a profit on their merchandise, whatever the risk.

A few weeks later news arrived that James, now in Chihuahua, had been arrested by the Mexicans as a spy. Then came rumors that an army under General Santa Ana had been formed to reconquer New Mexico. Santa Ana was a devoted patriot and seasoned commander who had led the Mexican army during the fighting in Texas in the 1830s. In a battle with French invaders at Vera Cruz in 1838 he lost his left leg below the knee; he sent the leg to Mexico City with a patriotic greeting as a sign of his devotion to the cause. Santa Ana would not be easily defeated.

Susan worried that if Santa Ana beat the American forces in the south, she and Samuel would have to flee to Santa Fe and safety at Fort Marcy. His victory would "inspire this fickle people with such confidence as to his superior and almost immortal skill that en masse they will rise on our heads and murder us." Suddenly the Mexicans were "fickle people." This is not the Susan Magoffin who had come to know and like individual Mexicans. For a moment, she is a member of a conquering nation, who is shocked that a defeated people might still be loyal to their native land.

The Magoffins were elated to hear a few days later that Doniphan had defeated the Mexicans at Brazito, outside of El Paso. The victory opened the way to El Paso, and Americans seemed in complete control of New Mexico. Soon, however, conditions changed once more. The Magoffins learned that a general uprising had been planned in the north by the Mexicans, with the intent of retaking Santa Fe and killing or expelling all Americans. Charles Bent, who had been appointed governor of New Mexico by General Kearny, learned of the planned uprising from friendly Mexicans. Governor Bent was able to thwart the rebellion by arresting seven of its leaders, but tensions remained.

On January 17, 1847, Governor Bent was in Taos, fifty miles from Santa Fe, visiting his family. Bent was one of the brothers who had built Bent's Fort; he had moved to New Mexico in 1829 and settled in Taos, marrying a Mexican, Marie Ignacia Jaramillo. Long a resident of New Mexico, he knew the country and its people well, but he was unprepared for the events now surrounding him. Early in the morning a crowd of Indians marched through Taos demanding the release of two men who had been arrested for robbery. The American sheriff refused, and the Mexican prefect called the Indians all thieves. Soon the sheriff and prefect were dead.

Meanwhile Charles Bent was at home with his wife, their three children, his wife's sister (who was married to frontier scout Kit Carson), and two other women. Warned that the crowd was after him, Bent dressed quickly and armed himself. He then tried to quell the rioters by reminding them of his friendship with them over the years. But they would not listen. They attacked the house and tried to dig in through the roof. Bent's wife and children begged him to defend himself, but he hesitated to fire, perhaps fearing he would only make matters worse.

A French Canadian neighbor and his Mexican wife had dug a hole through a wall dividing his house from Bent's. The governor's family escaped through the hole, but Bent hesitated and was shot by a Pueblo Indian. He crawled through the hole, and in his last moments he tried to write a note for his weeping family. Bent's attackers swarmed into the room, filling him with arrows and shooting him with his own pistols. They then scalped the dead governor and paraded their trophy around the village.

Susan and Samuel Magoffin were horrified by the news from Taos. "My knowledge of these people has been extended very much in one day," wrote Susan. She conceded that there were "some good people" among the Mexicans, but feared that most would "murder without distinction every American in the country if the least thing should turn in their favor." The Magoffins prepared hastily to leave San Gabriel. During their last hours in the village Susan looked at everyone with suspicion.

The Magoffins, their wagoneers, and another trader played a dangerous game of bluff, trying to demonstrate to the townspeople their confidence without provoking a confrontation. Samuel stood on the rooftop surveying the countryside; other men scouted the town; they all examined and fired their guns. At last they were ready to leave San Gabriel. "In truth we are *flying* before them," wrote Susan. That night the men remained on guard. In the Magoffin tent Samuel laid out a double-barreled shotgun and several pistols, including "one of Colt's six barreled revolvers." If they were attacked by Mexicans or Indians, Susan would stand beside her husband, gun in hand.

For the next few days, however, their greatest enemy was the land rather than its people. Deep sand clutched the wagon wheels. The winter nights were cold enough to freeze a cup of water in the Magoffin tent. Then came the Jornada, an eighty-mile stretch of arid land where mountains forced the wagon trail away from the Rio Grande. Most of all they worried about the Apaches, who made no distinction between Mexicans and Americans. They had attacked James's party and even raided Doniphan's livestock. Samuel warned her that she should not even venture two hundred yards from the wagons.

The Magoffins spent one night at Doña Ana, the one Mexican village between the Jornada and the town of El Paso. The danger from Indians had been so acute that the village, though Mexican, seemed a haven. It had been attacked recently by the Apaches, and as a sign of common cause against a shared enemy, Doniphan had given the people a cannon. Unfortunately, this gesture of friendship was wrecked by some wagoneers, who got drunk and stole the cannon and brought it into camp, claiming it was "unfit for Mexicans." The alcalde sent off a protest to El Paso, and Samuel took his side, insisting that the cannon be returned. Resentful, the thieves drove a spike into the cannon's touchhole so that it would not fire. Samuel apologized to the mayor, and took the names of the bigoted men who had ruined Doniphan's friendly gesture.

Farther along the trail the Magoffins passed through the battle-ground of Brasito, where Mexicans and Americans had fought only a few weeks before. Riding over the flat plain Susan discovered two cartridges, one Mexican, one American. Despite this sign of conflict, however, the Magoffins did not anticipate hostility as they entered El Paso. Samuel's friends in the city sent word that he should "come on without fear" and "that they have always been friendly to him and they still are." They move in with the family of a local priest.

The trader's wife was again at home among the Mexican people. But the war and the danger of American defeat could not be forgotten. Rumors reached El Paso that Santa Ana had assembled a great army to attack Doniphan and to recapture Texas. Susan and Samuel worried that they might be robbed, imprisoned, murdered. But living with a Mexican family, they did not see threats everywhere as they had in San Gabriel. In fact, they shared a unique bond with the curate's family. Samuel's brother James was a prisoner of the Mexicans — and the curate himself was a hostage with Doniphan, carried off with several other leading citizens to ensure the good behavior of the Mexicans in El Paso. "Our situations are truly similar," wrote Susan, "I shall regret deeply when we have to leave them; twould be injustice to say that I like one more than another, for I love them all."

On the morning of March 5, 1847, Don Ygnacio Roquia, a wealthy friend of Samuel's, came to the curate's house with news of the war. Don Ygnacio was one of the men Susan most admired in El Paso. She had visited his fine casa and saw his garden, where he raised oranges, figs, apricots, and almonds. His wife was "a lady easy in her own house," whose well-behaved children were studying English and French. Don Ygnacio was a dignified-looking man, who reminded Susan in appearance of George Washington. But on the morning of his visit to the curate's house he stepped through the door "with his hair somewhat on ends and his features ghastly." He took Samuel by the hand and led him from the room. Then with tears in his eyes he told his American friend that "he was a Mexican, and it pained him to the heart to know that the American army had gained the battle and taken possession of Chihuahua."

Visions of imprisonment and death faded from Susan's imagination, and she confided to her diary, "I am delighted with the news." But although she was relieved, she was not triumphant. A few days before, her Mexican friends had offered her consolation when it appeared that Doniphan would lose. Now she wrote in her diary, 'I would not for the world exult or say one word to hurt the feelings of this family."

Both families were soon reunited with their imprisoned kinfolk. With Chihuahua in his possession Doniphan released his hostages, and soon *El Señor Cura*, the curate, was home. In the meantime James had gained his release from the Mexicans by cleverly using his affable tongue — and by judiciously distributing some two thousand bottles of champagne. Following Doniphan's victory Susan and Samuel made their way to Chihuahua and the Mexican coast, and from there by ship back to the United States. Doniphan joined forces with General Zachary Taylor and defeated Santa Ana at the Battle of Buena Vista. General Kearny marched his army across Arizona to California and fought two small battles, consolidating American control of California. In New Mexico the Taos rebels were defeated in battle, and the leading conspirators were hanged.

The war came to an end in September 1847, when General Winfield Scott, after winning several battles in the environs of Mexico City, led the triumphant American army into the capital. In 1848 the United States and Mexico signed the treaty of Guadelupe Hidalgo, by which Mexico ceded the Southwest to the United States and received in exchange a payment for $15 million.

Few Americans questioned the justice of the Mexican War. Although some opposed annexation of northern Mexico, most, including the Magoffins, assumed that everyone would benefit from the new arrangement. But one day while she was still in El Paso Susan had been confronted frankly with the moral problem of America's invasion of Mexico. Don Ygnacio, the man who had brought the news of Chihuahua, told Susan he was an admirer of George Washington, "whose name is ever dear to the hearts of the American." This statement was pleasant enough, but then her Mexican friend said something disturbing that Susan carefully recorded: "He says the course Mr. Polk is pursuing in regard to this war is entirely against the principles of Washington, which were to remain at home, encourage all home improvements, to defend our rights *there* against the encroachments of others, and never to invade the territory of another nation."

She could find no satisfactory rebuttal to this argument, now that the invasion of Mexico was an accomplished fact. But the effects of the invasion were yet to be determined. Whether, as the United States claimed, its institutions could embrace and encourage men and women in all walks of life would depend on American willingness to be tolerant of people with different cultures. Susan Magoffin's experience showed the possibilities for both prejudice and accommodation. In El Paso Susan seemed to grow more tolerant, more understanding of all elements in Mexican culture. During her days of travel she had been unhappy that she could not attend church and carry out other traditional sabbath observances as in her Protestant home in Kentucky. She read the Bible quietly in tent or room, and tried to think about her soul and God. But religious observances were difficult without institutional support. On the trail the wagoneers seemed to swear less on Sunday, but no religious services were held. In Mexico on the sabbath church services were held, but otherwise it was business as usual. When Samuel himself sold goods on Sunday, Susan remarked, "It hurts me more than I can tell."

Finally on January 21, 1847, after more than half a year without attending a religious service, Susan began going to the Catholic church in El Paso. In her diary she struggled to explain why she had done something so unusual for a Protestant in an unecumenical age. She should not judge the Mexicans, she wrote, for "I am told to 'judge no man but to bear the burden of my brother.' " She must first purify herself before trying to reform someone else. At the least, she said, "they are sincere in what they do." And so she went to church and stood among a foreign people and listened to a foreign service. But it was all right. "This morning I have been to mass not led by idle curiosity, not by a blind faith, a belief in the creed there practiced, but because 'tis the house of God."

Susan could never have written those words a year before, could never have found this common bond between American Protestant and Mexican Catholic, but exposure to a new culture changed and broadened her. It was a small thing in the whole history of the Mexican War, but it was an example of the personal growth and flexibility that could provide the only possible justification for manifest destiny. President Polk and General Kearny might speak glowingly about the amalgamation of the Mexican and American peoples, but without growth in understanding and toleration between the two peoples, their words were hollow promises.

One of Samuel's best friends in El Paso, a dignified old man named Don Agapita, described Susan's experience well when he told her that on her journey she was "learning a lesson that no one could have taught . . . . but experience, the ways of the world." She thought about the words of this "philosophical" old man. " 'Tis true all he says," she wrote, "I have seen and read of Kentucky till I know it all by heart, but who could by telling me, make me sensible of what I have seen and felt since I left home to travel."

QUESTIONS

1. In 1846 New Mexico was distant from the United States, both geographically and culturally. Summarize the difficulties a traveler experienced in journeying from Missouri to New Mexico, and describe the most obvious cultural differences between the two regions. Consider particularly Susan Magoffin's experience.

2. In what ways did General Stephen Kearny attempt to persuade the people of New Mexico that he came as a liberator, not as a conqueror?

3. Why did Governor Armijo of New Mexico permit the Army of the West to occupy Santa Fe without a fight?

4. Why were some New Mexicans receptive to annexation by the United States, and how did they express their approval?

5. Why were some New Mexicans opposed to annexation by the United States, and how did they express their disapproval?

6. In what ways and for what reasons did American soldiers contribute to Mexican feeling for and against the American occupation? Did their behavior justify President Polk's claim that the United States intended to give the people of New Mexico "the privileges and immunities cherished by the people" of the United States?

7. Susan Magoffin sometimes treated the New Mexicans with friendship and respect, sometimes with hostility and contempt. Cite examples of each attitude and try to explain why her attitudes changed several times.

8. "Manifest destiny" is a complex idea. From your reading, how would you define it? What did it mean to Susan Magoffin? to General Kearny? to other American soldiers?

9. Was there a meeting of cultures in New Mexico in 1846 and 1847 — that is, did Americans adopt any Mexican ways, and vice versa? Or were the two peoples completely separated by their cultural differences and prejudices?

BIBLIOGRAPHY

BIEBER, RALPH P., EDITOR. *Journal of a Soldier Under Kearny and Doniphan. 1846–1847* (1935). Soldier's account of army life in northern Mexico during the war.

BRACK, GENE M. *Mexico Views Manifest Destiny* (1975). Mexican thoughts about American expansionism, 1821–1846.

CATHER, WILLA. *Death Comes for the Archbishop* (1927 and later editions). Hauntingly beautiful novel based on the life of the first American archbishop of New Mexico.

DRUMM, STELLA M., EDITOR. *Down the Santa Fe Trail and into Mexico* (1926, 1962). Susan Shelby Magoffin's colorful description of life on the Santa Fe Trail and in northern Mexico in 1846 and 1847.

MOORHEAD, MAX L. *New Mexico's Royal Road* (1958). Standard account of early trade on the Santa Fe and Chihuahua Trails.

SINGLETARY, OTIS A. *The Mexican War* (1960). Brief history of the political, military, and diplomatic aspects of the war.

SMITH, GEORGE WINSTON, AND CHARLES, JUDAH, EDITORS. *Chronicles of the Gringos* (1968). Documentary history of the Mexican War based on eyewitness reports.

WEINBERG, ALBERT K., *Manifest Destiny* (1935). Classic account of the philosophy and practice of manifest destiny.

13

PLANTATION LIFE

The Ordeal
of Slavery

For more than two hundred years slavery shaped the lives of black Americans, and yet the slaves' story is one of the most elusive strands in American history. Few bondsmen left personal records, and observers of the "peculiar institution" have argued for a century and more about the slave experience. Southern apologists claimed that the "comforts" of the slave exceeded those of northern free laborers, whereas northern abolitionists decried slavery as cruel and degrading. Twentieth-century historians have continued the debate, some holding that slaves were well cared for, others exposing the brutality of the system. The harshness of slavery varied from plantation to plantation; the Pettigrew plantation in North Carolina was one of the less oppressive. Its management reveals, however, the cruelty of slavery in even its most benign form.

In June 1856 William S. Pettigrew, owner of two plantations in Tyrrell County, North Carolina, went to Healing Springs, Virginia, leaving his land and slaves under the direction of two black managers, Moses and Henry, with whom he corresponded regularly. The letters exchanged by the three men provide a rare glimpse of slave society. On the surface they merely portray common episodes in plantation management, but read more closely they suggest the variety and complexity of a way of life that continually intrigues and eludes the student of history.

William S. Pettigrew was thirty-eight in 1856. A bachelor and a law graduate of the University of North Carolina, he had begun in 1838 to manage his two plantations, Magnolia and Belgrade, and their eighty men, women, and children. He usually supervised the plantations himself, but during the hot months of the year he vacationed in the mineral springs region of Virginia. He was there in 1856 when he wrote home urging Moses, one of his slaves, to "promote the welfare and credit of Belgrade" during his absence. He reminded Moses of the people's promise to be "industrious and obedient" and mentioned that he relied wholly on him to keep the plantation running smoothly. After sending his respects to an ailing slave, Moses' Uncle Charles, the master closed with the words, "Your friend, William S. Pettigrew."

Moses could neither read nor write, and so Pettigrew directed his letters to a neighbor, Malachi White, who read them to Moses and Henry, the other black manager. White also transcribed the slaves' replies, apparently catching the phrasing as well as the content of their messages. Moses responded to this initial letter on July 5, expressing his pleasure at hearing from the master and reporting on the fieldwork. In the past month the people had been busy, planting 270 acres of corn and harvesting another crop. His uncle Charles had died, but, Moses hastened to add, the elderly slave had been well cared for and "nothing but his time moved him away from us."

On the same day Henry wrote Pettigrew with a report on Magnolia. "The hands has bin faithful to their duty," he wrote, "an all has agreed wel together." His people had planted 210 acres of corn before turning their attention to the harvest. Henry said that all his people were well, but Arry, sister of the recently deceased Charles, was grieving and wished she could see Pettigrew. Another servant, Lizzy, enclosed a note with those from Henry and Moses declaring her affection for her master. "I shall be glad to see master come home when maybe to his convenance," she wrote. "Ef I never should see master no more I hope we shall meat in heaven."

Pettigrew replied to these letters on July 12. He was grieved, he said, not to have been home when Uncle Charles died. "It is ever a comfort to me," he said, "to be present when my people make their departure for the land of Spirits." Pettigrew reminded Moses again of the importance of the trust he had bestowed upon him. He had shown Moses' letters to a friend, Mr. Johnston, who was also interested in his work. "You see from this, Moses . . . ," wrote Pettigrew, "that should things take an unfavorable turn, in consequence of my absence . . . you and all your people would not only be disgraced in my estimation, but also in his."

Moses and Henry appear to have worked hard to avoid any such disgrace. Subsequent letters show them attending diligently to plantation affairs: planting corn, potatoes, and wheat; gathering in the harvest; threshing the wheat; building fences and clearing irrigation ditches. They worried over rats in the barn and vandals in the plantation houses. They minded Pettigrew's affairs so effectively that on a later trip he was willing to leave them in charge for a full year. When Moses died after many seasons of good service, Pettigrew wrote his sister, "He is entitled to all that any one can say in his praise; and, as to my own feelings, I shall ever regard it a duty and a pleasure to cherish for his memory the highest respect."

The relationship between Pettigrew and his two black overseers was the sort southern whites regarded as the natural outgrowth of slavery. The black was a servant, to be sure, but he was also a companion. He belonged to a cohesive community in which the master and the slave were interdependent. Moses helped Pettigrew act his "part amidst the toils of life." Pettigrew trusted Moses and rewarded him for loyal service. Their relationship was apparently one in which mutual trust led to mutual benefits. Pettigrew wanted to believe that plantation society was just. So too, perhaps, did Moses. Were they right?

Because the Pettigrew letters are mostly about the business of plantation management they emphasize — even exaggerate — the cooperative side of the master-slave relationship. But if we look more closely, we can discern other facets of plantation experience, including the master's ambivalent attitude toward the slave, the character of the slave community, and the means by which slaves were kept in their place.

What were Pettigrew's real feelings about these human beings whom he owned? When he wrote to Moses and Henry he emphasized the trust he had bestowed upon them. He stressed the mutuality of their relationship: any failure on their part would disgrace the plantation as a whole. Because they were his friends as well as his servants, he sometimes wrote them details of his travels, just as he might write a fellow planter. He told Moses that when he went from Healing Springs to White Sulphur Springs in Virginia the trip took "but five days on the way, which was expeditious for so long a journey." He always closed his letters with the phrase, "Your friend." When Uncle Charles died, Pettigrew spoke eloquently of his warm regard for the slaves. "Our lot having been cast together here," he said, "and feeling that I am a friend and well wisher both for time and eternity to every one of them [the slaves], it is my wish to see the last of them and to accompany their lifeless bodies to the grave, that final resting place for us all."

In such phrases Pettigrew evoked the image of an organic society in which mutual love, rather than the brute fact of ownership, held master and servant together. Other letters suggest, however, that Pettigrew's expressions of warmth may have issued from a calculated effort to increase slave productivity rather than from genuine affection for his servants. "It has been my effort," he wrote a white friend, "since my business has been so much increased, to stimulate the principal men to be faithful to me." Pettigrew "stimulated" his overseers with praise and with gifts such as boots, greatcoats, and whips that called attention to their special position on the plantations. Kindness to the slaves was, in part at least, a matter of good business practice.

Such presents reveal an important element in the master-slave relationship — the function of the master as provider. Moses and Henry received special rewards for their work, but all the slaves received some provisions. Common sense dictated that if the slave were to work effectively he would have to be clothed, fed, and housed. The Pettigrew letters refer to shoes, hats, and blankets purchased for the slaves; the blacks were fed, largely from the produce of their own plantations, and were given a few luxuries, such as molasses from the West Indies; they received medical attention when ill.

The extent of these provisions is difficult to determine. We do not know how much food Pettigrew actually gave his slaves, how many blankets they slept beneath, or how warm their clothing was, but we can comprehend the range of possible treatment by considering contemporary and modern descriptions of the slave's condition. The southern apologists for slavery argued that the bondsman was better provided for than his northern counterpart, the wage earner. South Carolina Senator John C. Calhoun made this point in the 1830s in response to northern attacks on slavery. Calhoun argued that inequality was an inevitable product of liberty and was "indispensable to progress." "There never has yet existed a wealthy and civilized society," he said, "in which one portion of the community did not, in point of fact, live on the labor of the other." Northern wage labor and southern slavery were products of common political and economic forces. But of the two systems the latter was more humane because the master cared more for the slave that the employer for the employee. "Every plantation is a little community," said Calhoun, "with the master at its head, who concentrates in himself the united interests of capital and labor, of which he is the common representative." It was true that the slave did not have as much liberty as other men, but "liberty," argued Calhoun, "though among the greatest of blessings, is not so great as that of protection." The northerner had liberty but no protection. His employer bought his services cheap and cast him out on the street when he became old or infirm. The slave, in contrast, received support from his master until death.

Other southern writers reiterated this fundamental point: slavery provided better for the laborer than did capitalism. George Fitzhugh, one of the leading writers on slavery, declared that the northern laborer was underpaid by the businessman and cheated by the merchant. He bore "the whole weight of society" on his shoulders. In contrast, the master cared for the slave. "We provide for each slave," said Fitzhugh, "in old age and in infancy, in sickness and in health, not according to his labor, but according to his wants." The southern poet William J. Grayson described the benefits of slavery and even imagined the northern laborer wishing he were a slave himself:

If bound to daily labor while he lives,
His [the slave's] is the daily bread that labor gives;
Guarded from want, from beggary secure,
He never feels what hireling crowds endure,
Nor knows, like them, in hopeless want to crave,
For wife and child, the comforts of the slave.

If William Pettigrew ever read Grayson's poem, "The Hireling and the Slave," he would undoubtedly have nodded in approval at its description of the benevolent master. Had he not done his part to provide for "the comforts of the slave?" He supplied his people with food, shelter, clothing, and medical care, and even set aside time for recreation. In 1856 he gave Moses a free hand to allow the people "such time on Saturdays as you think proper." He let them take holidays after the corn was harvested and the wheat threshed. He must have felt that he was just the sort of benevolent master who won the praise of Calhoun, Fitzhugh, Grayson, and others.

But other writers in this period painted a less favorable picture of the typical slaveholder's behavior. In the abolitionist view, the master-slave relationship resulted in continual mistreatment of the black. The master was not a benevolent guardian but a greedy opportunist. The slave was constantly abused, because he lacked the ability to bargain for fair wages or move elsewhere for better work. Henry Highland Garnet, a black abolitionist, described the southern masters as "heartless tyrants, who give you no other reward but stripes and abuse." Harriett Beecher Stowe, whose novel *Uncle Tom's Cabin* became the most famous

American indictment of slavery, described a slave who had earned $200 for his master but was allowed to keep only 50 cents for himself.

Clearly the bondsman could not sell his services as a free man might. He did, however, receive food, shelter, and clothing; and by working hard he could receive extra responsibilities and rewards — the whip was not the only incentive to labor. Some blacks became managers, drivers, house servants, or skilled craftsmen. Field hands often received small garden plots on which to raise their own crops.

Whether these "comforts" equaled those of the northern laborer is, however, another question. Modern historians believe that in many respects the slave was adequately maintained. The slave diet was generous and nutritious, the plantation producing beef, mutton, pork, chickens, milk, turnips, peas, sweet potatoes, apples, plums, oranges, and other foods. Slaves could supplement their diet by hunting and fishing and growing crops in their own gardens. The food provided many times the average daily vitamin supply recommended by modern nutritionists.

In other respects, too, the slaves were well maintained. The typical slavehouse in the late antebellum period was a cabin measuring about eighteen by twenty feet and divided into two rooms. These structures provided considerably more room than the tenement apartments inhabited by white laborers in New York a half century later. The slaves were sufficiently if not generously clothed, and they were given the best possible health care. As a result of good food, shelter, clothing, and medical attention, slaves actually enjoyed a higher life expectancy than that of urban white laborers in the late antebellum period.

Historians today generally agree that slaves were reasonably well maintained on most plantations, primarily because the slave was a valuable commodity. It was in the master's interest to keep the slave alive, healthy, and productive. But many scholars regard the picture of prosperous slaves as an exaggeration. Infant mortality was, for example, twice as high among blacks as whites, and many masters sought to maximize slave output while reducing costs for food and clothing. Most slaves were probably given only enough "comforts" to make them efficient workers. Pettigrew's slaves did not suffer from acute malnutrition, but significantly, the few cases of misbehavior among the slaves on his plantation usually involved food theft.

Along with its physical effect, slavery affected the social and psychological condition of blacks. To a degree, the slaves were able to preserve an independent culture even as bondsmen. The correspondence between Pettigrew, Moses, and Henry gives hints of a quasi-independent, semihidden slave community — of an Afro-American culture that existed mainly on its own terms, despite the fact of enslavement. The leading institution in this community was the family.

There are many references in the Pettigrew papers to family ties. Moses is saddened when his uncle Charles dies, and Charles's sister Arry on Pettigrew's other plantation also grieves. Moses has an aunt named Gilly and a cousin named Glascow. A slave named Affy has a son, Allen, and several grandchildren on the plantations. Undoubtedly there were many other kinship ties at Magnolia and Belgrade.

The character of the southern slave family has long been a matter of dispute among historians. It was once assumed that loss of personal freedom must have inhibited growth of strong kinship ties among the blacks, but scholars have discovered that on many plantations the slave family was a strong, vital institution. Not only did it provide for the physical needs of children, but it also "socialized" the young people, passing on to them a distinctive Afro-American culture. The young slave, in other words, absorbed his culture from his fellow blacks as well as from his white masters.

In its organization, the black family was not merely the mirror of the white family; it shows evidence of the continuity of African familial traditions in the New World environment. Slaves, for example, normally avoided marrying cousins, whereas their masters did not. They carried on the African tradition of assigning a special position to grandparents, naming children after them and allowing them to help raise the new generation. They also followed African tradition in honoring other kin, notably cousins, uncles, and aunts.

Certainly plantation life created special problems for the slave family. One could not easily visit relatives who lived on other plantations or write to kinsmen who had been sold to distant owners. Although masters generally respected slave marriages — in fact, the slave family was stronger in the United States than in many other New World slaveholding countries mostly because American masters encouraged slave unions — planter lust or hardship sometimes interfered with the black family. The incidence of sexual intercourse between masters and slaves is probably much lower than suggested by popular fiction, because the dominant moral code held that the planter should remain faithful to his own wife. But in many instances the planter's absolute authority over the slave proved an irresistible temptation to wander. In 1860 one slave in ten had some white blood. Sometimes planter-slave alliances ripened into love affairs; sometimes they led a promiscuous planter to form virtual harems of slaves; sometimes they constituted only fleeting alliances. But the possibility of such intrusion into their world must have had a demoralizing effect on slaves who wanted to control their own familial destinies.

An even greater threat to the slave family was the possibility that its members might be sold off the plantation. Economic necessity could compel even the most benevolent master to sell some of his slaves. In the late antebellum period the high price paid for slaves in the prosperous new southwestern states tempted many masters to dispose of their slaves for ready cash. The effects on a slave family were devastating. In one moment a human relationship nourished over many years might be destroyed by the inexorable decree of the slave market. The letter of a Georgia slave, Abream Scriven, who was sold from his Georgia plantation in 1858, reveals the human cost of such a transaction:

> My dear wife,
>
> I take the pleasure of writing you these few [lines] with much regret to inform you that I am Sold to a man by the name of Peterson a treader and Stays in new orleans. I am here yet But I expect to go before long but when I get there I will write and let you know where I am. My Dear I want to Send you Some things but I do not know who to Send them by but I will thry to get them to you and my children. Give my love to my father and mother and tell them good Bye for me. and if we Shall not meet in this world I hope to meet in heaven. My Dear wife for you and my children my pen cannot Express the griffe I feel to be parted from you all.
>
> > I remain
> > your truly husband until Death
> > Abream Scriven

The strong attachment revealed in this letter was common in slave families. One of the foremost reasons for fleeing enslavement was the desire to be reunited with kin sold to other plantations. After emancipation, the roads of the South were crowded with freemen seeking lost relations. And among slaves who were bereft of their kin, it was common to designate honorary uncles and grandparents to fill a familial role.

The strength of the Afro-American community revealed in the slave family was apparent also in black folk culture — religion, music, and folktales. Slave piety was so notable that whites sometimes chastened themselves for failing to match the religious fervor of the blacks. The actual character of slave religiosity is, however, difficult to determine. The Pettigrew correspondence is filled with conventional religious sentiments: Moses hopes that with "the help of God" the corn crop will be good; Pettigrew speaks of the grave as "that final resting place for us all"; and Lizzy writes that she hopes to meet Pettigrew in Heaven.

Beneath these rather common sentiments lay a strain of Christian piety that both supported and challenged the slave system. Christianity taught submission to authority and trained blacks to regard the hardships of this life as insignificant burdens on the road to a glorious life in heaven. The masters hoped that in such ways it would help the slaves accept their bondage. But Christianity also taught the slave his or her own self-worth. The notion of the spiritual equality of souls implicitly contradicted the idea that the slave was inherently inferior and destined to perpetual servitude. The most distinctive thread in black Christianity was a desire for release from bondage. Pettigrew's servant Moses bore the name of a biblical hero whom the slaves revered almost as much as Christ himself. The original Moses was the great secular deliverer; he had led real people away from real bondage. A powerful hymn celebrated his triumph:

> Go down, Moses,
> Way down to Egypt land.
> Tell old Pharaoh
> To let my people go.

Moses and other biblical figures were especially real to the slaves because theirs was an oral culture. Mostly illiterate, they imbibed their religion through the drama of sermons and songs.

Among slaves the Christian religion thus promised escape from bondage even while extolling obedience to authority. Other strains of black culture functioned even more explicitly to nurture a sense of Afro-American community. Historians have long suspected that some elements of African culture must have survived the violent uprooting and transporting of the slave. In a few regions of the South, distinctive African tongues, such as the Gullah dialect of the Georgia Sea Islands, endured the Atlantic crossing. Traces of black religion appeared on some plantations in the person of the conjurer, who could win favors for clients with magic. Black folktales and songs reveal that slaves created a distinct culture containing both European and African elements. Clever stories about animals, for example, subtly revealed the rapacity and stupidity of rulers and celebrated the trickster hero who managed to outwit his "betters" despite his apparent weakness.

If such tales circulated on the Pettigrew plantations — as indeed they must have — they did not find their way into the letters from Moses and Henry to their master. These planter-servant communications took place on the safe ground of common economic interest and abstract religious ideas. Pettigrew probably did not bother about what the slaves said to one another in their cabins. As long as slaves were obedient, it mattered little what ideas or dreams circulated in the hidden recesses of their minds.

If he had been asked to describe the black mentality, he would probably have said that his slaves were simpler and more emotional than white people. The black was regarded as racially inferior to the white. It was thought that God intended him to live as a servant to his master's will. The right-minded slave would be satisfied with the culture, the social role, and the daily bread his master gave him. His life was defined by the mutual obligations of black and white men — faithful labor from the servant, ample provisions from the planter.

Clearly, however, the slave was something more than the reflection of his master's will; he was not simply a tablet bearing the image etched upon it by his owner. But if he was indeed a vital human being, full of intelligence and resourcefulness, why did he accept his inferior status? Why did he not rise up against his masters? Certainly there were some rebellions — slaves who murdered their masters or joined others in flight or battle. In 1831 the most famous of these rebels, Nat Turner, led an uprising in which fifty-seven whites were killed. But such episodes were an exception to the normal pattern of black behavior under slavery. Revolts were far more common and bloody among the slaves in Latin America.

One explanation for the apparent black acceptance of bondage is that the slave system was so brutal that it completely warped the black personality, making the bondsman a childlike, irresponsible creature who identified perversely with his master. This interpretation might explain the rarity of slave revolts but hardly does justice to the slave personality or culture in the antebellum South. The strength of the black community belies the notion that slaves were totally demoralized by their situation.

Their "acceptance" of slavery was a practical necessity; even in the South they were outnumbered two to one. They were, for the most part, unarmed, and had little opportunity to communicate from one region to another. Acts of resistance were punished swiftly and brutally. Even lesser forms of resistance, such as running away, were dangerous. To escape they must make their way through a hostile country, hardly knowing in what direction the North was or what to expect there if they managed to arrive. Equally troubling, flight would separate them from the only black community they knew. If a slave sought to flee with wife, children, parents, aunts, and uncles, their capture would be inevitable. But if he left them behind, freedom would lose its luster. Resistance to slavery was not a practical option for most blacks.

But if open opposition was unthinkable, widening the margins of freedom was not. Even in the Pettigrew correspondence we can see slaves expanding personal initiative, sometimes even at the master's instigation. Pettigrew was clearly in charge of Belgrade and Magnolia, and Moses and Henry were his servants, but he realized that he could not obtain their best work by commanding them to work efficiently. He felt it necessary to flatter and reward them for their services. The relationship was similar to that between a manager and his hired men. Pettigrew frequently trusted Moses and Henry to undertake complex tasks. One summer he wrote Moses asking him to clear out a creekbed. He and Henry should decide what obstructions needed to be removed, what part of the plantation work force should be assigned to the project, and whether to buy extra ropes for the job. The very position of Moses and Henry on the Pettigrew estates — they were black men who ran their own plantations for months at a time — testifies to the willingness of whites to allow slaves to realize their full potential as long as that fulfillment served the master's needs. On such occasions it must have been convenient for owners to forget their pronouncements on black inferiority.

There were, nonetheless, episodes that continually defined the boundaries of slave behavior. In one case Moses acted on behalf of Pettigrew in limiting Henry's initiative. Henry had come to Belgrade and asked for some brandy, claiming that Pettigrew had said he might have some. But Moses told his owner that he had refused. "You know Master," said he, "that Brandy is a veary particular thing" — so "particular," it seemed to Moses, that it would never be allowed to a slave.

Slaves tested the limits of their freedom in many ways. A woman named Affy was allowed to visit a friend, but Pettigrew would not let her take her grandchildren along for fear that the journey might weaken their health. A younger woman, Venus, sneaked off to meet a man named Terry on a nearby plantation and was apprehended by a patrol at 2:00 A.M. Affy's request to travel with her grandchildren and Venus's efforts to carry on a romance were comparatively minor transgressions. Pettigrew was considerably more worried by the behavior of a slave named Frank Buck, who cut a trapdoor under the lard-and-meat house at Belgrade and feasted for several months before he was discovered. A few years later he stole $160 worth of gold and silver from Pettigrew and ran away with four field hands, telling suspicious whites along the way that he was on an official errand to capture a fugitive slave.

Pettigrew dealt with misbehavior in a number of ways. Sometimes a simple no or a scolding was sufficient. For more serious crimes he withdrew privileges — canceling the offenders' holidays or cutting off their molasses ration. When Frank Buck and his fellow runaways were apprehended — as inevitably they were — they were whipped and imprisoned.

When he thought it necessary, then, Pettigrew could apply force to define the boundaries of behavior on his plantation community. But he did not like to use force, nor did he like to think of his people as a community in bondage. As in any other society, punishment might sometimes be necessary to keep recalcitrant souls in line, but — as in a civil society — the fundamental unity of the plantations came about ideally from a sense of mutual obligation. Or so Pettigrew and thousands of other plantation owners liked to think.

Thus, his letters are full of allusions to the communal nature of his association with the slaves. Moses and Henry are his "friends." He wants them to promote the "welfare and credit" of the plantations. He speaks of "our lot having been cast here together." Frank Buck's transgression in running away with four other slaves seemed to him a disgrace upon the whole community. He recommended to Moses and Henry that they keep the slaves close to home for the immediate future on the grounds that "If I were they, I would be ashamed to be seen away from home after the plantation has been so disgraced by those criminals." We must depend upon one another, he seemed to say, to uphold the virtue of our little world.

Moses, Henry, and most of the other slaves appear to have acquiesced to a degree in this communal rhetoric. Moses apparently took pride in reporting to Pettigrew that the people "has been faithful and dutiful." The slaves told Pettigrew they wanted to see him, sent him their greetings, and hoped to meet him in heaven. "I take a delight in writing to master my love," says Moses, "all the people wishes their love to master hoping master is well."

Such expressions of affection for a plantation lord seem curious to a later age. We naturally listen to the words with skepticism and try to find a hidden meaning between the lines. The slaves would not tell Pettigrew so, but they would undoubedly have preferred to be free; and although probably he was but vaguely aware of it, they had many cultural and familial attachments that transcended the confines of the plantation. Yet the plantation was their home: it was where they worked, played, worshiped, reared their families. Real affection sometimes did develop between planters and slaves. And they both *wanted* to believe that it was a just society.

Blacks as well as whites tried to believe in the plantation utopia. Pettigrew, Henry, and Moses played the game as it was supposed to be played. They tried to believe that they lived under a mutually beneficial, even a voluntaristic arrangement. It is difficult if not impossible to discover the real feelings behind these professions of mutual affection. They may have been calculated to win favor. They may have been exercises in self-deception, each side wanting to believe that the system was just. Or they may have expressed genuine affection. Probably all three motives were at work.

But despite the rhetoric of acquiescence and communality, blacks never fully accepted slavery. Pettigrew must have sensed the frailty of the structure, its vulnerability to vital forces in a larger world. He tells Moses he prefers that his slaves not associate too freely with slaves on other plantations. "As long as there is a mingling-up of people on different plantations," he says, "there must ever be trouble."

Pettigrew wanted the plantation to be a static rural utopia. But the slaves knew a longing — which they themselves sought often to suppress — for a freer life: for a world in which Affy could show off her grandchildren to an old friend, Henry could buy his own brandy, and Terry and Venus could court as they pleased. They and the four million other slaves in the antebellum South did not talk of such things to their masters. They sometimes even sought to believe in the rectitude of their rulers.

If, however, you visited even such humane planters as William Pettigrew, you could hear the rattling of chains along with the professions of mutual affection. And if you listened closely to the slaves singing a familiar Christian hymn, you could hear the hidden sorrow and the passionate urgency that rumbled behind that mournful refrain, "Let my people go."

QUESTIONS

1. William Pettigrew often expressed concern for the welfare of his slaves. Cite examples and discuss whether his solicitude reflected genuine regard for the slaves or cynical manipulation of their feelings.

2. Pettigrew's slaves often expressed affection for him. Cite examples and consider whether their affection was genuine or contrived.

3. What, according to Pettigrew and other apologists for slavery, was the character of the plantation community?

4. William J. Grayson wrote a poem about the "comforts of the slave." What evidence supports and what evidence contradicts his view that slaves were well cared for? Even if it could be shown that slaves were better fed, housed, and clothed than northern wage earners, would slavery be preferable to freedom?

5. In what ways were slaves able to maintain control over their social and cultural lives? In what ways did slavery damage their families and traditions? What was the character and importance of the slave family?

6. If slaves didn't accept their condition, why weren't there more slave revolts?

7. In what ways could you hear the "rattling of the chains" on the

Pettigrew plantation? In what ways did Pettigrew's slaves show their longing for freedom?

8. "Liberty," John C. Calhoun argued, "though among the greatest of blessings, is not so great as that of protection." Would most Americans in the 1830s, or today, agree with Calhoun's statement?

9. What was "the rhetoric on acquiescence and communality"?

BIBLIOGRAPHY

BLASSINGAME, JOHN W. *The Slave Community* (1972). Description of slave society based largely on the slave narratives.

ELKINS, STANLEY M. *Slavery* (1959). Argues that slavery reduced bondsmen to childlike condition.

FOGEL, ROBERT W., AND STANLEY L. ENGERMAN. *Time on the Cross: The Economics of American Negro Slavery* (1974). Controversial study reporting material comforts of the slave.

GENOVESE, EUGENE D. *Roll, Jordon, Roll* (1975). Describes a "black nation" in the slave South based on familial and religious ties.

GUTMAN, HERBERT G. *Black Family in Slavery and Freedom* (1976). Extensive analysis of the black family.

HUGGINS, NATHAN I. *Black Odyssey* (1977). Evocative description of black experience in slavery and freedom.

JORDON, WINTHROP. *White over Black* (1968). Historical roots of American prejudice toward blacks.

LEVINE, LAWRENCE W. *Black Culture and Black Consciousness* (1977). Survival of African culture in black America.

McKITRICK, ERIC L., EDITOR. *Slavery Defended* (1963). Anthology of southern statements justifying slavery.

STAMPP, KENNETH M. *The Peculiar Institution* (1956). Fine survey of the slave system.

STAROBIN, ROBERT S. *Blacks in Bondage: Letters of American Slaves* (1974). Includes letters between William S. Pettigrew and his slaves, Moses and Henry.

14

THE CIVIL WAR

Two Soldiers
and Their Worlds

During the American Revolution, Loyalist opponents of independence had claimed that the colonists could never create a unified
nation because the economic and cultural differences between North
and South would lead to civil strife. But the two sections were able
to lay aside their differences while they fought the Revolutionary
War, drafted the Constitution, and began the new government.
Even as they cooperated in some enterprises, however, they disagreed over tariffs, slavery, and western lands, widening the breach
that Tories had discerned almost a century before. In 1861 antagonism between the two sections exploded into war, each side
believing in the righteousness of its cause. The Civil War revealed
the depths of sectional antagonism, but it demonstrated also the
underlying similarities between the sections. The careers of William Wheeler and Charles Colcock Jones, Jr., personify both the
brutality of warfare and the common humanity of North and South.

The Civil War occupies a unique position in American history. No event, not even the Revolution, holds a higher place in the national regard. Its battles were the bloodiest ever fought on American soil, and its people were at once the most human and resourceful of our heroes. The names of its events and leaders read like a patriotic litany: Abraham Lincoln, Ulysses S. Grant, William Tecumseh Sherman, Thomas ("Stonewall") Jackson, Robert E. Lee; the Gettysburg Address and the Emancipation Proclamation; the *Monitor* and the *Merrimack*; and the Battles of Bull Run, Antietam, Chancellorsville, Gettysburg, Vicksburg, and the Wilderness. The history of the war includes stories of recruitment, war industries, supplies, military leadership, politics, diplomacy, and civilian morale. It is really not one tale but many separate histories, each complex and elusive.

The Civil War can, however, be reduced to human scale by the very soldiers who fought in it. Each had his own history, personal experiences that reflected in some fashion the larger forces of the war. Although most soldiers left no record of their thoughts and activities beyond the brief notice they received in troop lists, casualty reports, and other public records, some wrote diaries and letters that allow us to observe closely their personal histories. Two such men were William Wheeler, captain of New York's Thirteenth Artillery and Charles Colcock Jones, Jr., lieutenant colonel of the Georgia Artillery. Their Civil War letters help explain why northerners and southerners took arms against one another and describe how they spent their days during the hard years of the war.

In spring 1864 William Wheeler was an artillery captain in a northern army marching toward Atlanta, Georgia, under the command of William Tecumseh Sherman. Wheeler had been in the army for three years and fought at the Second Battle of Bull Run, Chancellorsville, Gettsyburg, and Chattanooga. The army had become so much his way of life that after his infrequent leaves he actually enjoyed returning to camp. Recently back from a trip home he wrote his mother that he rejoined his men with "a quiet feeling of satisfaction and contentment, a happiness in being back at my work again."

In 1864 Wheeler was a seasoned professional, a soldier's soldier. We can understand him and his work best if we look at his early years as a civilian and as a raw recruit. William Wheeler was born in New York City on August 14, 1836. He developed an early interest in literature, reading when he was four and improvising stories to entertain neighborhood children when he was eight. Wheeler absorbed literature easily and could recall lines from Shakespeare, the Latin and Greek classics, and contemporary poetry. He developed a love of outdoors and became a skilled fisherman, catching seventy-two trout as a boy on a two-day trip to the Catskill Mountains.

In 1852, at age sixteen, he entered Yale College. His undergraduate letters combine prudery and playfulness. As a freshman he wrote home that four older boys had been "caught in the interesting occupation of cementing up the bell." His mother "need not fear" that he would be found in any such "scrapes." On a "stupendously cold" morning in January, he wrote her, "The fire itself froze the other morning. I would send you a piece, but . . . fear it would burn a hole in the paper." In fall 1854 when he was a senior, he attempted to grow whiskers; finding, however, that his beard's "powers of increasing were exactly the opposite of Jack's bean-stalk," he gave it up.

At college William Wheeler enjoyed his studies and nature equally. He excelled in classics and mathematics and formed a "secret society" for scholars. He observed closely the patterns of nature around the college — the spring when green and purple mosses came out upon the hills; the fall when the thick woods seemed painted by "unearthly artists, in earth-surpassing colors"; and the winter when he took sleigh rides over the snow through the valley between East and West Rocks, two hills that overlooked New Haven "like ermine-clad giants."

After completing his undergraduate program he studied law at Yale until 1857, then made a grand tour of Europe, a common post-graduate activity for well-to-do young men of his day. Wheeler's zest for life, his most appealing quality, was especially evident in his letters on the trip. His sailing ship, *Australia,* ran into a storm of rain, wind, and mountainous waves; while other passengers cringed in fear, Wheeler found that the threat of destruction gave the sea "a more sublime and lofty" character and reminded him of his "own littleness in comparison with this greatest of God's works." When the sea was calm on the long journey, he loved to watch the "snowy canvass" of the great sails, the moonlight's "flood of glory" on the water, and the glow of phosphorescence shining in the sea "like stars rolled out" of an angel's cloak.

Wheeler delighted in such scenes. He was drawn also to literary and historical grandeur. As the *Australia* sailed past Gibraltar into the Mediterranean, he thought of the great seamen whose keels had "furrowed" these waters. Here the fleets of Rome and Greece had fought, the Crusaders had sailed for the Holy Land, and Nelson had won the Battle of Trafalgar. And now along their path came William Wheeler, "not to strike a blow for Grecian or Italian Independence, but bound for Marseilles, in the merchant ship *Australia* consigned to Ribaud Brothers & Co., and oh! horror, laden with alcohol (I smell it now), stores, wheat, and bacon." Despite his amusement at the common circumstances of his arrival in Europe, Wheeler made the most of his year abroad, hiking through the Swiss Alps; studying in Berlin; and visiting Paris, Florence, and London.

He returned to America in 1858 and resumed his legal studies at Harvard. After graduating in 1860, he moved to New York where he took an apartment and studied for the bar, alternately reading Shakespeare's plays and legal tomes to fight the sleep-inducing effects of "cramming up the Revised Statutes" for his examination.

Wheeler was absorbed by the year's political events. In fall 1860 he was intensely interested in the outcome of the presidential election. Describing himself frankly as belonging to "the extreme Abolition edge of the Republican party," he worked hard for the election of Abraham Lincoln. As the outcome of the election became clear and the southern states began to move toward secession, Wheeler actually hoped for war so that slavery could be ended once and for all. If a civil war occurred, he wrote, "then the country will emerge from that chaos of fire and blood, fresh and free, its dross purged away, and its great sin expiated." As the conflict drew near he decided that he would join the army rather than hire a substitute, as many wealthy young men did. "I do not suppose that I am very well fitted for a soldier," he wrote, "but still I have a good deal of fight in me, and think that I shall never see a holier cause to fight for."

That spring, New York City was ablaze with patriotism, recruits marching up and down to the sound of fife and drum and the streets "a long arbor of flags." Full of excitement and hoping not to miss the first engagements of the war, Wheeler joined the Seventh Regiment in New York; purchased a uniform, blankets, and mess kit; and had his hair cut to regulation length. On May 9 he boarded the steamer *Mantanzas.* having written his mother, "For myself, I cannot see how a life could be more worthily given up, unless it were for God's sake, though is not this God's cause?" He was twenty-four years old, a practicing lawyer; a scholar proficient in Latin, Greek, Hebrew, German, and French; and now a soldier going forth on his greatest adventure.

The soldiers aboard the *Mantanzas* were crazed with exuberance, and Wheeler feared that "the younger ones seem to look upon the whole affair as a gigantic spree, and to form no true conception of the serious character of the undertaking." Yet it was Wheeler who led the men in giving three cheers when the steamer passed a ship bearing the Italian flag "under which Garibaldi achieved the freedom of Italy." Soon afterward he and the others cheered an English ship called the *Union* and joined in singing verse after verse of "The Star-Spangled Banner." The next day the spirit of patriotism was still ablaze as the ship streamed up the Potomac past Mount Vernon, her flag at half-mast, her bell tolling, and her men standing respectfully with heads uncovered, a traditional sign of respect for George Washington.

On May 14 Wheeler was stationed at Camp Cameron, the first of dozens of posts where he would spend the next three years sleeping in tents, makeshift cabins, and beneath the stars. When his regiment made camp on its long marches and countermarches in Virginia, Tennessee, and Georgia, the soldiers normally slept under canvas, a perfectly adequate arrangement when the elements were at rest. But there were nights when gales ripped through the camp and Wheeler's tent "rocked like a boat on the waves." In the winter the shelters became so cold that "the only way was to lie [in bed] and take it." After a particularly cold night Wheeler wrote home, "ten degrees below zero is not exactly comfortable in a tent." To make matters worse the fragile dwellings caught fire with alarming regularity.

The more resourceful soldiers made an occupation of improving their tents. Sometimes Wheeler had stone fireplaces built in his, using pork barrels as chimneys and lining the floors with boards. But such efforts were often frustrated by the need to move on, and moving frequently meant sleeping outdoors. Wheeler rather liked the camping out, even in the cold, when he could lie beside a roaring fire with the stars overhead. But when he had to sleep in the rain and the mud, then, he said, "the fun ceases to be perceptible."

The food was no better than the shelter. Men often had nothing more than crackers and coffee for breakfast and supper, with meat and soup for lunch. Worse, there were days of "salt horse and hard bisquit." On good days the diet might be improved with mutton or chicken purchased or stolen from southern farmers, but on bad days Wheeler had to make do with a handful of horse's grain, a meal he called "maize au naturel." Worn down by poor shelter and food, he wrote his mother that he had become "a shabby, muddy soldier."

Wheeler and others attempted to improve the tone of camp life with ceremonies, song, and even learning. On Christmas Eve in 1862, when the regiment was camped near the Stafford courthouse in Virginia, he went out into the woods and found "a most beautiful little holly-tree, with splendid leaves and full of berries," which he planted at the foot of a flagpole. In the war's early months, before he became disillusioned with the army chaplains, he organized well-attended prayer meetings at which the men sang "ever so many hymns." He enjoyed, too, the songs men sung by campfires. Wheeler's men, mainly German immigrants, sang fine old songs from their fatherland, while black servants sang camp-meeting tunes, "in a minor and melancholy key."

Such moments softened the hard outlines of camp life. Wheeler

Civil War encampment. Yankee and Confederate soldiers slept in crude huts of canvas and wood, often with pork-barrel chimneys.

sought also to uplift his surroundings by establishing a school for the soldiers. The schoolhouse was a collection of desks and chairs made from split logs and arranged around a tree; the teacher, an old corporal chosen by Wheeler; the pupils, "rough, wild" enlisted men, many of whom did not know how to read. Some forty men came to classes of their own accord, and Wheeler hoped they would soon sign their own payroll slips. But before he could strike a blow for literacy, the regiment had to move on again, leaving behind its latest encampment and Wheeler's improvised school.

Despite the disruption of each move, Wheeler generally welcomed the chance to break camp. "I am twice as buoyant, and hopeful, and happy," he wrote his mother, "on a hard march, as when vegetating in camp." Wheeler especially liked traveling through the mountainous parts of Virginia where the soldiers "went fishing, blackberrying, and cherry-picking, and where at times it seemed more like a charming summer picnic 'long drawn out' than anything else." Pleasant, too, was the train journey from Virginia to Tennessee on the Baltimore & Ohio Railroad, through the "mysterious lights and shadows of a perfect moonlight autumn night," and across Indiana where the citizens cheered the soldiers at each stop and ladies gave them cake, cold meats, doughnuts, handkerchiefs, towels, and soap. In such moments the whole war seemed a glorious adventure, made all the more exciting by "the inspiring prospect of a conflict with an enemy a few miles ahead."

Wheeler's regiment was never required to wait long for that next engagement. For two years they fought indecisive skirmishes and battles in Virginia. Then one day in 1863 the army began to move north, following Robert E. Lee into Pennsylvania. The men, who had lived for months amid the hostility of the southern populace, were stunned by their reception as they marched through Frederick County, Maryland. Children waved handkerchiefs and tiny flags; hotels were wrapped in red, white, and blue bunting; an old lady stood at her door handing out cups of cold water to thirsty soldiers; her gray-haired husband stood at her side, his eyes half filled with tears. "Good luck to you boys," he murmured, "God bless you."

On the morning of July 1 Wheeler's artillery battery was eleven miles from Gettysburg, Pennsylvania, moving along at a deliberate pace, when a messenger arrived urging speed. They flew toward the town, gun carriages rattling and bouncing over the stony road, food and kettles breaking loose from the caissons, and cannoneers running to keep up. When they reached Gettysburg, tens of thousands of men in gray and blue were gathering their forces in a vast pattern of artillery, infantry, and cavalry. Wheeler's battery rushed from one point to another in this scene of noise, movement, and confusion. Hurrying through town, they passed ladies waving handkerchiefs and cheering them on and stopped at a place called Cemetery Hill, where the Union forces concentrated their artillery.

During the next three days the two armies mauled one another with cannon, rifle, and bayonet. Lee unleashed the greatest artillery barrage ever known in America. "The air," said Wheeler, "was literally alive with flying projectiles." Cemetery Hill was hit with a hailstorm of shot, ranging from six-pound missiles the size of cricket balls to Whitworth rifled shot, so huge they gave "rise to the story of the rebs firing railroad iron." Most dangerous of all were the Confederate charges that drove right in among the Union ranks. When the enemy came close, and the Federal infantry drew back leaving the artillery dangerously exposed, Wheeler abandoned the large shells used against the Confederate artillery and aimed small canister shot at the infantry.

"Wheeler," said another officer, "which *are* the rebels and which are our men?"

"You pays your money," said Wheeler. "and you takes your choice."

The Confederates were driven back, then and in other efforts to break the Union lines. Both armies rested on July 4, and the next day Lee began the dismal march back to Virginia. He had failed to win the northern victory that would have meant so much to his cause.

William Wheeler's role at the Battle of Gettysburg was like that of hundreds of other junior officers. He stuck to his post, opposed the enemy advance, and kept up a strong fire. He was a minor actor in an epic drama. Yet he loved his role. "Somehow or other," he told his friends at home, "I felt a joyous exaltation, a perfect indifference to circumstances, through the whole of that three days' fight, and have seldom enjoyed three days more in my life."

Strange words, perhaps, for a man who admired the classics, led prayer meetings, and established a camp school. But battle had become a way of life to Wheeler. Not that he was unaffected by suffering; in his mind he carried images of the devastation of war: trees speckled with bullets and bored through by shells; a fellow artillery officer killed when a shell plowed through his horse; an infantry-man's leg, blown off at Gettysburg, whirling "through the air like a stone, until it came against a caisson with a loud whack." Worse still was the sight of his own men hospitalized with mortal wounds. One of the hardest to bear was a "fine-looking young Irishman, with a . . . deep susceptibility to both pain and pleasure," whom Wheeler visited in the hospital. "One of his wounds had affected the nerves," he wrote, "and the pain came in great wrenches and spasms that made him gnash his teeth and beat his feet on the bed in agony. I became so sick that I could hardly get to the door."

Despite his familiarity with the reality of injury and death, Wheeler appears to have had few worries about his own fate. He admitted that he felt anxiety at the approach to battle, before his guns were in place. He said that he "would prefer to be either in the midst of the affair or else entirely absent." When he had to set up his guns while the enemy was firing at him, he felt "unpleasantly"; but once the battery was ready and he was busy loading, aiming, and firing, his chief sensation was excitement. He enjoyed the challenge of his work as well as "the sense of bodily danger and of continual escape from it." In these engagements, death and injury were so common as to be unintimidating. At Gettysburg, he wrote, "the danger was so great and so constant that, at last, it took away the sense of danger." Wheeler even found that he slept especially well on the night before a battle. When conflict was inevitable, one might as well rest.

Different men accommodated to battle in various ways. Some were armed with the giddy assurance that they could never be shot. Others refused to speculate about their prospective fortunes. Wheeler's resolution came from another source — the certitude that he *would* be killed. In the first years of the war he had looked at the magnitude of the conflict and concluded that almost everyone who stayed in the army for the duration would die. In 1861 he wrote home, "This is emphatically a war deadly to officers, and I have fully made up my mind never to see any of you again." In the next year he predicted that "few of the army now in the field will ever see their homes again; the new conscripts will win the glory of finishing the war." He disliked thinking about the possibility of survival, because such imaginings weakened his resolve. "I prefer to accept the belief that I *must* fall," he wrote. "The question with us is not whether we shall die or not, but how we shall die and among what surroundings."

The expectation that he would die a soldier in the field intensified his relationship to the army. It was, quite literally, his life's work. "My battery," he told his cousin, "is my plighted bride." His weapons, a half dozen three-inch rifled guns, were to him "as a sweetheart, yea, as many sweethearts." When he lost one of his guns in an engagement at Gettysburg, he went out on the field after the battle, found the gun, and repaired it, glad in the recovery of an old friend. He was equally fond of his horse, who ate sugar from his hand, followed him like a dog, and bore the name Barry after Wheeler's artillery chief. Then, too, there was the pleasure of leadership. When he was elevated from the rank of lieutenant to a captaincy in 1863, he wrote home, "I like to have the command of men, and to say, like the centurion, 'Go! and he goeth.' "

As much as Wheeler enjoyed the craft of artilleryman, the war's purpose excited him more than its process. He called himself an "extreme Emancipationist" determined to see the end of slavery. Men fought in the Civil War for many reasons: some because they were drafted, others for adventure, others to save the Union. Wheeler, and soldiers like him, fought with the moral fervor of medieval knights on a Crusade, their goal the eradication of slavery. The war, he told his mother, "has become the religion of very many of our lives, and those of us who think, and who did not enter the service for gain of military distinction, have come more and more to identify this cause for which we are fighting, with all of good and religion in our previous lives." His hero was Grant, whom he called "a steam engine in pantaloons." He had no patience with men who gave sparingly for the cause and rejoiced when the timorous McClellan, a "softy warrior," was dismissed from command. Disgusted at the news of draft riots in New York City, he proposed a simple solution: he would set up his battery at a place on Broadway he knew where "the balls would ricochet splendidly on the hard pavement."

The Union cause simply must prevail. It was to him "the same that the quest of the Holy Grail was to Sir Galahad." He would endeavor, like Tennyson's Ulysses, "to strive, to seek, to find, and not to yield." After Gettysburg he acknowledged that the war might last many years, but he and his fellows would endure. "I am, in this matter," he said, "like St. Paul's Charity, ready to bear, believe, hope, and endure all things for the cause, knowing that if we do, we also, like Charity, shall never fail."

Wheeler was able to inspire others with his enthusiasm. He said little about his influence, but his men seem to have rallied around him in many circumstances: on the battlefield, in hymn singing, or in the creation of a school. When time came for reenlistment early in 1864, the men of his company wanted first to be reassured that Wheeler would stay in. When he agreed to do so, almost all of them followed him.

Wheeler's influence and his personal success as a soldier owed much to his devotion to his work and his cause. That commitment so hardened him to the attractions of home that he did not like to think a great deal about his civilian life. He even hesitated to visit his family, saying, "If I should go home, the parting would be most painful, the crust of insensibility and of absorption in my duty would be cast off, —I should be like a soft-shell crab, who had cast his shell prematurely."

He acknowledged, however, that when he was not absorbed by present duties, a longing for home swept through him. On a "beautiful Sabbath afternoon" in the South he thought of his mother walking through the autumn leaves on her way to church. He missed good conversation and domestic surroundings: "a quiet supper with a chosen crowd . . . and then a sensible chat over the apples and Madeira until the small hours." He begged his family and friends to fill their letters to him with the details of daily life. "It is the neat little touches thrown skillfully in," he wrote, "that make the home picture glow with life, and make the heart of the absent member beat warmly as he looks at it."

Affected as he was by memories of his home, he found himself sympathizing with the people whose lands the northern armies occupied. He could speak facetiously of "fried secessionists for breakfast," and he fired cannon shot at the enemy with unbridled enthusiasm. But when he came face to face with southerners his feelings changed. As the soldiers marched along, they often saw women "dressed in black and weeping as if their hearts would break." Wheeler sympathized with the plight of civilians in occupied land. In Virginia he sought to prevent excessive demands on the local farmsteads, interfering in one case, "in favor of a sheep, some bee-hives, and the potato patch" and winning in return an invitation to dinner. He was solicitous of enemy soldiers wounded in battle. At Gettysburg he walked among the southerners where they "lay scattered over the field in groups of twenty, fifty, or even a hundred." Wheeler brought water to one, propped another on his side, and rigged up a bed of straw for a third.

In such moments Wheeler was struck by the "common humanity" of Confederate and Yankee. He mixed easily with the people of Virginia and Tennessee, arguing at one moment with an old Presbyterian clergyman in Virginia about secession and at the next singing hymns at the piano with him and his family. He and his men often visited, played games, discussed books, sang, and ate melons with civilians, then ended their visits with a chorus of "The Star-Spangled Banner," which, he said, "ought to do a secessionists' ears a great deal of good." In Tennessee he spent a pleasant evening visiting a fine old house where an aristocratic young lady sang "Union songs, and secesh airs, darkey melodies and opera morceaux with equal facility."

It was a curious war, and Wheeler's life reflected all its ambiguities — the shabby encampments, the heroic aims, the brutal battles, the moments of reconciliation, the fugitive thoughts of home. Now in spring 1864 William Wheeler was engaged in a new phase of the conflict, marching south in one of the columns of troops that Sherman sent into Georgia. Soldiering was a way of life to which he had grown accustomed, and he operated with routine efficiency: bringing his battery into play in a series of engagements; writing home while bullets flew overhead; and enjoying, in moments of respite, the honeysuckles, jasmines, and roses of this fertile southern land.

A few miles away from Sherman's army another soldier, Charles Colcock Jones, Jr., was preparing to resist the invaders of his homeland. His background prepared him to see southern virtues that Wheeler could never perceive and to excoriate northern vices that Wheeler would never acknowledge. Jones was as dedicated to the Confederacy as Wheeler was to the Union. The two men were on opposite sides of a bitter struggle. Yet in retrospect, we can see that they shared many thoughts, aspirations, and experiences.

Jones was born on October 28, 1831 in Savannah, Georgia. His father was a Presbyterian minister who owned three plantations in nearby Liberty County. Jones grew up with many advantages and pleasures of plantation wealth: private tutors who nourished his interest in literature and history; lessons in riding and weekly "cavalry parades" with other children; opportunities to hunt duck, deer, raccoon, rabbit, and alligator in the countryside near his home.

During the 1850s Jones observed the North at first hand and so became aware of his distinctive southern heritage. He was an undergraduate at Princeton and studied law at Harvard, graduating in 1855, three years before Wheeler's arrival. Jones enjoyed his Harvard years — admired his teachers, indulged his "passion" for books, won

the respect of his professors and fellow students. At times he was positively attracted to New England, especially to "all the glories" of her
Indian summer. But he was reminded, too, of his attachment to the
South, finding tiresome the northern climate, with its sharp temperature changes, and disliking the noise of the local Fourth of July
celebrations, all firecrackers and rockets, instead of the fine orations he
associated with southern celebrations.

Jones was particularly repelled by the abolitionists, who abounded
in Massachusetts, even in the staid halls of the law school. He was
engrossed by the Burns case in May 1854. Anthony Burns was an escaped
slave owned by a Virginian, Col. Charles F. Suttle. A hearing to
determine whether Burns was in fact Suttle's property provided a focal
point for antislavery sentiment. After attending the hearing, Jones
wrote his parents that "Mob law, perjury, free-soilism, and abolitionism
are running riot." The courtroom was filled with armed men, and even
the attorneys carried guns and bowie knives. The mob in the street had
to be cleared every hour. Even then, the confused noise of the soldiers
and abolitionists nearly drowned out the voices of the litigants.

Jones befriended Suttle, the object of this vituperation, and found
him "a perfect Virginia gentleman, of high standing, well educated, of
fine, commanding, prepossessing appearance." The abolitionists considered him a vicious slavemaster bent on exploiting his fellow man, but
Jones came to admire him with "such an attachment as only a
Southerner can know for his brother Southerner." From such incidents
and such attachments Charles Colcock Jones, Jr., and thousands of other
southerners like him developed a sense of the beleagured righteousness
of their own region. Twenty years earlier he could have witnessed the
mobbing of William Lloyd Garrison by an antiabolitionist citizenry,
but the past two decades had seen popular sentiment swing against
slavery. Jones noticed with dismay that some of the bitterest
antisouthern diatribes came from New England's pulpits. He was
treated well enough by his classmates at Harvard, but he sensed that
he and his "brother" southerners were different from these harsh,
misguided northerners.

In 1855 Jones returned to Savannah and practiced law, soon
becoming a partner in the firm of Ward, Owens, and Jones. Like other
aspiring young attorneys, he engaged in civic affairs, joining the
volunteer Chatham Artillery Company and serving as a city alderman.
In 1858 he married Ruth Berrien Whitehead, whom he called "a noble
specimen of a young woman of the most generous impulses, and of
remarkably good judgment." Two years later he was elected mayor of
Savannah.

Jones's letters in this period do not mention the continuing
northern campaign against slavery, but his ideas about the institution

and about blacks continually appear in his correspondence. He and his family were exemplars of a benevolent, paternalistic relationship between the master and slave. His mother spoke of slaveownership as bringing "responsibilities not only for time but for eternity." The family owned 129 blacks in 1860. Jones's father was so effective as a Presbyterian evangelist among the slaves that his region was famed throughout the South for its Christianized blacks. He wrote two books, the *Catechism of Scripture Doctrine and Practice* (1837) and *The Religious Instruction of the Negroes in the United States* (1842), both widely used for evangelical work. The younger Jones inherited his father's sense of responsibility to the slaves. He opposed as cruel the reopening of the slave trade and was appalled when a southern commercial convention entertained such a notion. He believed that if slaves had to be sold at all they should be sold with their families and regarded slave trading as "the lowest occupation" in which men could engage.

His letters described scenes in which the lives of blacks and whites mingled in common sentiment. On June 30, 1858, he attended the funeral of the late mayor of Savannah, Richard Wayne, a solemn occasion at which volunteer organizations — the artillery company, the fire brigades, the Odd Fellows, the Irish societies, and other groups — marched through the streets past silent crowds and flags at half-mast. They formed a great procession a half-mile long, but what most impressed Jones was not the column in which he marched but the singing of hundreds of blacks from Savannah's Negro churches, who stood near the grave. As he and the other mourners entered the cemetery, the blacks began singing "that beautiful and solemn funeral hymn, 'We Are Passing Away.' " They sang with "a depth of feeling" that awakened "a sad echo in every breast."

In Jones's mind, master and slave in Georgia constituted a genuine community. Yet there was no question but that white authority must prevail. He disliked the arrangement that allowed slaves in Savannah and other southern cities to "live out," hiring their labor and seeing their masters only on payday. The practice, said Jones, "exerts a most injurious influence upon the relation of master and slave." If necessary he was willing to uphold slavery with the sword, as he tacitly admitted when he told his parents that the Chatham Artillery, which he had recently joined, was organized to "quell sudden insurrection or domestic lawlessness."

In 1850, when the memory of Nat Turner's rebellion was still fresh in southern minds, the blacks themselves seemed to threaten violence to the "peculiar institution" of slavery. But at the close of the decade the rise of the Republican party and the increasing stridency of the abolitionists suggested an even greater danger from the North. Private military companies such as the Chatham Artillery offered a means of preparing southerners for the eventuality of sectional warfare. In 1859 Jones and his company made an unusual out-of-state trip to Nashville, Tennessee, to encourage formation of a similar company there. His group had been "privately" assured that they would receive a warm welcome and made the railroad journey in force — fifty men in uniform with six cannon. They were cheered along the route, and in Nashville they were greeted by an enthusiastic crowd, including fifteen hundred children dressed in white who threw roses in their path. A series of banquets and artillery demonstrations highlighted their visit. Before they left, the gentlemen of Nashville had begun to form an artillery company of their own.

Within a few months the value to the South of such companies would become apparent. At the news of Abraham Lincoln's election, South Carolina seceded from the Union and declared itself an independent state. Charles Jones wrote his parents, "We are on the verge of heaven only knows what." At first, thought of secession may have frightened him, but he was soon a leader of the movement in Georgia.

On October 12 he presided over a secession meeting in Savannah. The crowd that gathered was too large for any hall, so that Jones and others addressed them from a balcony. The throng before Jones seemed to "sway to and fro on every hand like the sea lifted by the breath of the tornado." Mad with excitement, the people cheered and fired cannon and rockets when they heard the secession proposals. After the tumult quieted, Jones asked whether there were any nay votes. The throng was silent; then someone shouted, "There's *narra no,* Mayor Jones!"

Jones wholeheartedly supported the secession movement, believing that there could be no reconciliation between the sections. He wrote his father: "I have long since believed that in this country there have arisen two races which, although claiming a common parentage, have been so entirely separated by climate, by morals, by religion, and by estimates so totally opposed of all that constitutes honor, truth, and manliness, that they cannot longer coexist under the same government. Oil and water will not commingle. We are the land of rulers; fanaticism has no home here. The sooner we separate the better."

As mayor of Savannah, Jones observed the disposition of troops in the area and the strengthening of the city's defenses. He wrote with pleasure that "the ladies of Savannah" were busy making cartridges, bandages, and shirts. A spirit of sectional patriotism had swept the South, and his father declared the Union's opposition to secession to be "an outrage upon Christianity and the civilization of the age, and upon the great and just principals of popular sovereignty." He had no doubt that "The law abiding mass of the American people lies south of Mason's and Dixon's line." Father and son agreed that the Civil War had been brought on by a mass of lawless, godless fanatics. But they would prevail. "Heaven forbid," said the younger Jones, that the Yankees should "ever attempt to set foot upon this land of sunshine, of high-souled honor, and of liberty."

At this moment of buoyant optimism, tragedy struck Charles Jones in the death of his wife and his first daughter. He was despondent for weeks, haunted by the memories that filled his empty house. "Oh, my dear parents," he wrote, "What voices dwell in these vacant chairs, this silent piano, this desolate bed, these folded garments, these unused jewels, these neglected toys, these noiseless rooms." In his despair he had a prophetic sense that God might have taken them away to spare them from the "evil to come."

But in the summer months of 1861 his grief gave way to optimistic thoughts about the Confederacy. He welcomed news of the Battle of Manassas as a great southern victory. "Surely the God of Battles is with us," he wrote. His bereavement removed the sole impediment to his joining active service. He announced that he would not seek a second term as Savannah mayor at the expiration of his term on October 15 and accepted the rank of first lieutenant in his old company, the Chatham Artillery, now a branch of the Confederate army. He embraced the southern standard with his "whole heart," and he told his parents, he would gladly give his life in the "sacred cause."

At the end of October 1861 Lt. Charles Colcock Jones, Jr., moved to Camp Claghorn, on a bluff on the Isle of Hope nine miles from Savannah. The encampment was picturesque: pure white tents set amid a cluster of dark overhanging oaks, "burnished" guns gleaming brightly in the sun, a garrison flag waving overhead, a "bold river" flowing past, and the soft waves of the ocean sounding in the distance. This was one of several camps near Savannah. In the morning Jones could hear the sound of reveille from other camps along the river.

On November 7, a few days after Jones's arrival at Claghorn, the Union launched an attack from the sea on nearby Port Royal and the rich Georgia Sea Islands. Jones and his company expected to be moved at any moment to support the Confederate batteries on the islands, but within a few hours the Union fleet had swept around the island defenses and occupied Port Royal. The Yankees now threatened Savannah herself, and anticipating a deadly battle, Jones wrote his parents that he would gladly give his life in support of southern "honor, nationality, and principles" and in opposition to the "infamous pollution of a lawless and inhuman enemy." He anticipated that despite this initial defeat in Georgia the Yankees would find that "a people armed in the holy cause of liberty, and in such a country as this which we possess, are invincible by any force which they may send against us." Although Jones did not say so, his phrase derived from Patrick Henry's famous Revolutionary oration in which he said, "give me liberty or give me death." Jones, like many other southerners, believed that the principles of 1776 and 1861 were identical. And as the earlier patriots had, his people, too, would prevail.

Despite the proximity of the Union forces to Savannah, the battle Jones expected did not occur. The Yankees, controlling the seas, were impervious to threat on the Sea Islands and used their hold on this Atlantic outpost of southern plantation society as an opportunity to experiment with the reconstruction of black life through education and economic opportunity.

The proximity of Union forces to Savannah necessitated stationing batteries such as Jones's on the Georgia coast. Jones was offered the command of a volunteer company fighting in Virginia, but the threat to his native region kept him in Georgia. Small skirmishes occasionally erupted, and at times Savannah residents could see northern ships with the naked eye, but the wait for conflict stretched on month after month, and the situation acquired an aura of unreality. One day in early spring 1862 Jones rode out to an abandoned battery on nearby Skidaway Island. In the still evening the sea gulls and pelicans played above the gentle sea. The scene seemed "emblematic of perfect peace." But only a short distance away five Union ships stood in full view. When would the enemy attack?

For the present the artillery companies were left to the day-to-day work of camp life. Sometimes the men left the orderly rows of tents at Camp Claghorn and bivouacked in the country to practice the fatigues of march. One December evening they slept with only blankets in the cold clear air and awakened with frost on their caps and lumps of ice in their canteens. Sometimes they went farther afield and had to contend with bedbugs and crowded quarters. But, anchored as they were to their base near Savannah, they never had to endure the hardships of a long march.

Jones hoped for the opportunity to confront the enemy, but the Yankees at Port Royal seemed contented to stay on the Sea Islands, and the great engagements of the war took place in distant places. Jones was forced to follow the war from afar, drilling his artillery company and hoping for a chance to strike a blow for the cause.

He viewed the war with the strong religious sensibilities taught him by his Presbyterian father, believing that the South must recognize its dependence upon God in order to defeat the Union armies. When his state or the Confederacy called for days of fasting, Jones observed them strictly, halting all drills and encouraging his men to "feel their sins and their dependence upon God." Jones regarded southern defeats

as scourges from God, designed to purify the southern people and draw
their hearts to him. Despite their sins and temporary setbacks, they
were on the side of virtue and order, and in time God would punish
the North with a "day of retribution."

But after the defeat of General Lee at Gettysburg and the Union
victories on the Mississippi, the prospect of a southern victory began to
dim. Still the northern victories did not undermine Jones's sense of
Yankee villainy and southern rectitude. When the Federal navy bom-
barded Charleston, South Carolina, in August 1863, he was appalled at
this attack on a civilian population. "Can history furnish a parallel to
such an act of inhumanity?" he asked. He regarded the Emancipation
Proclamation as the "crowning act" in a "series of black and diabolical
transactions." He wrote his father that Lincoln intended to "subvert our
entire social system, desolate our homes, and convert the quiet,
ignorant, dependent black son of toil into a savage incendiary and brutal
murderer."

Believing, as most southerners did, that slavery was the natural
and proper condition for blacks, he thought the northern promise of
freedom misguided. Not understanding their own best interest, many
blacks would be attracted to the Union side. "Ignorance, credulity,
pliability, desire for change, the absence of the political ties of
allegiance, the peculiar status of the race" — all these factors would
make the slave unduly susceptible to northern enticements, contrary to
his best interests. He advised his father to offset the appeal of freedom
with harsh penalties for unruly slaves. Any black who incited others to
run away or acted as a spy should be summarily executed. Those who
sought the Union lines should be met with "terrible corporal
punishment" and imprisoned in the county jail. "If insensible to every
other consideration," he wrote, "terror must be made to operate upon
their minds, and fear prevent what curiosity and desire for utopian
pleasures induce them to attempt." In his anger at northern efforts to
undermine slavery he even suggested that Yankee captives should not
be treated as prisoners of a legitimate war but as robbers and murderers.

Before the end of 1864 Jones's characterization of the Yankees as
vandals was borne out by the behavior of many of the soldiers who
marched through his native Georgia with General Sherman. The necessity of obtaining food on the expedition and the animosity of some
soldiers toward the planters led to countless acts of violence and looting.
Among the victims was Charles Jones's mother, Mary. In January 1865
her house was repeatedly plundered. Union soldiers looking for food
and valuables broke open every room, closet, trunk, bureau, and box
in the house. They took grain, livestock, clothing, jewelry, cutlery,
and everything else worth carrying. She dared eat by candlelight only

before dawn, lest the invaders take her remaining food. The children could play outside only under close supervision; at the appearance of Yankee soldiers they would "rush in and remain almost breathless, huddled together in one of the upper rooms like a bevy of frightened partridges."

No person could have prevented the suffering experienced by the civilians on Sherman's route. But one of the officers who opposed the gratuitous destruction of southern property was William Wheeler, whose path almost crossed that of the other artilleryman, Charles Jones. One wonders what the two men would have thought of one another had they met. Both were lawyers, Harvard graduates, devotees of literature, sensitive officers, and artillerymen. Each believed he was fighting for God's cause against a sinful foe; but each was capable of forgetting party bias in the presence of another human being.

They never had the chance to meet. On June 23, 1864, Wheeler had moved his artillery company into position for another of the skirmishes that had become a routine part of his life. This engagement, however, was different. As he stood on the battlefield, giving orders, a bullet caught him squarely in the chest. In that instant he may have thought of his boyhood in New York, the ocean voyage to Europe, his years in college, his soldier's life, his family at home. Then the sound of battle faded, and he was gone.

Charles Jones survived the defeat of the South. His opportunity for battle came finally in December 1864 when he commanded the batteries that tried unsuccessfully to defend Savannah from Sherman. He must have known already that the Confederacy's end was near. His land had endured defeat after defeat, and food had been scarce for months. The North had been too powerful for a Confederacy that fought with fewer men, little industry, and no navy.

In 1865 Jones began the long work of accommodation to the new order of affairs. He counseled his mother to accept the fact that the slaves were now free. He found himself engaged in manual labor, loading cotton for shipment to market, his hands peculiarly hardened and tanned by the unaccustomed labor. He soon decided that he could not earn a good living in his homeland, because the plantation economy was devastated by Sherman's destruction and the effects of emancipation were uncertain. Legal and business opportunities in Savannah had become problematical, and in 1866 Jones joined a friend in establishing a law office in New York City, remaining in the heart of Yankeeland for eleven years. Eventually he returned to Georgia and became a lawyer and one of the state's leading historians.

If Wheeler had lived, he, too, might have combined writing and the law. The parallels between his and Jones's life are intriguing but not surprising. North and South might be "oil and water," as Jones had said. But ties of common character and experience bound the two sections together. It was curious but not entirely improbable that the story would end as it did — with Jones at work as a lawyer in New York and Wheeler lying at rest in the Georgia soil.

QUESTIONS

1. How did William Wheeler justify suppression of the South in the Civil War? What did he believe he was fighting for?

2. What were Wheeler's attitudes toward the following: the Union, army life, battle, the enemy, southern civilians, and home?

3. Describe Charles Colcock Jones, Jr.'s, attitude toward slaves. In what ways did he display warmth toward the blacks, and in what ways did he exhibit sternness? How did he explain the slave reaction to the Emancipation Proclamation?

4. What were Jones's attitudes toward these: the North, the South, secession, and the Emancipation Proclamation?

5. What connections did Jones and Wheeler make between their cause and God?

6. What were the main similarities and differences between Jones and Wheeler?

BIBLIOGRAPHY

CRANE, STEPHEN. *The Red Badge of Courage* (1895 and later editions). The classic Civil War novel, about a young man's maturation in battle.

FOOTE, SHELBY. *The Civil War* (3 vols., 1958-71). Beautifully written narrative history.

JOHNSON, MICHAEL. *Toward a Patriarchal Republic* (1977). Georgia in the Civil War; argues that Georgians seceded in part to protect slavery from local opponents.

KANTOR, MACKINLAY. *Andersonville* (1955). Novel about the notorious Confederate prison in Georgia.

MYERS, ROBERT MANSON, EDITOR. *The Children of Pride* (1972). Contains letters of Charles Colcock Jones, Jr., and his family.

MILLER, FRANCIS T. *The Photographic History of the Civil War* (10 vols., 1911). Largest published collection of Civil War photographs.

QUARLES, BENJAMIN. *The Negro in the Civil War* (1953). Black experience during the war.

RANDALL, J.G., AND DAVID DONALD. *The Civil War and Reconstruction* (1961). Good general overview of the times.

SHARRA, MICHAEL. *Killer Angels* (1974). Novel about the Battle of Gettysburg.

WHEELER, WILLIAM. *In Memoriam: The Letters of William Wheeler* (1875). Wheeler's letters as student, traveler, and soldier.

WILEY, BELL I. *The Life of Billy Yank* (1952), *The Life of Johnny Reb* (1943), and *Confederate Women* (1975). Stories of the common people of the Civil War period.

Index

To the student

We, as publishers, realize that one way to improve education is to improve textbooks. We also realize that you, the student, have a large role in the success or failure of textbooks. Although teachers choose books to be used in the classroom, if students do not buy and use them, those books are failures.

Usually only teachers are asked about the quality of a text; their opinion alone is considered as revisions are written or as new books are planned. Now, Little, Brown would like to ask you about this book: how you liked or disliked it; why it was successful or dull; if it taught you anything. Would you fill in this form and return it to us: College History, Little, Brown and Company, 34 Beacon Street, Boston, Mass. 02106. It is your chance to directly affect the publication of future textbooks.

School:

Course Title: _____

Instructor: _____

1. Did you like the book?_____

2. Was it too easy?_____

    Did you read all the chapters?_____

    Which did you like most?_____

    Which did you like least?_____

3. Were the questions useful?_____

    How should they be changed?_____

    _____

4. Were the bibliographies useful?_____

(over)

How should they be changed?_____

_____

5. Do you feel the professor should continue to assign this book next

   year? _____

   _____

6. Will you keep this book for your library? _____

7. Please add any comments or suggestions on how we might improve
   this book, in either content or format.

   _____

   _____

   _____

   _____

   _____

8. May we quote you, either in promotion for this book or in future
   publishing ventures?   _____ yes   _____ no

_____   _____
date   *signature*